IN ENEMY HANDS

Canadian Prisoners of War
1939-45

Brad 10⁰⁰

IN ENEMY HANDS

Canadian Prisoners of War 1939-45

Daniel G. Dancocks

Hurtig Publishers
Edmonton

Hurtig Publishers Ltd.
10560 – 105 Street
Edmonton, Alberta

Canadian Cataloguing in Publication Data

Main entry under title:

In enemy hands

ISBN 0-88830-240-1

1. World War, 1939–1945—Prisoners and prisons.
2. World War, 1939–1945—Personal narratives, Canadian. 3. Prisoners of war—Canada.
I. Dancocks, Daniel G. (Daniel George), 1950–
D805.A2I5 940.54'72 C83-091233-9

Printed and bound in Canada
by John Deyell Company

Contents

Acknowledgements

This book would not have been possible without the assistance and cooperation of a great many people and organizations. In particular, I would like to thank Mel Hurtig for taking a chance on an unknown writer, and the Canada Council's Explorations Programme for providing a substantial portion of the funding for my research. As well, my editor at Hurtig Publishers, Nancy Marcotte, did a marvellous job with my manuscript.

In my travels across Canada I met dozens of people, many of whom found time to talk to me in the midst of busy schedules; many others welcomed me into their homes, kindly offering lunch or dinner, along with countless cups of coffee and tea. Unfortunately, due to space limitations, it was not possible to include in this book all the former POWs who were interviewed. These people are acknowledged below, as are others who aided me in locating POWs to interview; those who provided me with personal mementos, photographs, letters, and documents; and those who helped me in numerous other ways.

Vancouver: Mr. and Mrs. Dave Lang, Art Deacon, Bill
              Laidlaw, Ken Johnston
Victoria: Bob Boyd, Bob Manchester
Sidney, B.C.: Norman Rubenstein
Calgary: Don Nelson, Gus Bitzer, Barry Davidson,
              Ken Hyde, Alex McQuarrie, Don Craigie,
              Beth Raugust
Stettler, Alta.: Jim Horne
Edmonton: Mr. and Mrs. Andy McCarroll, Sid Vale,

	Howard Donnelly, Russ Rogers, Forbes Morton, Art Crighton, Ross Elford, Gilbert Middlemass
Winnipeg:	Jim L'Esperance, Frank Harding, Harry Atkinson, Allister McDiarmid, Don MacDonald, Alec Henderson, Bill Douglas, Leo Lecky, Hayden Auld, Robert Dalzell
Hamilton:	Dr. and Mrs. Ron Bridges, Fred Milner, Tony Dydo, John Thacker, Jack Garety
Burlington:	Len Allen
Paris, Ont.:	Bill Larin
Toronto:	Jean Clark, Jack Gouinlock, Ed Patrick, Don Morrison, Rex Newman, Roy McLaren, Gordon Barnes
Marmora, Ont.:	Grace Leopold
Kingston:	Sam Ebsary
Ottawa:	Ed Houston, Daniel Despins, Bruce Robertson, Don McLarty, John Morison, John Aubry, John Nicolaiff, Al Aldridge, Peter Robertson, Gerald Cumming, Kate Wilkinson, W.A. McIntosh
Montreal:	Ken Gaudin, Dempsey Syvret
Quebec City:	Emile Beaudoin
Halifax:	Hec Cooper, Don Campbell, Arthur MacLeod, Bob Cole, Ian MacDonald

I would also like to thank James Lucas of the Imperial War Museum in London, England, for his interest and cooperation.

Throughout this project I received a lot of moral support from friends and relatives and I thank them all for it. My colleagues at CHQR in Calgary provided constant and much-needed encouragement, notably Andy Philip, Vern Koop, and Alice Brown. Last but not least are two special people whose input must be noted: Penny Allen, my typist (who received immense cooperation from her employer, Pan-Alberta Gas Ltd.), and my long-suffering wife Shiona, both of whom provided valuable comments and criticism along the way.

To my parents,
Bill and Lorraine Dancocks

Introduction

Canadian prisoners of war are the forgotten men of World War II. Much has been written over the years glorifying or vilifying Canada's military efforts, but the POWs have been largely neglected in the volumes of literature that have come out of the war. The irony is that many of these men spent more time as prisoners of war than they did fighting. For most, the POW experience was at least as memorable as any of the land, air, or sea battles in which they took part.

There were Canadian POWs in all theatres of the war, even where their numbers were relatively small. One estimate puts the total number of prisoners held by all participants during the final stages of the war at four million; Canadians accounted for fewer than ten thousand of these.[1] Most were either soldiers or flyers: 6791 of Canada's POWs were in the army while 2475 were in the air force. The Royal Canadian Navy lost only ninety-eight of its personnel as prisoners of war.[2]

Those are the statistics. It is sometimes easy to forget that the statistics are people. This book is about some of these ordinary people placed in an extraordinary situation as prisoners of war. They found themselves in a tight spot and they made the best of it. They did it with a sense of humour; when things got tough they helped one another, they pulled together. At a time when many were mere teenagers or in their early twenties, they displayed a maturity that belied their ages. Their conduct was a credit to their country. And they were so proud to be Canadian.

While Canadian prisoners of war have largely been ignored, this has not been the case with the POWs of other nations, particularly Britain and the United States. In Britain, a certain romanticism seemed to surround the ex-prisoners, and POW stories were very popular after the war. The public had an insatiable appetite for books describing real-life adventures as in *The Wooden Horse* and *The Great Escape*, and stories portraying prominent prisoners such as "Wings" Day and the late legless legend Douglas Bader.

While British POWs were getting their due, American POWs were the beneficiaries of Hollywood's distortions. The movie version of *The Great Escape* stressed the participation of Americans in the dramatic escape of seventy-six Allied air force officers from Stalag Luft III in the heart of Germany in 1944. In fact, American prisoners had little to do with it and no Americans went out through the tunnel. Several Canadian POWs did escape, and six of them were later shot by the Germans.

Television also got into the act, distorting the public perception of prisoners of war in the situation-comedy *Hogan's Heroes* of the mid-1960s. There is, however, some truth about prison life portrayed in *Hogan's Heroes* (although it would be difficult for the average viewer to discern possibility from absurdity) and you will find references to that series in this book. Perhaps the biggest irony about *Hogan's Heroes* is that, far-fetched as the program may have been, it is certain that the producers would have rejected many of the stories you are about to read on the grounds that they are unbelievable.

The lot of a prisoner of war has never been a happy one. Dating back to ancient times, prisoners have been at the mercy of their captors. They were routinely slaughtered on the battlefield until it occurred to someone that prisoners were valuable. They could be sold into slavery or, if they happened to be nobility or in some other way prominent, held for ransom. This carried on for centuries in European warfare. But wars got bigger and armies got bigger, and, most important, times changed. By the nineteenth century nobody sold prisoners of war into slavery (especially if they were white-skinned); butchering them was frowned upon; and it was considered unsporting to hold someone for ransom. More civilized alternatives evolved for disposing of prisoners of war. Prisoner exchanges came into vogue along with the concept of parole: sending prisoners home after getting them to promise not to fight anymore. However, exchanges could not always be worked out, and it was found that parolees too often returned to combat.

Without these arrangements, warring nations were stuck with their prisoners until the end of hostilities. To accommodate them, prison camps were established, but the earliest camps were far from satisfactory. The American Civil War, 1861-65, is a shocking example of the vulnerability of prisoners of war. Prison camps on both sides were atrociously inadequate and conditions were appalling: more than ten per cent (26,436) of Confederate prisoners in the North died, while nearly twenty per cent (22,576) of Union captives in the South perished during the war.

A major humanitarian step forward came in 1864 with the signing of the first Geneva Convention. (There would be four altogether, the most recent being in 1949.) This international agreement established the Red Cross movement. At first intended to ease the suffering of the wounded on the battlefield, the Red Cross also undertook to assist prisoners of war, initially during the Franco-Prussian War of 1870-71.

More progress was made just after the turn of the century. The Hague Convention of 1907 recognized for the first time the rights of prisoners of war and officially entitled them to protection. However, that agreement was primarily concerned with the choice of weapons and methods of warfare in that era; among other things, it forbade the use of chlorine gas as a weapon of war. It did not go into detail about specific rights of prisoners.

A breakthrough occurred in 1929 with another Geneva Convention, this one dealing solely with the treatment of prisoners of war. Following a general statement requiring that prisoners be treated humanely at all times, the Convention described at great length the ways and means of doing just that. POWs could not be coerced into giving information about their own forces; they were to divulge nothing more than their name and rank *or* regimental number. The Convention required that prisoners be given proper lodging with guarantees of hygiene, and that their quarters be insulated, heated, and well-lit. Provision was to be made for physical exercise. It specified the minimum food requirements for the prisoners. It put strict limits on the disciplinary action that could be taken against prisoners and their comrades for various activities, including escaping. The Convention stated that prisoners could be put to work as long as the work was not dangerous or related to the war effort; they had to be paid; the work could not be more excessive than that being done by civilians in the area. Officers could not be forced to work, while non-commissioned officers (NCOs) could work if they wished to do so. Responsibility for meeting these requirements was given to each protecting power, the nation holding the prisoners.

In theory at least, prisoners of war in World War II should have been the best-treated in history. And many were. Certainly servicemen captured by the Allies were well cared for; German POWs held in Canada, for instance, were so impressed with the treatment they received that many opted to immigrate here after the war. Unfortunately, the same cannot be said for Allied POWs in enemy hands.

Although Japan signed the 1929 Geneva Convention, its government did not ratify the agreement. Therefore the Japanese felt no obligation to live up to its terms. In 1942, Japan's foreign minister graciously announced that his country would indeed comply with the Geneva Convention, but there was a catch: *mutatis mutandis,* "with the necessary changes." It was the loophole that opened the door to outrageous abuses. The reason for this was *bushido,* the centuries-old code of conduct espoused by the military, and the military dominated every aspect of life in Japan during the war. *Bushido,* among other things, equated compassion with weakness. To the Japanese mind at that time, a soldier's greatest calling was to die on the battlefield. Surrender was unthinkable. The Japanese soldier, if captured, was required to commit *hara-kiri* or face disgrace in the eyes of his family and his emperor. And the Japanese expected this not only of their own troops but of enemy soldiers as well, so it is not surprising that the Japanese viewed prisoners of war with utter disdain. Without the Geneva Convention to protect them, Allied servicemen who fell into Japanese hands were treated in the most callous, cruel, and contemptible manner.

The German attitude toward the Geneva Convention, while unquestionably better than that of the Japanese, was nevertheless ambiguous. As one former POW, Ross Elford of Edmonton, put it, the Germans were "in the Geneva Convention, supposedly; you were supposed to be treated like a noncombatant, but they didn't always follow that Geneva Convention too closely. If it was convenient, they would." The Germans could be unpredictable and that often made it difficult to deal with them. By and large, prisoners of war in Germany were relatively well-treated (except Russians, who were terribly mistreated), and life could be bearable as long as the POWs received more or less regular deliveries of mail from home and Red Cross food parcels. Unfortunately it was not always possible to get mail and Red Cross parcels to the prisoners, particularly in the latter stages of the war. As the POWs found out, the Second World War was "total war" and they sometimes suffered as much as the civilian population amid the devastation inflicted on Germany.

With the efficiency for which they are famous, the Germans devised a system for handling prisoners of war, a system that was designed for simplicity but which turned out to be rather complicated. (This was in sharp contrast to both the Japanese and the Italians, who generally segregated officers from other ranks but beyond that did little to sort out their POWs.) The Germans gave each of the armed services responsibility for its own prisoners. The Wehrmacht processed all army prisoners (the basic camp in this setup was called a Stalag or permanent camp), the Luftwaffe looked after air force POWs (these camps were labelled Stalag Luft), while the Kriegsmarine handled naval prisoners (there was one camp mainly for navy personnel, Marlag und Milag Nord, in northwestern Germany).

The Germans also believed in segregating officers into separate camps (each of these was called an Oflag). While these were primarily for army officers, it was not uncommon to find some air force and navy officers there as well. Air force officers and NCOs were kept apart, either in different compounds within the same camp or in separate camps altogether; for example, Stalag Luft III evolved into an officers' camp while Stalag Luft VI was an NCO camp. The system was not without its inconsistencies. Stalag VIII B, nominally an army prison camp, contained a compound for air force NCOs and many air force prisoners ended up at another army camp, Stalag IV B, supposedly on a temporary basis, but they remained there until the end of the war.

Any number of nationalities could be found in these camps, and here again the Germans tried to segregate their prisoners. Russian POWs were always kept in a separate compound and the same was usually true of Americans once they started arriving in large numbers. Most camps had a so-called "British compound," but this was a clearing house for all Commonwealth (including Canadian) prisoners, along with Czechs, Free French, Poles, Yugoslavs, and others. Eventually the system began to break down under the sheer weight of numbers of prisoners coming into Germany. By war's end, it had collapsed in chaos, just like the rest of the country.[3]

The Germans loved to tell prisoners, "For you, the war is over." POWs in Germany heard that expression over and over again. As far as combat duties were concerned, it was true, the war really was over. But in many other ways, the POWs were still fighting — fighting to retain their sanity and dignity, fighting to stay civilized and to maintain discipline. They were fighting for survival; instead of doing it on a battlefield, they were doing it in a prison camp. It was a fight the POWs did not always win.

It is not the intention of this book to glorify prisoners of war. At best, life in a prison camp was just bearable. At worst, it could be degrading, depressing, debilitating. By the time you have finished reading *In Enemy Hands*, you will have an idea of what it was like to be a Canadian prisoner of war. Although many were serving in British units at the time of their capture, everyone interviewed for this book was a Canadian.

This is an oral history detailing the experiences of men who lived in enemy prison camps, some for as long as five years, others for as little as a few weeks. For those of you who have never read an oral history, it is much like sitting by the fire listening to your grandfather recall his past. Although the grammar and vocabulary may sometimes offend you, remember that what you are reading is based on unrehearsed, completely off-the-cuff conversations. The stories are compiled in more or less chronological order or, in places, according to subject.

Detailed knowledge of World War II is not essential to understand the stories; a brief introduction to each chapter gives the necessary background and keeps the anecdotes in perspective. Where necessary, footnotes are employed to provide additional information or, in a few instances, to correct or clarify a statement made by one of the POWs.

To be sure, a lot of the stories in this book are grim, but they are not as grim as they could be. Time has smoothed out some of the rough edges. Now, when these men gather for reunions, they tend to recall the good times they had as POWs; the bad times, while not forgotten, tend to be left unspoken. Still, the emotions are there and the memories are often painful; eyes watered and voices choked during many of the interviews.

Nearly four decades have passed since the end of the Second World War. The ex-POWs do not want or need sympathy at this late date. It is enough that, after all these years, Canadians are finally made aware of what these people experienced on our behalf.

Footnotes

1. This figure does not include any civilians or merchant marine seamen who were captured. For the purposes of this book, only those who were serving in the armed forces at the time of their capture will be taken into account.
2. These statistics came from the Directorate of History at National Defence Headquarters in Ottawa. Obviously, with only ninety-eight POWs, the navy is not very prominent as far as this book is concerned. As a result, the

uninformed reader could be left with the mistaken impression that the RCN contributed little to Canada's war effort, when in fact it played an enormous role. This is not the place to go into details; suffice it to say that the RCN was the third-largest navy in the world when the war ended.

3. It is essential that the reader recognize the difference between prison camps and the most notorious product of Hitler's Germany, concentration camps. Prison camps housed captured members of enemy armed forces, and POWs had certain rights which the German authorities acknowledged. Concentration camps, on the other hand, accommodated the so-called "undesirables" of German society: political prisoners, Jews, convicts, even the mentally and physically handicapped. Concentration camps had two main purposes: to provide a pool of slave labour and, later, to provide a vehicle for extermination of Jews and others considered to be subhuman. Unlike POWs, inmates of concentration camps had no rights whatsoever and suffered unspeakable privation. Aside from Russians, it was unusual for POWs to be incarcerated in concentration camps, although one notable exception is covered in Chapter XI.

Part One: Europe

I/The Early Days

Most of the Canadians captured in Europe during the early part of the Second World War were airmen. The reason is simple enough: the war would be more than two years old before Canadian soldiers would fight a major battle against the Germans. With our army on the sidelines until then, it would be up to Canadian fighter pilots and bomber crews to carry the war to the enemy.

World War II started with Germany's invasion of Poland in September 1939. Britain declared war September 3; Canada followed suit on the tenth. But after the Blitzkrieg knocked out Poland, there was a lull in the action — the so-called "phony war" — as the participants awaited the inevitable German invasion of France and the Low Countries. That did not happen until May 10, 1940, but once again Germany's Blitzkrieg tactics proved irresistible. The Netherlands surrendered May 14; Belgium did likewise May 28; France capitulated June 22. These events left the Germans unchallenged in Western Europe. Unchallenged on the ground, that is; in the air it was a different story. It was in the air that Germany suffered its first setback, the Battle of Britain, fought in the summer and fall of 1940. And it was in the air that the Germans could be given a taste of their own medicine as the British mounted retaliatory bombing raids on targets in Germany.

So it was that aerial warfare assumed critical importance, and Canada came to have a vital role in it. Canada was home to the British Commonwealth Air Training Plan, a program that eventually trained 131,533 flyers from all over the world. More than half of them were Canadians and many saw active duty. By war's end Canadians would make up one-quarter of the Royal Air Force; despite an incredible expansion by the Royal Canadian Air Force, more Canadians flew with RAF squadrons than with RCAF squadrons during World War II. In addition, there was a smaller number of Canadians who went overseas before the war broke out, enlisting in the RAF on short service commissions. As a result, Canadian airmen, unlike their counterparts in the army, saw plenty of action right from the beginning, first in Europe and later in North Africa.

Inevitably, many of these Canadians were shot down. Those who weren't killed soon discovered one disadvantage of waging an offensive air war: they found themselves in occupied territory and, unless they were among the handful of Allied airmen to evade capture, they ended up in prison camps. There most would remain until the end of the war, not knowing when or how it would end.

Flight Lieutenant Art Deacon, 242 Squadron, RAF

We were flying Hurricanes. The day we were shot down, May 28, 1940, we were doing a patrol. It was our third trip that day. There were four or five of us, and we ran into twenty, twenty-five [Messerschmitt] 109s. They got into their protective circle, and the only way you can get them is to nip in and get one and get out before somebody gets on your tail. Well, I did this. I'll never know for sure that I got the guy, but the pieces that were flying off it was good enough for me. And I tried to get out the other side, but I got hit by the guy behind me.

This was just off the Channel there, just off Ostend. So I thought, "Maybe I can get to the coast." I put the nose down and threw off the escape hatch, threw the hood back, and undid my harness. I thought, "Well, if it catches fire, I'll jump. If it doesn't, I'll ride it down." And I just barely made the coast, and I pulled back on the stick. Nothing happened. I just went straight in. And when I came to, I was in a potato patch. Never forget it. I was in the garden of a hospital.

Somebody came and took me in, and they patched up my leg and my eye. I asked, "Can somebody take me back to

British lines?" And somebody said, "Well, we have capitulated." May 28. So I said, "My gosh, I've got to get out of here." And the doctor said, "My son was killed yesterday. He's about your size. Would you like to get into civilian clothes?" I said, "Yes, anything to get me out of this situation."

So he took me over to his house. I threw away my identity disks — one of the most stupid things I ever did — and got into a nice brown suit and a brown hat, over top of my bandages. I was going to head for the coast. At this time, of course, I wasn't aware that there was an evacuation going on, or would be going on, at Dunkirk.

So I started walking along, and I spent the first night in a haystack in a farmer's yard. Next morning I got walking again. I could hear gunfire. Along comes this motorcycle, two Germans in it. They started shouting and screaming at me. So one guy went off and came back with sort of an open, troop-carrying vehicle. They poked a gun in my back and said, "Get in." And in the back they had a cross and a couple of shovels.

Off we went. We got out on a country road, and they stopped. I was about to say, "Look, I'm an RAF officer." I turned around, and they had started to dig a hole. Here was a dead German! I just about passed out! Anyway, they got finished burying this guy and got back in the vehicle, and they took me back to the same hospital.

That night the doctor said, "I'll get you onto a bus. We have a lot of wounded going up to Antwerp." So I got on this bus and went up to Antwerp. Went around to the American Consulate there and said, "I'm an RAF officer and I want to get back to the lines. Can you help?" They said, "No, no. Absolutely not." So I went to a park, wondering, "What can I do next?"

I stopped this fellow walking by and I said, "I am an RAF officer. Can you help me?" He said, "Yes," and took me to his house. By this time, my eye was swollen and my leg was bothering me. So after a couple of days, this fellow said, "I'd better see if you can get fixed up at the hospital."

[A nurse] took me in and they patched me up. Just as I was going out the door, a civilian said, "Would you step in

3

the office for a minute?" So I stepped in the office, and here's a German standing there. He said, "For you, the war is over."

I was in civilian clothes, of course. They said, "If you're an RAF officer, where's your identity disk?" Well, I'd thrown them away. The interrogation went on for some time. To me, it was quite obvious that I wasn't a spy, but they didn't seem to agree.

I guess I was in there a couple or three hours, and then they took me to a civilian jail in Nürnberg. I was in a room with a Jewish schoolteacher. At that time, you see, we had no information whatsoever about prison camps. I just thought if you were a prisoner, you were put in jail. They kept me in that jail for about three weeks.

Finally they said, "We will send you to an army camp." And I got on a train and got down to a place called Laufen[1], in Bavaria. This is where the 51st Highlanders[2] were. One hundred and twenty-seven to a room. Three-tier bunks, in blocks of twelve, with three lavatories. And everybody had dysentery. God, what a place!

Then a Lieutenant-Commander Buckley — he was Fleet Air Arm, but he still had his uniform on — finally prevailed on the Germans to take us to Dulag Luft, which was the assembly camp for air force prisoners. And then we were sent up to the camp on the Baltic at Barth, Stalag Luft I.

Pilot Officer Don MacDonald, 21 Squadron, RAF

I got shot down June 11, 1940, about seven o'clock in the evening, in a daylight raid on Saint Omer. Blenheims. I managed to get out, landed by parachute. Unfortunately, the parachute was hit by bullets too and it broke when it hit a tree, and I made, oh, the last sixty feet without a parachute and I landed on a concrete road. Which is not something I recommend.

When I came to, my hips were all mucked up, paralyzed. And a whole bunch of Germans were right there. I was taken to a field where I met a German general who asked me a lot of stupid questions, man-to-man sort of nonsense about what squadron I came from and how many were in my aircraft, which I didn't give any answers to. And then I was taken into

4

a field. There was about six or eight German soldiers with rifles, and in front of them was a tree and bullets all across it, chest high. Which I automatically took for a firing squad tree. We'd been told that they were not taking prisoners of war. Doesn't make you feel too chipper.

And all the time I was talking to this junior officer, who was a cocky little stinker. He kept manoeuvring me around to get me in front of this tree in line with, in my mind, the firing squad. All of a sudden he says, "You will stand here." I thought, "All right, you bastard, if you think you're going to see me scared, you're crazier'n hell." I was; I was scared spitless. And of course, the German orders and the British orders sound exactly the same: "Ready, aim, fire!" And I heard the "Ready," I heard the "Aim," and I heard the bolts in the rifles go. And then I heard another word, and I didn't feel anything. I thought, "Hmm, if this is dying, it's pretty easy." And as I looked over my shoulder, it was the perimeter squad going on guard duty!

The next morning we were taken to a field where I joined, oh, six, eight thousand people, British soldiers who'd been taken at Dunkirk. And we started marching. We would march for two or three days at a time, and be within a mile of where we started from. All the Germans were doing was keeping us moving. And that night, my leg seized up, and I was in a sick bay for about four days, in Neufchâtel.

Well, a couple of days later, they put me on the road again. We'd march, oh, twenty-seven, thirty kilometres a day, which is not difficult to do when you've got a bayonet sticking at your tail end. Finally, we got up to a place called Hulst, in Holland. And we were put into a boat with a whole bunch of Frenchmen. At that stage of the game, the British and the French didn't get along too well.

We went up the Rhine, and then we were stuck in a sort of a train and taken up to a place called Barth, which is a way up in the north end of Germany. I got there, I'd say, around the first of August.

Flying Officer Jim "Pappy" Plant, 58 Squadron, RAF

We were briefed for this raid on Krupp's marshalling yards —

5

these are the railyards — on the night of June 20, 1940. It was a beautiful night, a full moon, and we had no difficulty identifying the target. We were hoping to make one run over the target, but our bomb aimer only got four bombs off. We swung around and came back over the target a second time. And this time we were hit. The port engine caught fire. The skipper, George Walker, gave the order to abandon aircraft.

Then you're sitting there in your parachute, you're swinging down. I watched the aircraft. It was in a long, low glide, and it was going like a blowtorch by this time. There was a party the next night at the mess that I was going to miss, and that was one of the things I was thinking about.

I made a rather hard landing, but I was all right. You were always told to get rid of your 'chute first. So I rolled it up and stashed it under a haystack. I was in a field, and I started walking toward what looked like a gate. And as I was going through the gate, there was this German party coming up the road, and I was picked up by them.

They were from one of the flak batteries that had been firing at us. They took me back to their concrete dugout and gave me a very cursory interrogation. They wanted to know if I was wounded, that was about all. They offered me a cigarette and a drink and a sandwich. I was then taken to Luftwaffe headquarters in Essen. Again here, the interrogation was very brief. I just gave them my name and my rank and my number.

I was picked up again later in the morning and driven to Dulag Luft, which was just outside Frankfurt am Main. A Dulag is a transient camp and Luft indicates it's air force. So all air force prisoners were first brought to this place and this is where they were interrogated. From there, they'd be moved in groups to one of the permanent camps.

By this time, there's a certain amount of shock about the whole thing. You're put in solitary for a time, and after a while this civilian came in. His name was Eberhardt, and he spoke fluent English. He had all the RAF colloquialisms. He threw down a package of Players on the table. He said, "Now, I've got a form here I want you to fill out." They wanted to know the squadron number, type of aircraft, your base, and your target. I gave him my name, rank, and num-

6

ber, and pushed the sheet back to him. After a bit, he said, "It really doesn't matter." And he sat down and filled in most of those questions! He had my squadron, my station, he knew the station commander's name. That was the "interrogation."

From Dulag Luft, I went to Spangenberg. Spangenberg was designated Oflag IX A. This is an officer's *Lager*, or camp. And it was an old castle, a beautiful setting near a place called Kassel. It's on high ground, with the wood and village down below. It had been built, I think, around 1200, and it had housed prisoners in earlier wars; we weren't the first ones. When I got there, in July 1940, they had a real mixed bag: army, navy, and air force. It had a moat all the way around it, and instead of the drawbridge, it had a permanent bridge with a guardroom on the other side of the moat. German quarters were inside the castle itself.

There was not a great deal of recreational space. The only exercise you could get was to walk around the moat, about three-quarters of the way around, so you could almost make a circuit before you had to turn around. Down in this moat, which was dry, they had these wild boars as a deterrent to escaping. We used to amuse ourselves by throwing rocks at these things and getting them to stampede around.

When the Blitz started in 1940, they were overwhelmed with all sorts of prisoners. And there simply wasn't enough food to go around. But I was at Spangenberg for only a couple of weeks. They called us out on parade one morning and picked out many of us air force and said, "You're going to another camp." It was a place called Stalag Luft I, at a place called Barth, up on the Baltic. It was a very isolated spot. It was a very small camp, there were only three huts, and each hut would hold maybe one hundred, one hundred twenty-five people.

When we got there, the French were occupying one hut, and the other two huts, they put the British in. Shortly afterwards, they moved the French out of there, because there was a certain amount of ill-feeling. When we arrived, here were the French with all their suitcases and their uniforms — they'd never fired a shot in anger. They waited on their aerodromes when the Germans took over France, and they were there with their bags packed! They had all the comforts of home, literally. So when we came in, and we looked like a bunch of scarecrows, all we had was what we were shot down in.

It was a very poorly-organized camp. Again, the rations were very poor and there was no Red Cross. This is where most of us got our first real taste of hunger. The German rations were two thin slices of bread, plus a dab of margarine, and you might get a slice of sausage or a dab of jam, and that was about it.

They were pre-fab huts. They were wooden, and we started out with about four in a room. And the rooms were roughly twelve by twelve. When we first got to Luft I, there'd be four men in a room: two double-decker wooden bunks, a small table, and stools. As the camp became crowded, we went up to six in a room, and that meant another bunk. And this began to get a little cozy. Then we got eight in a room, then twelve. So what we did was make triple bunks.

In each hut, there was a small kitchen and a sink, a cold water sink. And they used to use briquets for the stove. Now you only got so many briquets per day, you didn't have the stove going all the time. The climate there is not unlike Calgary's — it may not get quite as cold, but it got pretty darn cold at times. Each hut had a small stove. With typical German thoroughness, every degree the temperature dropped, you got an extra two briquets when you drew your rations. They're not your ordinary barbecue briquet. These briquets were about six, seven inches long, oval-shaped, and about two inches square. They used to bring these things to the railway, and then our people would go over and help unload them and haul them over to the camp.

Flight Lieutenant Anthony Pengelly, 102 Squadron, RAF

(Pengelly was shot down November 10, 1940, following a raid on Berlin.)

It was a moonlit night. I took my 'chute off and buried it. It was quiet as the devil. All the stars were out, and being very optimistic — which you are at twenty — I was going to head

head west and walk to England. Probably try walking on the water!

So I started to walk [down] the road. I'm afraid I didn't even know which side of the road they drove on in Germany, and I was walking, as it turned out, on the wrong side of the road. And a bloody silly volunteer policeman was riding his bike — without a light because there was an air raid — and the two of us met. Forcefully. And he wanted to know what the hell I was doing. I didn't really want to have a long conversation with him.

He was joined very shortly afterwards by a police car with a policeman in it. So they then got in touch with the local Luftwaffe station to say they'd found a clown in blue. They then took me in a truck to this air force station.

They gave me a once-over-lightly interrogation, very once-over-lightly: name, rank, and number, and that was it. And they told me that they'd found two of my crew. They put me on a train and took me to Frankfurt am Main, the air force holding camp which was called Dulag Luft. They put me into the buildings outside the camp itself. Put me in a cell with a long hallway outside. There were no windows in the door, but there was a window looking out over the woods, and I could see barbed wire.

They brought in some coffee and some bread and said that I would be seen by one of the officers shortly. So, somewhere around two in the afternoon, an absolutely charming German officer came in. I was pretty scruffy by this time. I hadn't shaved and I was still in my flying clothes. He looked like he'd just stepped out of a tailor's shop. Terribly polite. Called me by name. Asked me, "How's life in 102 Squadron?" Of course, I hadn't told him the squadron. And then he started to tell me little vignette stories about different people on the station to show that he knew everything, and therefore he didn't really need to know anything. Very smooth. And he had English cigarettes which they had captured at Dunkirk. This chap had been a history professor in Austria. His major was English history, and he'd travelled extensively in England. And he knew everything about Four Group and about 102 Squadron. Which was a little disarming to me.

We'd had no training in this at all, at that point in the war. Every time he got to what I considered to be security-conscious information, I told him I didn't have to tell him that. No problem. He said, "That's all right, I'll find out some way or other. We're shooting lots of you chaps down." He knew turnover figures, casualty figures, reinforcement figures. He knew that I had flown to Italy, and only five of us had done that.

When he figured that he either wasn't going to get any more information from me or he didn't need any more, he said, "That's fine. You'll be here for a little while, and then you'll be going into the camp."

About five in the afternoon, a guard came along and took me into the camp. And of course, anytime anybody moved from the interrogation centre into the camp, everybody in the camp came to the gate to see if it was almost certainly going to be a friend. The Senior British Officer was a Wing Commander Day. He was my flight commander and he was at the gate at Dulag Luft. And of course, he recognized me. Which is one of the ways that they provided a secure camp. In most instances, a chap who was shot down would be known by somebody in that camp. Wing Commander Day was the Senior British Officer, and he knew me, therefore I wasn't a phony, you see.

Pilot Officer Bruce Campbell, 97 Squadron, RAF

I was shot down in July 1941. Our target for the night was the Ruhr Valley. We were going in on Düsseldorf, big marshalling yards. This was very early in the war, and we didn't have radar, as such. As a matter of fact, we were being fed Brussels sprouts and special pills and eating carrots to improve our night vision!

We were flying at a height of about eighteen thousand feet. And we were picked up by the cones of the searchlights. What they would do, they would pass you from one cone to the next, trying to track you. And once you got caught in those lights, it was very difficult to get out of them. Getting caught in the lights was quite an experience because it lit up all the cockpit, even at that height.

I had gone down into the bomb bay to fuse the bombs because, as an observer, I was in charge of bombing. I was just getting ready when we were attacked by a night fighter. It knocked out our communication — and, I found out later, it killed the rear gunner and the wireless operator — and the plane started to go into kind of a glide.

The intercom was out, but I could smell smoke. So I got ready to bail out. There was a handle that you twisted and a door would open up. You had a chest 'chute, and you'd just fall out. I remember trying to get this door open and just a portion of it would open. I could see, down on the ground below, fires and everything else. But I couldn't get this door open. I lived my whole life over again. And all was peaceful.

The next thing that I remember, I was falling through the air. It was a moonless night, no sign of aircraft. And as I went to pull [my 'chute], I said to myself, "I've got to hang onto this, because you'll be fined if you don't return it." This was a standing joke on the squadron. You could be fined two shillings or something if you didn't return the 'chute, and if it didn't work, you could just return it and get another one. The things you think of in that situation!

I hit the ground with an awful thud. It was pitch black, way out in the country. I went to take a step and I found I had lost a shoe. I prayed, was the first thing I did. And then I kind of collected my wits, and just when I was doing this, I could hear the planes. They'd been to the target and they were on their way home.

This would be about two o'clock in the morning. I took a bearing on the stars — I didn't have a clue where I was — and I walked all that night, roughly westward. Towards morning, I came to a wheatfield where there were stacks of hay. So I just got into one of the haystacks and fell into a sleep, to be awakened by women singing, working in the field. So I stayed hidden and rested all day, and started off again that night.

The morning of the second day, I came to this big walled farm. I turned my tunic inside out and I knocked on the door. I didn't have any papers or anything, so the only thing I could do was pretend I was French. The door opened, and I was brought into this courtyard. I took off my tunic and showed them my Canadian epaulets. This lady, Mama Maria, wanted to help me but she didn't want me to stay there for fear of reprisal. She gave me a suit and a pair of her husband's shoes. This is where I discovered I had landed in Belgium, just about five or six miles from the border with Holland. And Mama Maria suggested I would have better luck travelling in Holland.

So I swam across the Meuse River and into Holland. I got help through the churches and I was living off the land, eating raw potatoes and rhubarb and so on.

I was making for Eindhoven, where the Underground was established. I had stolen a bicycle, and I was riding down the autobahn. I must have been looking pretty rugged, because I hadn't washed properly and I certainly hadn't shaved, and I had my battledress on and this suit over top and I was sweating away. And I met this fellow on the road. He says, "You're not French" in perfect English. And he pulled out papers to show that he was a member of the Underground.

He says, "It was your appearance that gave you away." So he took me down a lane to a big farm, and he told a story in Dutch to this lady. She came out and put her arms around me and kissed me. There were three children, I think. Then we went into the barn and my friend said, "You need a good rest. Then I'll make arrangements for you to get washed and shaved." And I think he fell asleep before I did.

I was awakened by the screams of this woman who had befriended me. My friend had disappeared, so I ran out into a wheatfield. And I just got down in the field when this woman was pulled out by some German troopers. And she was put against the wall and she was shot. And the children were put into a truck and taken away.

I was stunned. I was just lying there when I heard, "Psst, psst!" And I looked up a tree and here was my friend, he was looking right down on top of me. He said, "I've got some bikes ready. Let's get moving."

So he led me down another lane, and we went into this house. He shoved me into a filthy bathroom. I'd just started to shave when my friend came running down. He said, "The Dutch police are coming. We've got to get out of here."

We ran out into a field with the Dutch police pursuing us.

And they fired a few shots, and I stopped. One of the Dutch police could speak not-too-bad English and he apologized for frisking me, and he found some sandwiches the lady had prepared for me. So then, a short time later, we formed a parade with two Dutch policemen — they had big plumed hats and they had blue tunics and white pants, they looked very picturesque — then me on a bike, two more policemen, then my friend, and two policemen.

So we got to the local jail in this little town, and the Chief of Police could speak very good English. And his first words to me were, "Too bad your friend was not a true friend." He was a German agent, and they were testing the loyalty of various people. They had their doubts, see, about this particular woman, and he took me there and he saw the reaction. So it was through him that she was murdered. And of course this German spy was actually going to use me to lead him to Eindhoven and, through me, get to the Underground. So I was kind of thankful that I got caught when I did.

I was taken to Dulag Luft, at Frankfurt. I was walking around in the compound when I was approached by a German *Unteroffizier* who called me in to listen to Lord Haw Haw[3] — how the Germans were going to be in Cairo by Christmas, and our losses were terrible, and things looked pretty bleak. "We have six names of prisoners of war who have been captured today. But before these, let us tell you of the German victory at . . ., and of the British losses at . . . ." And, of course, the embassies would listen to these radio broadcasts. Also, the International Red Cross at Geneva.

So I was invited into this sort of a rec room for the Germans, and they were listening to this. And all this conversation of Lord Haw Haw's was in English. And then I heard my name: "Pilot Officer Bruce Campbell of Montreal, Canada." And it was picked up in London and it was immediately sent to Ottawa, and I think my parents got it within hours of the time that it came out. It was a great relief to me, because I'd lost my brother. My brother was nineteen, and he was the first Montrealer killed in the air force. He was with the RAF.

Of course, nobody knew what a prisoner of war was, at that time. I understand there was a big celebration in the

13

squadron because I was its first prisoner. I guess I was lucky becoming the first prisoner because, of the group that I went over with — I think there were about forty of us — only about four of us came back again.

Sergeant Stew Saunders, 405 Squadron, RCAF

I was on 405 Squadron, which was the first Canadian bomber squadron formed. I was shot down on September 7, 1941.

We were hit by flak over Berlin, and both motors quit. We went into a dive, right over the city. So I told everyone to get out. We had a crew of six, everyone was saved. The rear gunner came down in the centre of the Olympic Stadium grounds. He was lucky the police got to him before the civilians did.

I stayed with the aircraft. Someone going out of the aircraft had pulled my 'chute, so the 'chute was all over the inside of the front of the aircraft, and I couldn't see myself trying to gather this up and then jump. So I had to stay. I got down to about two thousand feet, and I got one motor back. I suppose the pressure of the dive started the prop going again. So I was able to level the aircraft out and continue flying.

I took what I thought was a course for Sweden. However, I had no idea where I was. I guess I flew close to an hour, and I was slowly losing height. I passed over a small island, and I thought, "Well, I'm not heading out to the ocean," so I turned back and decided to crash-land on this island.

I came down in a sand dune. I scratched the back of my hand, that's all that happened. So I suppose I sat there five minutes or ten minutes, trying to collect my thoughts.

Our instructions were to blow the aircraft up. You were to use an axe, get out on the wing and cut through the tanks, and then throw a match in. So I got the axe and tried to chop the gas tanks, and these were lead. I couldn't even make a dent in the damn things! So I got the Very pistol and six cartridges and fired these at the fuselage. They started a great fire, and it blew up.

So, not knowing where I was, I wandered around and found a road and walked into a little town. One of the first signs I saw in a store window was Persil, which was at that time English soapflakes. And I thought, "My God, where the hell am I? I must be free." Anyway, I go down a little further, another store, and there's a big picture of Hitler. So I realized then that I was still in Germany.

At that time in the war, we didn't have escape equipment of any kind. We had no maps [or] money, absolutely nothing. And being on an island, where the hell am I gonna go anyway?

It turned out it was the Isle of Sylt[4]. At that time, the Germans had a radio station on the island. I was walking through this little town — this is about three, four o'clock in the morning — and some guy shouts at me. He had a double-barrelled shotgun, and he took me to a police station. And they in turn got in touch with this radio station. And they came and picked me up, took me up to the radio station, kept me there overnight. And the next day, a Luftwaffe officer came to take me back to the mainland, down in the interrogation centre.

We had never had any kind of briefing on becoming a prisoner of war. Back at the squadron, no one ever talked about being a prisoner. Either you finished your tour, or you were killed — there was no in-between. So I had no idea what was going to happen.

We were at Dulag Luft for about three weeks, and then they took a bunch of us to Lamsdorf[5]. And the people in Lamsdorf were all prisoners they'd taken at Dunkirk, permanent British army types. Very rough characters. The air force were in their own compound, a camp within a camp.

I was in that camp about a year. We had a lot of army fellows who didn't want to go to work. They wouldn't let the air force out to work because we had the ranks of sergeant and up. If you wanted to work, you could volunteer, but they couldn't force you to work. But the first air force guys that were in the camp, they let them out on a few work parties and they all buggered off, they all escaped. So they decided that no air force people could volunteer to work. So the only way you could get out of the camp, other than going out through the wire, was to change over with an army guy. You took his rank and so on, lived with the army guys, and he went into your compound and lived there.

I became a fella by the name of Charles Reader, who was a New Zealander. I used to get his mail and he would get mine. And we would attempt to answer and I'm sure, back home, people must've suspected something because the handwriting wasn't the same. His girlfriend used to write me, and I'd just write back and say whatever I thought seemed appropriate!

Pilot Officer Don Lush, 33 Squadron, RAF

I was shot down October 5, 1941, in the Middle East, not far from the border of Egypt and Libya. I was escorting a "Tec R" machine — technical reconnaissance, photographic type of thing — over the Sidi Omar area. And we hit a sandstorm that was up to, oh, ten, fifteen thousand feet. And I lost the "Tec R" machine — this is well behind enemy lines — and the understanding was, once you lose the machine, for whatever reason, you make your own way back to base. Which I did, but I felt rather frisky that day and once I got out of the sand, I went low and started to strafe some German 'dromes and emplacements on the way back to base. I pulled up and gained height, back to about fifteen thousand feet again, and the first thing I knew, I was being attacked. Cannon shells started going through the port wing, and I could see the tracers going by me. The aircraft looked like it had pretty well had it and could catch on fire any time. So I turned her over and pushed the stick forward and flipped out.

I landed not too far from the Halfaya Pass and I was picked up in, oh, about fifteen minutes by an Italian armoured patrol. Then a German patrol showed up and claimed me. And that's when I realized that I had been hit in the leg, and they took me to a German dugout for the night. Then they took me up to Bardia, to a hospital where they took out the flak.

I was there for three or four days, and just about every night, we were bombed by Wellingtons. Being twenty-one and not knowing what things were all about, I found the Germans pretty honourable in the early days. And they looked on the whole thing as kind of a game. They were pretty confident. When the Germans first caught me, they

16

couldn't understand what the hell I was doing over there as a Canadian. So I found myself quite a novelty in hospital.

I met Rommel in hospital in Bardia. He just dropped in on one of his flying trips, and he heard they had a Canadian air force guy in hospital. And he came in and shook hands and wanted to know how I was, how I was being treated. Spoke great English. And of course, he was looked on as God by the Germans. And I was very impressed with him.

Then they flew me by Junkers 52 to Athens. And that was a flight I really dreaded because I knew that was a favourite run for our fighters.

I was in hospital for four or five days and I found out that in the next room was a South African army type who'd been wounded and captured. And we managed to talk to one another through the windows, and we decided one night to try the old trick of throwing some sheets out the window and try an escape. We were only on the third floor. Well, he went out first and I could hear his boots going across the courtyard, and he disappeared. Then I went out. And by the time I got to the ground, there was three or four Germans waiting for me. He was picked up within a matter of hours, too. So then they put me in solitary confinement, in a kind of cellar, where I spent my twenty-first birthday. I was there for a couple of weeks, I guess.

From there, they took me by truck all the way up to the north of Greece, up to Salonica. There were a couple of German soldiers going back to Germany on leave, and they took me under their wing. They took me all the way through Serbia and all the way to Germany. It was about a three-day trip, I guess, four-day trip by train. Things got a little tougher after that.

So eventually we got to Barth. That was the winter of '41. That's also where I met some Canadians for the first time since being captured.

Pilot Officer Daniel Almon, 274 Squadron, RAF

We were stationed in the Middle East. We were flying Hurricanes, escorting and shooting up convoys, troop concentrations, in the desert. The day I got shot down, we were

17

escorting our bombers that were bombing a concentration of German armoured vehicles under Rommel. There were twelve of us, and we were attacked by somewheres in the vicinity of fifty Me 109s. Unfortunately, I got caught by one of them who came up underneath me and shot me down.

I had to bail out, and I was wounded in the ankle. It was a well-known fact that the Germans used to shoot guys out of their parachutes. So I did a delayed drop — what I thought was a long time, and I guess it was, too — I think I must have gone ten or fifteen thousand feet before I opened my 'chute. And I came down amongst some Italians. And when I came to the ground, there were about five of them coming running towards me. And the first guy that got to me got my watch.

Anyway, we did get to a base hospital in the desert, a tent hospital somewheres. And the first night, we got bombed by our bombers and they set practically all the tents on fire and killed a fellow in the cot next to me. The Italians were really upset and they threatened to shoot me because our fellas had bombed and shot up a hospital which, they said, was clearly marked with red crosses on the roof.

[Eventually] I got on the hospital ship to Italy. I didn't get any treatment until I got on the hospital ship. The nurses and doctors on that hospital ship told me that I was very lucky that I didn't lose my leg, and the only thing that saved it from gangrene setting in was that my wound was just crawling with maggots, and they said that this ate out all the poison.

I got to Italy. We landed at Bari, and we went by train up to the northern part of Italy — a hospital train — to a place called Piacenza. It's up near Milan. I went to a military hospital there and I was in there, I think, around three months.

It was mostly Italians and Germans in that hospital. I think I was the only Canadian in the hospital. I believe there was a couple of English fellas too. I was a bit of a novelty, I was a Canadese.

They were extremely short of drugs, and I had an X-ray there and the bullet was still in my foot, they found out. They had to operate on it there, to get it out. And they operated on me with no anaesthetics. So I had the bullet removed.

I was sent to the camp, I think, in March 1942. P.G. 59[6], in Sevigliano. We were extremely short of food in that camp. It was a starvation diet, and people were continually hungry. There was no facilities of any kind. We had no library or recreation. There was nothing to do except walk, and we had recreation football once a week. I was in that camp a year and a half. I can't think of anything that happened in that camp except being hungry.

Flying Officer Brian Filliter, 418 Squadron, RCAF

(Filliter was shot down April 12, 1942, over Holland. He was badly injured while bailing out of his burning aircraft. After several days on the loose, Filliter was finally picked up by the Germans.)

They took me off to jail in Amsterdam.

When I was injured, I also cracked a tooth and it became ulcerated. The whole side of my face, you know, went up like a balloon. I could only speak out of the corner of my mouth. This turned out to be a little bit of a blessing because they interrogated you many, many, many times. Because my face was swollen, I was able to put on a little bit of an act, you see. Anyway, I managed to hold through these three or four days that they kept me there. Then I was in hospital for about a month. They treated us quite well in hospital.

Then I got to Dulag Luft. And there was a very handsome English squadron leader there. "Won't you come and have a cup of tea with me, and a cigarette?" So I whipped over to his hut and, sure enough, he had tea and cigarettes. We had a very casual and informal chat. He said, "I've been out of it, I got shot down a couple of years ago. I'm not familiar with what's going on. What were you flying?" "Oh, Bostons." I told him a lot of information that I withheld all the time I was in hospital, all the time I was in jail. And this guy — he was English — was in the pay of the Germans. So everything I managed to withhold all this time, I gave away anyway.

I heard later on that they lined him up and shot him in the cold, grey light of dawn, after the war.

So, anyway, from there I finally went to Stalag Luft III.

19

Pilot Officer Don MacDonald, Stalag Luft I, Barth

We coped. It wasn't easy. It was damn hard, as a matter of fact. And had anybody, at that time, told me we were getting along fine, I'd have fed him his teeth, because we didn't figure we were getting along too well.

But each and every one of us helped the other guy. I suppose the Canadian boys helped the British, because we didn't have the strain on us because our families were not being bombed. Because some of them had such damn bad problems. They didn't know where their families were, they didn't know whether they were even alive. And we really didn't start getting letters until well into '41. I didn't anyway. And then they were always six to eight months late.

Sergeant Stew Saunders, Stalag VIII B, Lamsdorf

I think the thing that got to most of us was the fact that we didn't know when we were going to get out. If you were shot down, you're taken prisoner, and they said, "Two years from now, you're going home," you could look forward to that date, knowing that you're going to go home. The first two years that I was there, of course, things were going against the Allies. The Germans were doing well in North Africa, and they were going into Russia, and so on. And it could be pretty discouraging to hear this news and it's only natural to wonder, "How the hell are we ever gonna get out?" In actual fact, a lot of us wondered, "Are we even going to win the war?" All of us would say, "We'll be home for Christmas," whether you really believed it or not.

Flying Officer Brian Filliter, Stalag Luft III, Sagan

Things you really missed were things like toothpaste and brushing your teeth, the little things you take for granted in everyday life. But you were pretty well reliant on prisoners who had been there to help, and they're very, very good. They tried to help the new prisoners.

I think that, initially, you're very depressed and down-hearted. The first reaction is, "I'm gonna escape and get back and do another two tours and kill all the Germans and be a

20

hero." Then after a while, you realize it's pretty hard to get out of the place. And then you become depressed: "How am I ever gonna get out of here? Are we even going to win the war?" Because at that time, you know, things weren't looking too good for our side.

It takes about six months to gradually reconcile yourself to your fate. Then it takes a year for you to realize also that, hey, you're not gonna get home for Christmas.

As soon as you can say to yourself, "I'm only gonna take one day at a time, and I'm gonna have something to do tomorrow," and look forward to it and just take it one day at a time, then you're a lot better off.

Footnotes

1. Oflag VII C/H.
2. This is a reference to the British 51st (Highland) Division. Most of this division was captured during the Fall of France, in June 1940.
3. Lord Haw Haw was the derogatory nickname given by the British to one William Joyce. Joyce was an American-born British Fascist who volunteered to do propaganda radio broadcasts for the Germans during the war. After the war, Joyce was convicted of high treason. He was executed January 3, 1946.
4. This island is in the North Sea, just off the border between Germany and Denmark.
5. Stalag VIII B.
6. P.G. is from the Italian phrase for prison camp, *campo concentramento prigionieri guerra*.

II/Disaster at Dieppe

Until the middle of 1942, the war had been a frustrating experience for Canada's army in Britain. The First Canadian Division had arrived amid much fanfare in December 1939, with the Second Division arriving the following summer. The reinforcements poured in steadily and in April 1942, the First Canadian Army was formed, under the command of Lieutenant General A.G.L. McNaughton. McNaughton proudly likened his newly-formed army to "a dagger pointed at the heart of Berlin."

But so far the dagger had drawn little blood. One brigade of the First Division landed in Brittany at the height of the Battle of France in 1940, but the Canadians spent only two days there before being withdrawn without having seen any action. During the desperate days that followed, since the British army had abandoned most of its equipment in the Dunkirk evacuation, the Canadians were virtually the only fully-equipped troops in Britain. At the time, a German invasion of Britain seemed almost certain and, had it materialized, the Canadians would have played a major role in the defence of the island. But the invasion never took place, and the Canadians seemed doomed to a bleak future of endless route marches and interminable training.

Canadian troops could have been put to good use in the desert fighting in North Africa. But Canadian policy, most stubbornly and determinedly articulated by General McNaughton, was to keep the army intact and under Canadian command rather than employing it piecemeal wherever and whenever the Allies needed reinforcements. As a result, the Canadians languished in Britain, reluctant spectators to a war they had volunteered to fight. Their frustration grew as the war intensified. They booed Prime Minister Mackenzie King when he toured Canadian bases in Britain in August 1941. On top of that, there was rising public pressure at home, especially after war broke out in the Pacific. Newspapers across the nation were clamouring for Canadian troops to get into action. Canada's honour was thought to be at stake and there was an escalating chorus of calls for the commitment of Canadian troops somewhere, anywhere, against the Germans.

Elsewhere, events were unfolding that would soon affect the Canadians. In mid-1942, the Soviet Union was bearing the brunt of the Nazi war machine, and the Russians were far from satisfied with the aid being provided by the western Allies. The Soviets wanted more than material help; they wanted something to distract the Germans, preferably an invasion of the Continent. The British Chiefs of Staff balked, and rightly so, at the suggestion of an invasion. They did not have the expertise to conduct such a massive and dangerous operation, and they had no real idea of the strength of the German defences along the coast of France, Belgium, and Holland. So, while rejecting an invasion, the British war planners did come up with a proposal for a major raid on the French coast. On April 30, 1942, the project was offered to the restless Canadians who, not surprisingly, embraced it enthusiastically.

The planners had selected the small French port of Dieppe as the target for a "reconnaissance in force." It would be carried out by the Second Canadian Division under the command of Major General J.H. Roberts. Under heavy security, the Canadians immediately began intensive training in amphibious landings, on the Isle of Wight. The raid was tentatively scheduled for early July, but a number of factors combined to force its cancellation.

The Canadians were surprised when the raid was suddenly resurrected and rescheduled for August 19. The final plan called for minimal air and sea support for the raiders, the intention being to rely on the element of surprise. British commandoes were to land first, on the extreme flanks, to neutralize the German coastal batteries at Varengeville-sur-

Mer to the west of Dieppe and at Berneval to the east. The Canadians, who made up the majority of the raiders, were to attack Dieppe frontally, with flank attacks designed to encircle the town. On the right, the Queen's Own Cameron Highlanders and the South Saskatchewan Regiment were to land at the coastal village of Pourville and seize the headlands overlooking Dieppe on the west side. The Royal Regiment of Canada was to land simultaneously on the left, at Puys; its job was to take the eastern headlands that dominate Dieppe and the main beach. Half an hour after the twin landings on the flanks was to come the main assault on Dieppe itself, carried out by the Royal Hamilton Light Infantry and the Essex Scottish Regiment, with the Calgary Tank Regiment in support and les Fusiliers Mont-Royal in reserve. All this was to take place just before daybreak; the plan called for everyone to be withdrawn later in the day.

If nothing else, the Dieppe raid showed the Allies how *not* to launch an invasion. The tragedy of August 19, 1942, undoubtedly paved the way for the many successful amphibious landings that followed, culminating in the vital Normandy invasion two years later. But the Canadians paid a heavy price for those lessons. Of the 4963 Canadians who took part in the raid, less than half returned to England. Nine hundred and seventy lost their lives. And 1946 Canadians became prisoners of war.

Major Allan Glenn, Calgary Tank Regiment

There were no alternatives in the planning itself. The Calgary Tanks were in support of the infantry units. My "C" Squadron, we were in support of the Essex Scottish. Colonels in charge of units, and I as a lowly major in charge of a semi-independent tank squadron, were included in these planning conferences. So I knew of all the plans that were going on, what was being discussed, and the changes, and all the rest of it.

Our colonel was Colonel Andrews. He was a Permanent Force officer, a professional soldier, and a good one. So, after these planning sessions, we'd get together. There were three squadron leaders and the colonel, and we'd discuss this in privacy. And this was the thing that struck everyone: "What do we do if we can't get through?" There were so many things that didn't mesh, that didn't make sense, really.

Private Alfred Moody, Royal Regiment of Canada

Our briefing was very lackadaisical. For a raid where you're supposed to go in and come back out, you should be briefed to the very last second, in my opinion. You should know what you're gonna do every step of the way, and have alternatives — if this can't be done, you go this way instead. Nothing.

Everybody was seemingly under the impression that we were going to sneak in there at dark and sneak up the cliff and take these jokers by surprise. No way. And anybody that would think that way in the first place is crazy.

Private Gren Juniper, Royal Regiment of Canada

Actually, we were supposed to go to Dieppe a month before we did. We were taking our training on the Isle of Wight. Then, there, we boarded the ships and we were floating around in the Channel, waiting for weather conditions favourable for the paratroopers. Well, finally, on the sixth day, they decided they weren't going to use the paratroopers because the weather was just terrible. And in the meantime, we were just wandering around the Channel.

So they cancelled the raid. So we went ashore, and then we went back to England. And some of the guys went on leave, which was a mistake because everybody was talking about this thing, you see.

Private Bill Olver, Royal Regiment of Canada

Then when we come back from leave, they start training us again. And then they tell us we're going on a King and Queen's Inspection. And then they tell us when they get us on the boat again, we're going back to Dieppe. Well, jeez, you could've heard a pin drop.

Trooper Forbes Morton, Calgary Tank Regiment

I remember my first thoughts when I heard we were going

25

back to Dieppe: "No, not there!" I just had kind of a gut feeling that it must have been publicized, and the Germans must have got hold of it.

Major Allan Glenn, Calgary Tank Regiment

So, we knew the Germans had to be awful goddam dumb, to get away with that. We had no security.

And then, the day we were taking off, Johnny, the colonel, came around to each of the landing craft. He said, "Well, Al, this is it, I guess. Be seeing you, I hope." But he was a sad boy. He didn't think the plan would work. He was killed that day.

Corporal Bill Dignam, Canadian Provost Corps

I was very calm coming across the Channel. And I spoke to the Royal Navy skipper running the TLC. I said, "Well, what's the projection here?" He says, "We expect to lose eighty per cent of everything that's on the water today." I said, "Jesus Christ! Eighty per cent?" I couldn't believe it.

Corporal D.D. Johnstone, Queen's Own Cameron Highlanders

We landed at a small seaport town called Pourville. The Jerries opened fire while we were still at sea. A number of us landed, a number of us were blown out of the water. Our company commander got clipped across the face, wounded quite severely. The company sergeant-major got hit in the stomach. He died.

We went inland a short distance, and we crossed over this river at a small bridge. And then we came back across this bridge and remained there for a short time. Then we took off into the town. And men were getting hit, killed. They were dropping off pretty quickly. And we got mixed in with the South Saskatchewan Regiment, or parts of it.

Casualties at this time were very heavy.

Private Gren Juniper, Royal Regiment of Canada

Our regiment was late in landing. They landed us at Puys. About a mile out, I saw the red flare. That's the signal that enemy troops are approaching. And I heard somebody say, "They know we're coming." Then I could hear all the machine gun fire.

I was sort of excited. I wasn't exactly scared because I didn't realize what it was all about. But we were sort of excited as the Assault Landing Craft got close to the shore.

Private Alfred Moody, Royal Regiment of Canada

We were late getting in, and we hit a terrific crossfire. That I do remember. How anybody could get through it and still live, I still don't know. When that ramp went down, I looked out there and I saw all these little white things going by. Every one of those was their tracer bullets. For every one you saw, there was four or five you didn't see. I saw guys falling, and I said to myself, "This is sheer madness." For a moment I hesitated. But you gotta go, boy. And away I went. Straight out onto the beach, as we were told to do, and flopped down, and give covering fire. Covering fire for what, I wouldn't know. You couldn't see anything except the odd muzzle flash from a machine gun. And that's what we fired at.

Private Peter Macleod, Royal Regiment of Canada

First thing I remember after I left the boat, I got hit in the eye. I got to the wall, and then I was hit again in the leg. And after that — all hell had let loose, of course — I put the bandage on my leg. And my eye, it was gone. And I got hit in the head when I was tryin' to fix up my eye. Shrapnel in the eye and the head, and a bullet in the leg.

Private Bill Olver, Royal Regiment of Canada

Our platoon was on the left flank. The sergeant rushed us up to the wall. He got a bangalore torpedo and blew a hole in the wall. There was six of us got through before the Jerries started to open fire.

The lieutenant, Wedd, ran through the hole and right up to this ten-foot barbed wire fence. There was myself, with a Bren gun, and Carl Walsh, my Number Two. Carl Perry, with a rifle, and there was Gord O'Connor, he was with wire-cutters. Then Corporal Hillier came through the hole. I

27

remember the lieutenant yelling for the wirecutters, and instead of Gord O'Connor getting up, my Number Two gets up. Now why he got up and run — because he didn't have any wirecutters, he had the ammunition for my Bren gun! He went to jump over the concertina wire — there was a roll of it before you got to the barbed wire fence — and he got caught. And he couldn't get off, and he was pullin'. I can still see him. Then the Jerries let him have it, just cut him down. As soon as he relaxed, his uniform let go of the wire and he fell over.

We never heard another word out of the lieutenant. Carl Perry, his left arm was dangling. So there was only Gord O'Connor and myself still in one piece. I turned around, and Corporal Hillier was laid out there as dead as a doornail. Just then, everything went black. Somebody'd thrown a smoke cannister over. We just grabbed Perry, Gord and I, and threw him over that wall. It was about a seven-foot drop. Then him and I just took a running dive and back onto the beach.

Private Gren Juniper, Royal Regiment of Canada

I'm a two-inch mortarman. I decided to fire a couple of smoke bombs. Well, my Number Two man, I don't know where the heck he got to, but he wasn't around. I had all my bombs in my pack. So there was a fella beside me. I told him to get me a couple of smoke bombs, but he got me a couple of high explosive bombs. Well, I called him everything under the sun! Then he got the smoke bombs I wanted, so I fired them off. I don't know where they landed.

So that was my war effort. It cost the government thousands of dollars to train me, and that's what I did. Fired two smoke bombs!

After that, I got hit in the side. I thought my whole damn side was ripped up. God, it really hurt! So I thought, "That's me. I've had it." I had a shell dressing, and I put it [on]. And I was laying up against the sea wall, and I got three machine gun bullets in my ankle.

Private Bill Olver, Royal Regiment of Canada

I thought it was just a disaster. You know, you couldn't get off the beach. And the bloomin' Jerries were firin' at you, and you couldn't see anything. All you could see was the little slit in these pillboxes. Up on this corner of the beach, to our left, there was a pillbox, and he had a view of the whole beach. They could have slaughtered the lot of us. The only thing that protected us from the front was the sea wall.

(With only partial success at Pourville and complete failure at Puys, the main attack on Dieppe now began.)

Corporal Bill Dignam, Canadian Provost Corps

We were quite a fair way out in the water and, all of a sudden, tracers started, all different sizes of tracers. Then there's the realization, boy, this is no practice, we are really playing for keeps. The crap's starting to fly pretty handy, see. Now that the realization is there, you want to get on the shore just as fast as that bloody boat can go, you know.

Corporal Al Comfort, Royal Hamilton Light Infantry

I expected to meet a hail of fire, but for some reason, the Assault Landing Craft I was in wasn't fired on. Every man disembarked without being wounded. I landed on the gravel and ran up the beach. The noise was indescribable: rifle fire, machine gun fire from both sides, and shells being lobbed over.

I was in the medical section, and my first patient was Buddy Fry. He had a serious hip wound. And I was the next casualty. A trench mortar shell must have landed very near me. I don't remember being blown up in the air, but I remember coming down. Shrapnel had wounded me in both legs and the hip. I also remember that I screamed. I am a firm believer of the Bible. And I remember I cried, "My God, my God, my God!" And I feel because of my plea that the pain left me and my wounds did not bleed much.

So, I was wounded, and I had to dress my own wounds. Then a man from Dundas, Jim Sample, came to me. He had a head wound. As I was approaching him, I definitely remember seeing little spurts on the gravel. It was machine gun fire. And it took me right through the left shoulder. But I didn't feel it, in the shock, I guess. So Jim Sample and I looked for shelter, and we saw an Assault Landing Craft beached farther down. So we proceeded in the sea. The only shelter we could find was under water. It hid us a little, but it didn't protect us. And I also remember seeing, like a heavy rain on a mill pond, the bullets splashing on the water. And it was blood red. And bodies floating around. We were so shocked, I believe — it was our first time under fire — that the fact that our buddies were being killed, heads off and legs off, it didn't impress us like it should have.

Anyway, we were able to get down the beach and took shelter behind the Assault Landing Craft. There, my legs began to stiffen — I was wounded in both legs and the shoulder — and I couldn't move. But wounded men came to me. I remember one, Johnny Sharp, came to me with a slight head wound. In order to be sheltered from the rifle fire, he crawled right up, sat in front of me and was lying on my breast. And while he was there, a shell landed near, and a piece of shrapnel went right in his abdomen and up at his heart. He did live for a while. But if he hadn't been there, that would have been my piece of shrapnel.

Corporal Bill Dignam, Canadian Provost Corps

I went up the ramp and just took a dive straight off it into the water. I guess it was up to about my waist. Then I started for the beach as fast as I could. I flopped on the beach. I'm a bit winded, a little excited. I don't know where I heard it, but it must have been from my Dad in the First War — I grabbed a couple of pebbles and jammed them in my mouth. Because now, my mouth is pretty tacky and sticky, man, and dry. So I moved these marbles around to create the saliva, and I felt better.

It was just blazing all across in front, coming at us. The beach went up a fair elevation and all of a sudden here was something suspicious. You got the idea it became quite a good hump in front, which wasn't in any of the detailing at all. It was a small wall, they told us, and some concertina barbed wire on top of this wall. But the engineers would blow a hole in the wall to give easy access, not for the troops so much as for the tanks.

Our intelligence was lousy. I don't know where they got their information from, but it was lousy. Good God, instead of a two- or three-foot wall, this sucker is a way up there. It's an enormous wall. And then I realized that the Germans had scooped out all that portion of the beach, bulldozed it back towards the water. So that when the troops come in, they've got to come up on the rise and the boys facing us just pick 'em off. They had their machine guns on a fixed line of fire, and one overlapped the other. They started firing at ankle height, for God's sake, and about every six inches on up. They just sat there and sprayed 'em back and forth.

At one stage in the game, honest to God, I thought I was the only person alive. You know, I couldn't see anybody else.

Major Allan Glenn, Calgary Tank Regiment

We had the Churchill tank. They were forty-five tons. We were assured it was a good beach, not too steep. The beach consisted of stones. You couldn't pick worse terrain for a tracked vehicle. You turn the vehicle a little bit, the stones are rolled into the track, and if you get too many going through at once, you break your track.

Captain Fred Woodcock, Royal Hamilton Light Infantry

I was blown up. My landing craft was Number Seven, on the extreme right flank of the town of Dieppe itself. We felt that there was an underwater charge still there, although the beaches were supposed to be cleared. And we sank in, oh, I imagine, a foot of water. Only two of us survived.

I was blinded, one eye literally hanging out on my cheek. And no feeling. Fortunately my face was above water. I didn't know that I was all smashed up otherwise. Self-preservation takes over, you know. You realize you've got to get out of there. So I got out of my web equipment. We all wore an ordinary Mae West. I was blowin' away on that, and I guess it was as full of holes as I was, because I didn't get anywhere.

And the tide went from under my chin down to my lap, sitting in the landing craft. Then someone came in and got me out of there. Bandaged me up, because I was hit in the small of the back, my right shoulder was all smashed away. I

31

was partially paralyzed down the right side, both ear drums perforated.

I remember him doing something to my head, then passing out and coming to, and he asked me, "Can you run?" Well, it was one arm over his shoulder, and we went down the beach to another landing craft that had been driven too hard ashore. And I got in, and I put my head down on someone's thigh. I don't remember anything after that.

Private John Kozakewich, Royal Hamilton Light Infantry

The Germans started dropping mortar shells on us, so our officer said, "Let's get going!" So we started heading for the Casino. All at once, I get bullets hitting all around me and I got hit. A bullet went right through the wrist and knocked me over. I got up again but before I got too much further, a mortar bomb went off, and I got shrapnel in my shoulder.

There were some corpses there on the beach. So I pushed one on top of another, for a little cover.

Corporal Al Comfort, Royal Hamilton Light Infantry

So, we were sent into a slaughter. Even reinforcements were sent in after, and they were slaughtered. We had steel boats, and the Fusiliers Mont-Royal came in as reinforcements in wooden boats. I laid there and watched the machine guns just sow a pattern right down the sides of those boats. Almost all of them must have been killed.

Private Geoffrey Ellwood, Royal Canadian Corps of Signals

I was attached to the Essex Scottish. We were the rear link communications for the battalion headquarters, back to the brigade. Our orders were to stick like glue to the colonel. Wherever he went, that's where we went. We got up under the sea wall, and the colonel pulled out his little maps.

Our brigade headquarters didn't land, they remained on the ships. And we had very, very poor communications. The messages we were asked to pass back were usually verbal. An officer would shout to you, tell you what to say. Or one of the officers would come over and take the set and give "sit reps."

It was an accurate picture of what you could see, but it wasn't really a realistic picture of what was going on. Because we didn't know what was going on. Our battalion headquarters was under the sea wall, and we were pinned down. Over the sea wall was a flat promenade of about a hundred and fifty yards. Stick you head up and it was gone. You couldn't move.

We'd been there for quite a few hours, and by this time we're getting to suspect that there's a possibility we may not get out. We saw the landing craft trying to come in and pick us up. The artillery on the headlands were shooting at them, hitting the odd one. Eventually they went back out and stayed there.

A lot of the fellas, hundreds of them, decided they were going to swim out. They'd strip off their clothes, and out they went. Actually, it was a solid mass of heads.

This was the real horrifying part of the whole episode, actually. You could see the bodies twitch as the snipers were hitting them. And then the Germans sent over three bombers very low. You could see the bomb bays opening, and they dropped myriads of these little tiny bombs, just spread them amongst these guys that were swimming. And they started exploding, and there were parts of bodies flying up — heads, arms, legs. This brought everybody back to shore. And afterwards, the bodies and debris were washed ashore. A good six or eight feet along the water's edge was just bodies and parts of bodies just floating there.

Sapper Des Ewins, 7 Field Company,
Royal Canadian Engineers

That's another thing you remember. A sea full of blood. It's damn near impossible to describe. They'd be machine gunning the fellas in the water, and the water come in just blood red.

Corporal Earl Summerfield, Royal Hamilton Light Infantry

The last boat that I seen, I go to get on it, and I get a hold of the kedge rope, you know, that's the rope hanging out the back with the anchor so they can back off shore by winding it

33

up. I figured this was no good, so I started swimming back to the beach.

I remember a destroyer[1] there, firing at the cliffs just above the Casino. I heard the explosion, and the next time I looked, that destroyer was gone. But there was bunker oil on the water. All the guys ahead of me were in it. It just sounded like a slaughterhouse. You know, the guys get in the bunker oil, and even their Mae Wests wouldn't hold them up. They'd go for a bit, then start to scream, and drown. It was just luck that the bunker oil floated past me.

And I swam into the beach. I was tired, beat. So I got into a mortar hole and laid down.

Corporal Bill Dignam, Canadian Provost Corps

When it all ended, I was standing with Brigadier Bill Southam. And he had taken off his steel helmet, and he'd put on his 48th Highlander glen. He said, "Dig, I guess it's all over."

I started then to see guys who'd been in the water for bloody hours. They just had their underwear shorts on. They were coming in, wounded and otherwise. And the Jerries, the real sharpshooters with telescopes, were picking these guys off. They didn't really have to kill the guys. Some were hit, and some just played possum and lay there on the beach.

Private Bill Larin, Royal Hamilton Light Infantry

I don't know just what time it was. I estimate it was eight or nine hours we were there on the beach. You lose all track of time.

I think I felt a sense of relief because it was over. We didn't know what was ahead of us, but at least we were alive.

Private Geoffrey Ellwood, Royal Canadian Corps of Signals

We noticed this group of people starting to walk up the beach. And they were carrying a cane with a white flag. When I saw that flag, the bottom fell out of my world. Two of us stood up and looked over the sea wall. I don't think they were ten feet away from us, a long line of Germans, all with their weapons pointed at us.

34

We put our hands up and went around the edge of the sea wall and up there. Just as we were getting in amongst them, one of them sort of went berserk. I guess maybe he'd lost somebody close to him. He had his weapon by the barrel and he was swinging it at our fellas and pounding them. The German officer yelled at him two or three times, and then just took his pistol out and shot him.

Private Lou Pantaleo, Royal Regiment of Canada

Then the word went up that we were surrendering. I became very frantic. A feeling of shame, a feeling of fright. In all the time we were training, the thought of becoming a POW never entered my head at all. I was nineteen at the time.

Sergeant Tommy Cunningham, Calgary Tank Regiment

I don't think the average guy who went on Dieppe had any conception of having to face surrender. You're young. You think you're well trained. You're going to do this thing, and do it well, and it was an adventure. And, all of a sudden, the balloon bursts.

Trooper Richard Clark, Calgary Tank Regiment

Some of the guys didn't want to surrender. Some guy put up a white flag, and one or two of them said, "Shoot the bastard!" They didn't want to surrender. They wanted to finish it here. But they did give up, and rightly so. There was no way out.

Corporal Al Comfort, Royal Hamilton Light Infantry

I expected they would kill us. And I hoped they would shoot us. I didn't like the idea of cold steel in my belly. But the Germans were not antagonistic at all. As I understand it, they were front line troops, recuperating. They knew what the score was. No one was abused. And those who could walk, walked to the Dieppe hospital. On one occasion, the bandage on my right thigh slipped down, and one of the Germans took his field dressing from his pocket, walked out to me, and applied his own dressing. Compared to what I expected, it was a relief.

35

Private Bill Olver, Royal Regiment of Canada

This German officer waiting for us as we came off the beach, he says, "What happened? You're four days late!"

Major Allen Glenn, Calgary Tank Regiment

This is one of the comments I do remember one of the Germans made. "If we knew there were so many of you coming, we'd have been prepared."

The French nurses at the hospital at Dieppe told us they'd been getting up at four o'clock in the morning for the last four or five days. They were expecting us.

Captain Fred Woodcock, Royal Hamilton Light Infantry

I came to underneath a canvas. All the rest in the landing craft were dead and I was marked as dead, too. I fought out from underneath the canvas. There was about three or four parties of souvenir hunters came along. One of them gave me a boot in the ribs. The only bit of equipment left on me was my binoculars, and they were all tangled in underneath the bandages. Another guy tried to break the strap, and he was yankin' me off the floor of the landing craft, but it wouldn't break. Not a word spoken. You could feel the cutting of a knife and then the strap slithered from around me. And then he was gone. And I don't remember another thing until I came to in a hospital in Rouen.

Sapper Wally Hair, 2 Field Company, Royal Canadian Engineers

They marched us into the centre of town, around the hospital. And I must say, the Germans treated us with great respect. They treated us as fighting men. At the same time, they had their famous saying, *"Für euch ist der Krieg zu Enden.* For you the war is over." If we heard that once, we heard that thousands of times.

Private Geoffrey Ellwood, Royal Canadian Corps of Signals

They were bringing up the bodies. They had a flatbed truck

and they were bringing up these carts with the bodies on them. It was all our fellas. The part that just fascinated me was the fact that all these bodies piled up just like a haymow, and the blood was running off the side of the truck and dripping on the ground.

Private Gren Juniper, Royal Regiment of Canada

Then the battle was all over. I'm laying amongst a whole bunch of bodies. Then they started to take the prisoners up this ladder that was up against the wall. Up until this time, I didn't see any aircraft at all. Then they came, wave after wave after wave. Machine gunning. Our planes. After it was all over!

Then, of course, the Germans stopped helping the wounded. So they left us there all day and didn't start moving us until dusk.

Then finally some of these old guys, Germans, four of them, they put me on a stretcher and they lifted me up over the wall. And then they put me and another guy on a truck, tied us on there, and then they went like a son of a gun to try to get us into Dieppe hospital. But it was full. So they took us to the railway station and put us in a boxcar. And throughout the night, they took us to Rouen. The hospital was actually a monastery that had been turned into a hospital.

Oh, gosh, the place was full. I was in a sort of hammock affair, double. I was on the bottom and there was another fellow up on top. We were like that for a couple of weeks, and then finally they got rid of some of the wounded, and they moved us into a regular ward, and we were on regular beds then.

Doctor Heinkel was looking after us, and he was rough. He was a Prussian. And he had these fencing scars on his cheek. Thick lips and big chin, high forehead, receding hairline. He was ugly. But he was a great man. He performed an operation on me without an anaesthetic. All he did was pour some disinfectant on my foot, where he was going to make the cut. I think there was one of our guys holding my hands back of my head, and then there were two orderlies on my feet.

37

Corporal Al Comfort, Royal Hamilton Light Infantry

A piece of shrapnel passed through my left leg and entered the inside of my groin. The Germans put me on a table [in a hospital in Rouen] and three Canadians held my hands and feet. No anaesthetic was used. The doctor reached in with forceps and dragged the shrapnel out. And when I screamed, he said, "*Ruhe Mensch.*" Means "Quiet, man." Then he forced a large pair of forceps, like tin snips, through my leg from the back right through to the front and drew a gauze bandage through and cut both ends off. Then he wrapped my leg with paper bandage. Then he slapped me on the rear and said, "*Gut, gut.*"

We were in Rouen a few days. My wounds were septic by this time, and the infection soaked through my mattress and dripped on the floor. I remember holding the sheets down tight to keep the stench from choking me. Then we were put in a hospital train to go east into Germany, a place called Obermassfeld.

We expected German nurses or German orderlies to take us off the train. But they were all British fellas, Limeys. They had been captured in '40 with the BEF, and they were staffing a hospital. All British doctors, too.

That was the first time I got a proper dressing on my wounds. I laid in bed until almost Christmas. The wound on the inside of my leg, my groin, was even at that point [so large] my hand wouldn't cover it.

Red Cross parcels were there from Geneva, and with the supplement of German rations, the food was reasonably good. The first Sunday I was there, we had a roast. But it was horsemeat.

Captain Fred Woodcock, Royal Hamilton Light Infantry

At Rouen, they patched me up. Then I boarded a hospital train to Kloster Haina, where there was a lot of blind from Dunkirk and Greece and Crete. Going to the bathroom was agony. I finally let go, and I was lying in that canvas, stretcher-like bunk up there, and I was literally rolling in lovely warm water, you know. About ten days after I got hit, we got to the end of the line, which was Obermassfeld.

I was operated on by Colonel Tucker. He was an orthopaedic surgeon. Henderson was a brain specialist. Duffie was ear, nose, and throat. They operated on me that night, about ten or eleven o'clock. The next morning before seven o'clock, I was being carried out of there to be sent to Kloster Haina. The surgeons said, "He won't survive the journey. He won't live."

It was a lot later when one of them, I think it was Tucker, came through wanting to know where they'd buried me. They told him: "Buried? He's not buried. He's upstairs!"

Sapper Wally Hair, 2 Field Company, Royal Canadian Engineers

Then they marched us out of Dieppe. I happen to be trained in explosives, and our job was to blow up cranes around the Inner Basin in Dieppe Harbour. We were marched by these cranes. And they'd been sabotaged in 1940! They'd never been used since. So our intelligence wasn't too hot.

Major Allan Glenn, Calgary Tank Regiment

Before the raid, I was shown an aerial photograph. At the end of one of these streets on this new photograph, here is something. It actually looked like one of our metal granaries, you know, on a farm? So this was a great concern, what this new structure was. We were told it could be some big gun emplacement, so watch out.

So, anyway, after it was all over, I walked past it. It was a latrine! And it was riddled! I tell you, you couldn't put your hand on it where there wasn't a hole. I think everyone in the outfit had taken a shot at it. I even had to laugh then. I couldn't help it. That was their "secret weapon"!

Private Geoffrey Ellwood, Royal Canadian Corps of Signals

As we got to the other side of town, there was this white church over on the left side of the road. It was a formal wedding. And the bridal party came out of the church. And they were in tuxedos, tophats, long gowns, the whole thing. And they stood out there, and the women were all crying and

39

looking at us. This, right in the middle of all this fighting, you know.

Corporal Leo Lecky, Queen's Own Cameron Highlanders

They started to march us through the city. We got to the outskirts, and we come through one very small village. And mostly women were lining the streets as we marched by and some were coming out with pitchers of milk, and fruit, and they were being swatted aside by the German guards. This one woman had been very roughly pushed aside. She had a basketful of tomatoes. And then she got the idea — we didn't quite grasp it at first — she started calling us all names, dirty names, in French. "You swine Canadians!" And she was throwing these tomatoes at us. And the Jerry guards were laughing like hell. But our boys were catching the tomatoes! That dear old woman, she really used her noggin. And the guards laughing at us did not realize that actually we were getting the food that they were trying to stop.

Lieutenant Jack Dunlap, Calgary Tank Regiment

We were all marched out to a small town called Envermeu. We were taken from Envermeu to a camp at a place called Verneulles, which was northwest of Paris. It had been a transition compound, where they interrogated prisoners and segregated them. And you did all your filling out of the forms for notifying the Red Cross.

Private Geoffrey Ellwood, Royal Canadian Corps of Signals

The chaps that were taken away to be interrogated said the Germans were very, very nice to them. Take them into a room, sit them down at a table, give them a cigarette. Ask where you come from, your unit. Of course, we were told to give them our name, rank, and number, and no more. They'd tell you your commanding officer's name. They could even tell you who your sergeant-major was. Things like that. They knew so much about us.

Lieutenant Jack Dunlap, Calgary Tank Regiment

We were there almost a week. We were marched through

town to a railway siding and put on a train. The officers were segregated from the men for the journey into Germany.

Private Geoffrey Ellwood, Royal Canadian Corps of Signals

They put us on these little European boxcars. On the side of the boxcar, it had "Forty men or eight horses." Of course, to us, this seemed a little crude.

They just took us in bunches and put us in. Well, this little Scottish fellow and myself got stuck together, and they put us in a boxcar with thirty-eight Frenchmen, these French Canadians, FMRs. And I thought, "Holy smokes. I don't speak any French." The few words I had gathered in school didn't mean too much.

I come from London, Ontario, which is a WASP area. It was just a fantastic experience to get into this boxcar with all these Frenchmen. One of them would translate it in English to us, even if it was just a conversation between two of them. And there was one there who was always saying, "Speak English, speak English." I have never seen consideration like they gave us.

We stopped at one point. The Vichy French separated the French Canadians, called them off to one side. And each Frenchman was given a present from the French government. Canned food, bread, cake, this sort of thing. We assumed this was supposed to start dissension among us. I would say probably less than a third of our group were French Canadians. But the whole works, when they came back, they just pooled the whole thing and split it with everybody.

And I found this all the way through. Whenever things got difficult and tough, the Canadians would stick together.

Trooper Sid Hodgson, Calgary Tank Regiment

It was tough on those boxcars, it was really tough. There was no place to go to the bathroom — just a tub that was sloppin' over and stinkin' like hell. And sweat and dirt. And a dry loaf of bread. We each had a loaf of bread. And how the devil could you eat it? You didn't have enough water even to wash it down. I don't think I had half a dozen bites out of mine.

41

Corporal Leo Lecky, Queen's Own Cameron Highlanders

And finally we reached Lamsdorf, which was the railroad station about a mile or two from Stalag VIII B.

Stalag VIII B was where a lot of British prisoners of war were, from the BEF, the Dunkirk boys. And they gave us one wonderful welcome. When we got off the boxcars, we were in pretty bad shape. More or less staggering along. Until we saw the gates of the camp. And then one of our regimental sergeant-majors, I think it was RSM Beesley, shouted out, "Let's show these Limeys what Canadians are made of!" So, to a man, we marched into that camp, arms swinging. Well, you should have heard the shouts from the boys that were there. Shouting and hurraying and clapping, and cigarettes started flying at us.

Private Geoffrey Ellwood, Royal Canadian Corps of Signals

This was a very, very large camp, and it was a predominantly British. And [the British POWs] told us that you had to be registered, and when you gave your rank, name, and number, be sure that you're an NCO. Because as an NCO, corporal or above, by the Geneva Convention, you can't be made to work. If you're a private, they can make you go on work parties.

They marched us into this compound, and took us one at a time to a photographer. They hung this board around your neck, scribbled a number on it in chalk, and took your picture. And we all registered as corporals. Of course, we had no badges of rank. And the Germans made a few snide remarks about "How come all the NCOs lived and all the privates got killed?" There was one private, he registered as a sergeant-major! And it was a long time afterward before I found out he was really only a private.

We didn't know it at the time, but they submitted this registration to Geneva, back to the Canadian government for confirmation. And the Canadian government confirmed everything we put down.

Major Allan Glenn, Calgary Tank Regiment

[Oflag VII B] actually had been a permanent barracks for the

German army. Four or five two-storey concrete block buildings, regular barracks. And of course, there was a perimeter fence around it, with lots of barbed wire.

We were in there three, four days, and all these Limeys were put in with us. The Germans had broken up a camp north of us. Altogether, there was about twenty-five hundred officers in that camp. But these Brits, you know, [if] there's three of them, they'll organize something. They got that camp humming in no time. And it made it a lot easier for us. They told us how to make heaters to cook our food. We got clothing from the Red Cross because they had connections, we didn't.

Lieutenant Jack Dunlap, Calgary Tank Regiment

We were given our first letters to write home, and this was well into September. The big worry you had all through this time was your family. You knew you were all right, but your parents didn't. My wife didn't know, because the first message she got was that I was missing in action. It wasn't until the documentation goes through the Red Cross, and the Red Cross notifies the British, and the British notify the Canadians, and the Canadians send all the information home, and it took a while to get that through.

And we just settled into camp life.

(Settling into prison life would not be easy for the Dieppe veterans because they soon found themselves at the centre of an international controversy. The bodies of a few German prisoners were found on the beach at Dieppe following the raid; they had had their hands tied. The Germans also discovered a complete copy of the operational orders for the raid. They were enraged to find one clause requiring the raiders to tie the hands of prisoners wherever possible, supposedly to prevent them from destroying documents. In early September, the Germans announced they would take reprisals against the Dieppe Canadians for this violation of the Geneva Convention. They changed their minds when the British War Office issued a statement cancelling the tying order.

On October 4, British commandoes raided Sark in the Channel Islands. Here again, the hands of a few German prisoners were tied. This time the infuriated Germans would not be satisfied with rhetoric from the War Office.)

Trooper Jack Whitley, Stalag VIII B, Lamsdorf

We were called out of our compound one morning, marched into a vacant compound. And while we were being marched down there, they posted guards all around the perimeter of the camp, with machine guns and everything else. They had guards inside the camp, and we wondered what was going on. They called for the first twenty to go forward. And as soon as they said that, I think it ran through most people's mind — I know it did mine, 'cause I heard a lot say, "the dirty bastards"— they thought they were going to shoot the first twenty. I'm glad I wasn't in the first twenty!

Private Geoffrey Ellwood, Stalag VIII B, Lamsdorf

They took us one group at a time. Amongst ourselves, we said, "Well, let's show these sons of bitches how Canadians will die!" We've got our chests stuck out, and we marched right in.

They got us inside, and they made us line up. They'd taken the string off the Canadian Red Cross parcels, and one fellow had all these strings over his arm, and the other fellow was tying them up. The relief was so great, we started to laugh. They were giving what they thought was one of the greatest insults you could give to a soldier, by tying his hands. And we stood there laughing! But the relief was so great, because when we went in there, we were marching in to die.

Trooper Jack Whitley, Stalag VIII B, Lamsdorf

Well, the camp commander came down and read out a letter he had from Berlin saying that we would be tied up in retaliation for prisoners that we had tied up at Dieppe.[2]

Corporal Leo Lecky, Stalag VIII B, Lamsdorf

We tried to explain that we were just following orders. It was

44

purely an information raid, actually. And one of the objectives was to try and get as many German prisoners of war as we could. Now, being a commando raid, a lot different from an ordinary campaign, you can't expect any reinforcements. We could not afford to waste men for escorting prisoners of war back to the beach. So the army high command had issued us with these lengths of light cord, which we carried hooked on our belts. When we captured a prisoner, we tied his hands behind his back. That way, one man could march, well, a hundred or more. There was a few provosts back on the beach and they were to take charge. Now they were throwing these prisoners into the landing craft to be brought back to the mother ship and consequently back to England. Well, what was happening, our landing craft were being knocked out of the water like crazy. The boats were being sunk and the German soldiers were drowned. So we tried to explain that it was as much their fault as ours that these men got killed. But, no, that didn't go.

Trooper Forbes Morton, Stalag VIII B, Lamsdorf

About three o'clock the next morning, they woke us up and said that, through the generosity of the German people, they were going to untie our hands so we could sleep. So consequently we were tied up from eight in the morning 'til eight at night.

During the course of a month, a month and a half, our wrists got ulcerated with sores from the rope burns. I'm still bothered by poor circulation in my hands because of that.

Corporal Leo Lecky, Stalag VIII B, Lamsdorf

The most humiliating and embarrassing thing was, they left two of our medical orderlies per hut untied. And anytime we had to go to the bathroom, we had to ask them to take us. Now the embarrassing part is to ask another man to take down your trousers and to wipe your bottom. It was very embarrassing, although the boys that were detailed for this would say, "Don't worry about it, don't worry about it." But it is embarrassing.

We were that way approximately two months. And then

one day they came along and took them off. But then they snapped on handcuffs.

Well, the handcuffs were not bad, actually, we did not get that terrific tightness, and the sores around our arms had a chance to heal then. Not too long after, one of our ingenious boys discovered — in a Canadian Red Cross parcel, we had a can of New Brunswick sardines — the key that would open the sardines would open the handcuffs too! So what we used to do, we would post a guard at the front entrance and a guard at the rear entrance — we took turns — we'd take off the chains and wear them around our necks inside the huts.

Trooper Fred Tanner, Stalag VIII B, Lamsdorf

You'd pick the lock, put the cuffs in your pockets with the chaining across the front of you. So when you saw a German coming, you'd just slip your hands in your pockets, and it would look like you were still chained.

Sergeant Tommy Cunningham, Stalag VIII B, Lamsdorf

Toward the end of the chaining, everybody had their own tag on their handcuffs. Two German guards would bring down a big wooden box, and all the chains were laid in it, so the guys would just root through and pick out their chains and chain themselves up. This one day we had a new guard and, boy, was he a wiseguy, going right by the book. He was going to personally chain everybody up. So he'd chain one guy and away he'd go. They'd take off their chains and sneak them back into the box. He'd chain up fifty guys, and there'd still be the same fifty guys in line waiting to be chained up! And we got lots of time, we could have been there all bloody day. So he gave up. And that kid cried. He actually cried.

Corporal Leo Lecky, Stalag VIII B, Lamsdorf

One boy decided he was going to go sponge off his body in the ablution hut. And he took all his clothes off, and he was washing himself down, with his chains hanging on the side of the tap. A German officer and two guards walked through, and the only thing this boy could do was grab the cuffs and click, click, put them on. The German officer got about three steps past, then all of a sudden he stopped dead in his tracks, and he looked. Here is a naked chap with his handcuffs on! But he told them he had found a little piece of wire to get the cuffs off. I guess they believed it.

Trooper Forbes Morton, Stalag VIII B, Lamsdorf

And if you were caught without your chains, their favourite torture was to stand you to attention with your hands tied behind your back for four hours. Either up against a wall or the barbed wire. All depends on how mean they felt. I was caught a couple of times.

Lieutenant Jack Dunlap, Oflag VII B, Eichstätt

Over a period of time, the German surveillance lessened. They were getting fed up with it as well. One day they just didn't show up with the chains, they weren't brought into the camp at all. Then the barricades were taken down, and we were free to go any place in the camp.

Trooper Forbes Morton, Stalag VIII B, Lamsdorf

On October 8, '42, they tied our hands. This carried on till December 2, '42, when they chained us. And we were in chains from December until November 21, '43.

(Although the tying and chaining episode lasted thirteen months, it was more of an inconvenience than a hardship. Still, these conditions made it that much harder for the Dieppe Canadians to adjust to life behind barbed wire.)

Trooper Forbes Morton, Stalag VIII B, Lamsdorf

A daily ration, if we had to exist on German rations alone: in the morning, they'd give you a cup of ersatz coffee made out of burnt barley and chicory. Then about ten o'clock, they'd give you two or three small potatoes cooked with their jackets on. At noon you'd get a cup of turnip, mostly, and horsemeat soup, and they didn't care if the turnips were good or bad. Then about three o'clock, you'd get a loaf of bread for ten to twelve men. And then about three times a week, you'd get, oh, twenty-five men to a pound of margarine. And the odd day, maybe you'd get a spoonful of liverwurst or artificial jam. For suppertime, you'd get a cup of mint tea. Well, it wasn't bad for shavin' in, that was the only thing it was good for!

Sapper Wally Hair, Stalag VIII B, Lamsdorf

The huts were long, narrow. There'd be an "A" end and a "B" end, in between which there was a cooking room and a washroom. Washtroughs is what they were, with taps above. But nine times out of ten, there was no water. Your huts were made out of concrete. The floors were right on the ground, with no basement or anything, so they stayed pretty cool. We had two stoves in each hut, one at each end. They were an upright stove. They didn't throw much heat, really.

Corporal D.D. Johnstone, Stalag VIII B, Lamsdorf

The Geneva Convention said the prisoners had to get so much water per day, and so much light, electric lights. And the Germans were very kind about that. In the daylight, when we didn't need light, they turned the lights on. They stayed by the Geneva Convention. And then at night when everyone was sleeping, they turned the water on. When nobody could use it.

Major Allan Glenn, Oflag VII B, Eichstätt

One thing about most everybody in the camp, we'd shave about every other day. With German blades, that was kind of a torturous thing. And you kept your leather clean. A lot of fellows'd even get a shine on their boots — I don't know how they did it with that German polish they had. Mind you, as far as uniforms are concerned, it was all bits and pieces, unless there was a special parade. So we looked a pretty raggedy bunch, but personal cleanliness was a pretty high order.

Sapper Harold McConnell, Stalag VIII B, Lamsdorf

It taught us to look after our companions. We found there was a lot there that we could help. Even if it was counselling. I remember a young fella who stayed pretty close to me. He was about three years younger than I was, and he thought I was helping him quite a bit. You know, we talked a lot and we discussed different things about our families and stuff like that. But, really, he was helping me just as much as I was helping him.

It was a long struggle to get through. Thank goodness we only had two and a half years. I don't know how we'd've made it longer than that. Rations were poor. I think it was said that we got about four hundred calories a day.

I think religion was important. I think silently, quietly, they said a lot of prayers. I know I did. A lot of guys have told me they went to bed crying at night and saying prayers. The loneliness was terrible.

Lieutenant Marcel Lambert, Oflag VII B, Eichstätt

The first many months, I was drifting. I found it hard to adjust. That first winter was a tough, tough winter, morale-wise. War news was bad, God it was bad. Then came along '43. Then the Eastern Front: Stalingrad. Somewheres around the early part of January, the *Völkischer Beobachter* came out with a big black border: "The war for the Sixth Army has ended." The *VB* was a national newspaper that came into camp occasionally.

Then we noticed quite a difference in our treatment. Things such as paroled walks and visits to the cinema. You went out on walks during the afternoon or the morning.

Trooper Sam Dunn, Stalag IX C, Molsdorf

I don't think many of us ever thought we wouldn't end victorious, even at that time. But it was the time element. We knew that to beat Germany, there had to be a Second Front, had to be an invasion of some kind. And we didn't know how long it would take to build up a big enough force to be able to land on the coast of France. Because we were pretty sure, all of us, that the actual Second Front would start in the same area as where we landed. We thought we could be there five years. Could be ten years, or even fifteen. And that was what bothered me. Not the fact that we wouldn't get out, but when. You know, when they send you to jail, you even know that you're going to be there five years, or ten years. But we didn't know that. The uncertainty was the worst part. It was a real strain on you.

Sergeant Tommy Cunningham, Stalag VIII B, Lamsdorf

This one work party we were on — these were old and established, they'd been there for literally years — boy, could those guys screw the dog! It was unreal. It's harder not to work than to work, but they made a study of it. God, they could do less work in eight hours, they were past masters at the art. They have to go to the can. Tomorrow they're sick. They wouldn't do a thing. We got to be pretty good at it too. We didn't exactly bust our butts. See, the whole object of being a prisoner of war, as I see it, is, to the best of your ability, bug the Jerries!

Trooper Jack Whitley, Stalag II D, Stargard

A lot of people went out on the work parties just to escape. The work parties were also better as far as food goes. If you were gonna do labour along with the Germans, well, I guess they had to feed you a little bit more, and the rations were a little better. We still got Red Cross parcels out there too, off and on. The work parties also gave us a chance to steal food, too.

Private Bill Douglas, Stalag II D, Stargard

I went from VIII B to II D up at Stargard. And from there, I went on a work party on a farm. That was an experience too. There was about thirty of us, and we got out and mingled with the people. We used to go on parade every morning and we'd get certain jobs to do, like driving the horses or cutting hay or planting potatoes or hauling potatoes. All kinds of work. Carrying flour, whatever. Farm work. And it wasn't bad. It kept us in fair shape. But we didn't do the things we were supposed to do, most of the time. We were either slacking off or throwing something in the mix or some darn thing, just to keep them annoyed.

Out on the work party, we bought a German shepherd from a farmer. Four, five, six months old. Just a ball of fluff.

And one day, one of the fellas wasn't feeling too good and he figured he'd go on sick parade. So the guard come in and started to shake him up, and that little dog went right for his throat. The Germans took him away from us, and they killed him out in the field somewhere.

We could have got another one, but after that we said, "No, what's the use?"

Footnotes

1. HMS *Berkeley*.
2. British Prime Minister Churchill immediately responded to this action by announcing that German prisoners in Britain and Canada would be shackled. Churchill did so without consulting the Canadian government, which opposed the retaliatory move; the Canadians went along with Churchill's decision in the interests of Allied unity. German POWs in four camps in Canada were selected for shackling on October 10, 1942. In one camp, in Bowmanville, Ontario, the German prisoners staged a three-day riot to protest their treatment. To their credit, the Canadian authorities never seriously enforced the chaining procedure. The shackling order was eventually cancelled December 12, 1942.

III/The Bomber Offensive

The next large group of Canadians to be captured were part of
the strategic bomber offensive against Germany. This offensive started in March 1943, and it resulted in a dramatic
escalation of the war in Europe. The bomber offensive involved massive and continuous air raids carried out by the
Royal Air Force at night and by the U.S. Army Air Force by
day. The decision to intensify the air war was made by British
Prime Minister Churchill and American President Roosevelt
when they met in Casablanca in January 1943. The bomber
offensive had a twofold purpose: to cripple the enemy's
capacity to produce war material and to break civilian morale.

Of course, the bombing of German targets was nothing
new. It had been a more or less regular feature since 1940, but
the offensive launched in 1943 was different. For the first
time, air power was seen as an integral part of the ultimate
victory over Germany and incorporated into the Allied war
aims. There were other differences between this offensive
and the earlier air attacks. The 1943 raids were, with few
exceptions, unprecedented in scale, involving hundreds of
aircraft every time; production of new bombers was just now
reaching the point where the Allies could make good the
losses a campaign of this type entailed. They were also using
better planes, with the pre-war Wellington and Whitley having been largely replaced by the more modern "heavies," the
Halifax and the Lancaster. Before 1943, the technology and
methodology of night bombing had left much to be desired. A
1941 British survey found that bombing at night was very
much a hit-and-miss proposition — mostly miss. The survey

indicated that only one-third of crews were dropping their bombs within eight kilometres of their targets; only one crew in ten managed that feat in the heavily-defended Ruhr Valley, the industrial heart of Germany. As a result of these findings, bomber crews were reorganized for greater efficiency and a Pathfinder force was created to mark the bombers' routes and targets with flares. This was followed by technological advances in navigational aids, such as the Gee system, Oboe, and H2S.

Canadians made a major contribution to the bomber offensive against Germany. January 1, 1943, saw the formation of Six Group, with eleven RCAF bomber squadrons under Canadian command. Six Group was not autonomous; it operated as part of the Royal Air Force. And thousands of Canadians continued to fly with RAF squadrons, as they would throughout the war.

The first phase of the strategic bomber offensive lasted just over a year, from March 1943 until March 1944. At that point it was geared down, the Allies shifting the emphasis of their aerial operations to support the impending invasion of France. There was another reason for easing up: losses in aircraft and manpower were unacceptably high. In fact, casualties in this period were simply staggering. At one stage, only twelve per cent of aircrew could expect to complete the thirty missions that constituted a tour of operations. The ranks of the prisoners of war residing in Germany swelled accordingly. However, these POWs went into captivity with an advantage over their predecessors, one of attitude. Although the time factor was still in doubt, they knew the Allies would win the war.

Pilot Officer Harry Jay, 408 Squadron, RCAF

April 15, 1943. It was our first official raid. The raid was on Stuttgart. We were in a Halifax from which all of the guns had been taken. Some whiz kid in London decided that the Halifax would go a few knots an hour faster if it didn't have an upper turret and it didn't have guns in the front turret, so the only weapons on the plane were the ones I had in the rear turret. My skipper was Lee Usher, an American.

We were coming home over France. The mid-upper gunner, who'd spent the last several hours on his stomach looking through a blister in the belly of the aircraft because his turret had been removed, said suddenly, "Skipper, don't take any evasive action because there's another Halifax down below." Whereupon I depressed my guns and tried to look out of the back end of the turret. And all I could see was the twin fin and rudder of an Me 110 which was flying formation with us just down below! I reported this to the skipper and he tried to speed up a little bit so that I could get a shot at this aircraft.

I fired, and the tracers indicated I was missing. And suddenly he was right behind us, shooting. And the brightness of the flames from the guns after all this darkness just blinded me. I just kept firing into the middle of all this. I don't know that we ever did get him or not, but it seemed like we had because he went down. In any event, he'd hit us. He'd knocked out an engine. The skipper said, "I think we'd better put our 'chutes on."

We went on for half an hour when the guy looking through the blister in the belly said, "Here comes another one!" It suddenly came up and went at us from the back. And this time, he knocked out our plane. The skipper said we had to get out. In my panic, I jammed the 'chute on over my intercom cord, which was still plugged in, so if I'd jumped out, I would've left my head in the plane.

I calmed down at that point, took my 'chute off, took my helmet off, put my 'chute back on. And all this time, you could feel the aircraft going down. So I opened the doors, put my leg on the seat and proceeded to try to get out of the airplane. And I got out into the slipstream, but I couldn't throw myself because one foot wouldn't come, with those felt flying boots that we had at the time. So I went back in the plane and took both boots off. And I jumped out in my stocking feet.

And I was so relieved to be away from that feeling that any moment the plane was going to hit that I forgot for a second to do what I was supposed to do. I was just falling in the dark, a very great sense of peace and quiet. I had forgotten to pull the rip cord! So I pulled the rip cord. And the ground comes up pretty quickly! I rolled over and I was on the ground, unhurt.

But I knew instinctively where I was: in the middle of a German aerodrome, a night fighter aerodrome! I was way out on the tarmac of this thing. I ran across the tarmac to the nearest building. I stumbled around the edges of the building for a quarter of an hour, I suppose, and came around the end of one building and found myself only about sixty yards from the front entrance of the aerodrome, where the drop bar was.

And the guard had slung his weapon over this drop bar, pointing in my direction, and started screaming in German. If you know anything about Germans, you know how they can scream when they get excited. I didn't know what he was saying. I only knew that I was scared to death. So I yelled, "*Kamerad!*" I don't even know where that word came from, I must've seen a movie or something. I decided that he probably wanted me to come closer, so I walked over. A patrol showed up and I was taken into their custody.

[At Dulag Luft] we were met by a very pleasant guy speaking English. The door was opened for me, and I walked into a tiny little cubicle with a window which was all covered with wood. And the door was slammed. And I didn't know where I was, why I was there, or what was gonna happen. That was solitary confinement, and I think I was in there for seventeen days.

And every now and then, some phony Red Cross man would show up. Then, when we got over the period of not getting sucked in by the phony Red Cross, we'd be taken out of that building and across a little compound to another compound, where we were properly interrogated by pros. I think I was there three times in this period and never got past the name, rank, and number bit.

Until the last day. He was very serious in his demeanour. And he described to me how Lee Usher, the skipper I told you about, was in the hands of the Gestapo. And he went on to assure me that the Gestapo was much worse than I'd ever imagined. I'd never admitted that anybody was my skipper, but he just told me that Lee Usher'd been picked up in civilian clothes, and the Gestapo were treating him like a saboteur and not as a member of a bonafide military service.

And until they could establish that he was a member of such a service, he couldn't get Lee Usher into this relatively less mean system of being a prisoner of war. But he could get himself very much chewed up by the Gestapo.

So there I was, barely twenty-two, and the decision was mine. Was I going to do something to identify Lee Usher, or was I to go on talking about name, rank, and number? I thought about it for a minute, and then I said, "Well, may I talk with so-and-so and so-and-so," the flight engineer and the mid-upper gunner. They were in the same interrogation centre that I was, but we'd never given any indication that we belonged to the same crew. They were brought over. I explained to these other two young men what he'd said to me. I asked them what I should do, and they said, "Well, you're the officer, you decide." So I turned to the major and I said, "We really don't have much of an alternative, you know, Lee Usher's a friend of mine. So what do we have to do to prove who he is?"

So [he] started asking questions: What was your squadron? What was the squadron leader's name? Where were you raiding? Where was your station? And I told him all that. And then they got to the business of a black box, about which I knew bugger-all anyway — some sort of navigation device, very modern equipment. And I said, "We don't even know what you're talking about. And, in any event, whatever it is, it's got nothing to do with proving that Lee Usher is a member of the air force."

So he said, "That's fine. You'll be released now and leave your solitary confinement and go across the road to the holding camp, and then go on to a proper prisoner of war camp."

Well, I said that I'd like one favour. I said, "Lee Usher's a friend of mine, so I would like to wait in the holding camp until he shows up." And he said, "Fine, we can do that."

And, true to his promise, I stayed in that holding camp until Lee Usher showed. But the trouble was, he didn't show up for quite a while. So after about six days, and a couple or three drafts of prisoners had come in and been taken out, the camp administration — who had all volunteered to stay and administer that camp — had decided that I was some kind of

56

a phony. And everyone stopped speaking to me. And it was very unpleasant, and I went for several days in that limbo, with increasing suspicion building up.

One evening I was sitting up on a top bunk alone, and I heard somebody say, in the corridor, "Does anybody know Harry Jay?" And it was my skipper. And he had been in the hands of the Gestapo, in Paris — all that part was true.

So we then went out on the next draft and went to Stalag Luft III. It looked like a crazy place to me. It was all sand, and the roughly nine hundred prisoners in our compound were all more or less undressed and lying around in the sun. Those that couldn't stand the sun had made hats out of Red Cross boxes, cardboard.

That evening, I went into a room with my skipper. We were accepted very kindly by a room of Britishers. We were given spare toothbrushes, and whatever anybody had, they shared it. We settled down, and the first night, talked to people — very carefully, in the beginning, because they never knew whether a new prisoner was a plant. And in a very subtle way, we were being interrogated by everybody, to make sure that we weren't phony.

The next night I was invited to go down and have a cup of tea in another room. In that room — I don't know whether it happened to me or happened to somebody else and it was so real that I remember it as my experience — I had tea with a skull on the table. They pretended that the skull was a departed prisoner of war pal whose ration they were still drawing. So they kept his skull around, because they thought it was rather mean to be eating his ration without having him at the table! And I began to believe that everybody was slightly insane. But they weren't, of course.

Flight Sergeant Carl "Soggy" Norton, 408 Squadron, RCAF

It was the night of May 4, 1943. I was flying a Halifax. The target was Dortmund. We were on our way to the Ruhr, and I got shot down in Holland by a nightfighter. The pilot was killed, the engineer was killed, the mid-upper gunner was killed. The aircraft was spinning, and I had stupidly not put my seatbelt on, and I was up on the roof. It was my job to open the trap door. Anyway, the plane levelled out and I managed to jettison the trap door, and the three of us got out.

I came down in northern Holland, near Leeuwarden. There are almost no trees, the land has been reclaimed from the sea. So I spent the night wandering around. And they don't use fences in this part of Holland, they use ditches. And this horse kept following me. And it sounded like the whole German army was behind me. He'd whinny, and I'd throw a clump of earth at the son of a gun to chase him away. The next time I turned around, the goddam horse was behind me again. If you're frightened anyway, the last thing you need is this goddam big horse clumping behind you. [Finally] I jumped a ditch and got rid of him.

I was wandering around in red carpet slippers. I used to wear them under my flying boots. When I jumped, I lost one boot, so I threw the other one away. So I was wandering around in these slippers. Hell of a looking sight!

At daylight, I met a farmer. He turned me over to the milkman who picks up milk along the canal. So he's feeding me and giving me milk, and I'm giving him these Canadian cigarettes. Then he turned me over to this guy on a diesel-powered canal barge. He gave me some more milk — I had goddam milk coming outta my ears by that time — and he hid me under the tarpaulin that he covered the milkcans with. I really thought that I was with the Underground. Anyway, he took me down to a place where the canal and the railroad met, and there was a phone booth there. And he phoned. You know, I still thought I was on my way home.

So sure enough, along comes a big policeman, about six-foot-seven, in a black uniform. He put me in the car and drove me right downtown and turned me over to the Jerries. They put us on a train to Amsterdam, and we spent two nights in the Amsterdam prison. There was all kinds of names of different airmen who'd carved on the wall "Kilroy was here" bullshit.

Then they moved us from there to the interrogation camp at Frankfurt, Dulag Luft. I spent a couple of weeks in isolation while they tried to get whatever information they could. The sons of bitches told me more than I knew! This guy — I couldn't believe this — he said, "You're from 408 Squadron."

Of course, they find that out from your wrecked aircraft. He brings out a big book, *408 Squadron*. He's got goddam pictures of me playing football with Toronto and Ottawa, from the Canadian papers!

They had a goddam clipping service, and they clip everything and get it through a neutral country, anything to do with the services in Canada and the States. And they just accumulate this stuff. We had a service paper, *Wings Abroad*. It was supposed to be restricted. Shit, he had every goddam copy of it!

So from there, I went to Stalag Luft I, Barth. We stayed there that summer, and in the fall we moved out of there, up to Stalag Luft VI, up in East Prussia.

Warrant Officer Ross Elford, 35 Squadron, RAF

I was shot down on the night of May 12, 1943, on a raid to Duisburg in the Ruhr Valley. We hit the flak about ten minutes before the target and bailed out at about twenty thousand feet. Not too much time to think, just hit the silk and that was it.

It was at night, very dark, and when I collected myself after a parachute drop of about fifteen minutes in the dark, I knew I was in German territory. I tried to contact other members of the crew, but it didn't work. We had a signal system by whistle, but you're spread out on the ground — thirty seconds in the air, and you could be two or three miles apart.

After burying my 'chute and sort of collecting my wits, I decided that if I headed west I would be heading for Holland. I holed up in some bushes and was lucky as hell, because when an aircraft went down in Germany at that time in the war, they used to form a circle, come in toward [the middle] trying to pick the people up if they were close enough to the wreck. These people went down the road right by me. That's the first German, or Hun, that I saw, and I was somewhat terrified: big jackboots and rifles. Anyway, I stayed there all day, and then I travelled every night.

I don't know how many days went by before I realized that I was in Holland. I would hole up in barns or haylofts during the day, stealing food along the way. Once into Holland, they used to milk their cattle at night and leave it in little carts, and you'd get lots of milk. In the escape kits you had pills for purifying water [and] Dutch courage pills. If you popped a couple of those, they were uppers, and I guess you'd take on the whole German army!

I finally made contact with a farmer. This guy could speak English. He'd spent some time in Winnipeg, immigrated in the thirties, then went back. Anyway, he suggested I head for a small village. Cora, I think. There was supposed to be a church and monastery there, and this was known around the district as the Underground movement.

I didn't have too much success at Cora either, and I kept going, and about the end of May I came to this village of Diepenheim. I made contact with this fellow on the edge of the village and he must have had something to do with the Underground because everything was very secretive. They can't jeopardize the links of the Underground for just one person. And then they got word that the Gestapo were into the link, so I had to leave that.

But I got caught by the Gestapo. And that's when I thought I'd had my time, because the Gestapo considered me to be a spy, and they were ranting and raving. They were really fanatical Nazis. Shoved a big Luger in my stomach and were gonna pull the trigger because I couldn't identify myself. But eventually my story must have been believed.

With these Gestapo characters, I was shipped up to the Gestapo barracks in Amsterdam. Spent a couple of weeks there in solitary confinement. Darkness.

Eventually, from that Gestapo barracks, they took me by train down to Dulag Luft in Frankfurt. They knew I was from a Pathfinder squadron. We used to be the markers, mark the target. We had the H2S system on the aircraft at that time. It was a combination of television and radar. It would send you back a picture of the ground, and right through the clouds you could see the streets and the rivers. And we used to bomb like that, and they couldn't jam it. They were really wanting all the information they could get out of anybody off Pathfinders about this H2S system.

In Dulag Luft, the guy who did the screening on me used

to be an embassy man in Liverpool for twelve years. He almost had an English accent. He could speak better English than I could. I wouldn't give him any information, so he finally said to me, "Here, have a look at your squadron." Tossed this book on the desk, and it had our squadron crest on the front of it. I looked in the book and it had everybody's name and squadron leaders. He had our pilot's name, and our crew. Had aerial photographs of the squadron. I couldn't contribute much to their book. Their intelligence was fantastic. Hell, I'm supposed to be suffering through this bloody Gestapo bit where you don't say anything but your name, rank, and number. And here they had all the info anyway!

Flight Sergeant Bob Masters, 51 Squadron, RAF

It was Midsummer's Night, the shortest night of the year, 1943. The target was Krefeld. We got hit by flak and lost both port engines on our Halifax, so we had to bail out. I landed at a place called Mol, in Belgium. I stayed hidden all day. I cut my rank and all my badges off my uniform. And it was around six o'clock I decided I couldn't stand this anymore. I was holed up in a little clump of trees miles from nowhere.

So I got onto a little bit of a cobblestone road. And I came to a village pub with a whole bunch of bicycles parked outside, so I wandered in there. And I didn't fool anybody, not having any insignia. They all recognized me right away. Boy, women were swarming all over me and the guys were wringing my hand off my arm! Till one of them came to his senses and said, "We'd better get this guy out of here." They stuck me in the back garden between a row of peas, brought me a pint of beer and a piece of hard bread.

Anyhow, he came back in a few minutes, and he said, "Okay, we've got to flow away." I got on the back of his bicycle. I was put in touch with a family, I moved to about three or four families within a matter of three or four days. And then I stayed four days with a fellow in Mol proper. Then I went to Turnhout, which is north of Mol, and I stayed there until my identification was verified.

And as soon as I was verified, then I was supposed to be returned to England, and they had two or three groups that they used. And the first stop was Brussels.

And things were starting to come unstuck for these people. Jerry had sent through a handful of Gestapo agents, you know, fellas that had grown up in the States and passed without any trouble as American or Canadian airmen, or Englishmen, for that matter. I was on my way to Rochefort to be taken by a fishing boat out to a rendezvous with a submarine. And I was halfway down the line, I was in a town just before crossing into France, and the word came back to turn me around, that the group that had gone before me had all been gunned down. And of course that means that everybody that had anything to do with that had to disperse because their cover was completely ruined.

I guess I was in Liège when I was working for a fellow who ran a piston ring factory half a block from the Fabrique Nationale, a huge arms factory in Belgium. And I worked for him there for a time, ostensibly working in the factory. But what I was doing in fact was handling stores of food which was being sent to these various Underground groups. Then I got the job servicing handguns. You should have seen some of the weapons that came in. Some of the stuff went back to the Franco-Prussian War.

I didn't get too involved in the actual terrorist activities, although this was specifically a terrorist group. One thing we tried to do was divert the gassing vans that they used to use for the little kids. It was always a guessing game. There were several places where we knew they went, lime pits, and they turned the exhaust at the back of a closed van loaded with these little Jewish kids. We'd try to outguess them and ambush the truck. The only attempt that I was involved in, we missed entirely. Too bad for the kids.

This Underground group was made up of cells. The cells were made up of five people, with one cell leader who had contact with nine other cell leaders. I don't know how high this pyramid went, but it did embrace the whole of Belgium. If you were working with somebody, you never knew whether he's in the cell or if he's an independent. All I knew is that there was a top committee of five people, but we didn't even know what city they were in. There was an espionage group. There was a terrorist group, assassins and saboteurs. There was a group involved with repatriation of

Allied airmen. And all this was done under this one organization that I was with.

We had houses we'd go to from time to time when things got tough. They'd be empty houses, but if we could get to them and into them without being seen, we could hang up in there for maybe four or five days provided we never showed our heads above the window sills. And you want something boring, you lie on a mattress for four days.

I moved into a house with a widow. And when I was there, I met an Englishman who was from the same group that I had been with, that is, Four Group. He got shot down three months after I did. And an American. And the three of us stayed upstairs in Madame LeGrande's meatmarket.

[One] morning, the gal that worked in the meatmarket down below came running up the stairs. And the next thing you know, Madame LeGrande says, "Get out of here, everyone!" The Gestapo was banging on the front door.

Well, I dragged on a pair of pants. And there was a little balcony from the second-storey bedroom, and it looked over a courtyard. And the girl downstairs had a dog. And it was a question of going over there in my sock feet, over the balcony, and trying to hit a clean spot on the cement. I made it, but Harry didn't. He got out, but he didn't hit a clean piece of cement. We went out the back garden gate, we went through somebody's house. There was another "safe house" down the road a piece, and we got down in the coal cellar there. I guess we were in the cellar until midnight. We broke curfew that night and moved from there to another place, and the following day we went to the south end of town.

[After several close calls with the Gestapo] the Underground took us down to Paris. We were trying to get through to Switzerland. We got to Besançon. We had some contacts, but they all fell through. Across the river, we could see Switzerland. I guess we were walking about thirty-six hours. There was snow on the ground, it was cold. It's December 23.

And we got picked up. We ran into a motorcycle *Feldpolizei*. Wehrmacht. And they didn't buy our little story at all. So they threw us in a civvy slammer.

I had to tell them who I was. Now at this point, I had been on the loose for more than six months. But they didn't realize that. They thought I was from a crew that had been shot down just three days before.

And then from there I went to Dulag Luft. I was at Dulag Luft four or five days. And from there, I went to Stalag Luft VI in Heydekrug.

Flight Sergeant Bill Rowbotham, 434 Squadron, RCAF

I got shot down on November 18, 1943. It was our fifth trip from Yorkshire. Our target was Mannheim. We were on Halifaxes, and we flew around eighteen to twenty thousand feet. We were crossing the Ruhr Valley. There was a lot of flak and we got shot up. I think we lost a motor or two and there was a fire on the wings, so we bailed out. We all got out except the pilot.

It was fall weather, and it was kind of misty. I landed on the side of a hill not far from the River Rhine. After I buried my 'chute, I started walking. I hadn't got very far when I heard a couple of dogs barking. And then I could see a fence and then the outline of some buildings.

That's when the guys appeared, a couple of German Home Guard. They took me inside the house and shortly afterwards a car came along, picked me up, and took me to Cologne.

It wasn't very long before they took [me] to Frankfurt. That was their interrogation centre. This was solitary confinement, with cells maybe eight feet wide, nine feet long, eight feet tall, with a little gate in front. They used to turn the heat on and off, to get a response out of the prisoners, I guess. Freeze 'em for a while, then turn the heat on. You know, it just dazed you when they turned the heat on. You felt pretty weird, pretty faint sometimes.

Their main effort was to find out all about you, where you came from, where you were flying to, what bombs you were carrying, who your crew were, and this sort of thing. Of course, when you didn't tell them what they wanted, they'd rant and rave and insult you: we were murderers, we all came over from America as murderers and gangsters. You do get a little scared when a guy rants and raves the way this interrogator did. Then he orders you back to your cell, and they shut the heat off so you freeze, then they turn the heat up and you faint. After that, they drag you back. That lasted ten or twelve days.

Warrant Officer Keith Pettigrew, 77 Squadron, RAF

I was on my fifth trip, and we're on Berlin. January 28, 1944. We had some problems with the aircraft, and we arrived late over the target. Anyway, we went in and bombed the target. And we were about thirty miles, I'd guess, northeast of Berlin when we got hit. About four years ago I found out about a weapon the Germans had called *schräge Musik*, "slant music," and it was two upward-firing guns on a seventy-five-degree angle in a blister at the back of an Me 110. And then they'd line up underneath you and the pilot had a prismatic sight, and they could fire a blast at your wing, set the gas tanks on fire. At that time, we didn't know about *schräge Musik* but I really believe we did get that.

I landed in a field. And because of the fires in Berlin, it was like evening in the city; you could see. I twisted my leg pretty badly when I landed. I started walking north, with the idea to get to Rostock and then try to get onto a Swedish liner. And if I knew then what I know now, I'd have just sat down in the field and waited till morning. Because I spoke no German and didn't have a clue as to anything about evasion.

It started to get light, so I decided to look for a place to put down for the day. And I picked a drainage ditch, under a corduroy bridge that some farmer had built. I couldn't've picked a colder place in Germany! I was a little emotional and I didn't get much sleep that day.

I woke up about six-thirty, and I started going north again. To give myself something to walk on, I put my flying gauntlets on my feet. And I'd like to have seen some German the next day tracking these flying gauntlets! I'm sure the tracks looked like something from the Black Lagoon.

I walked till about nine that night, and my leg was pretty swollen up. And I finally came to a farmhouse, and I decided that was it. I went in and gave myself up. I had a three-day growth of beard, I'd cut myself under the eye when I bailed out, there was blood down my face. And the arms of my battledress jacket were torn open at the shoulders from the force of the parachute opening. I'd been laying in the bloody mud all day, and in the straw, and I had these gauntlets on my feet. My hair was all mussed up. This woman came to the window with a lamp — she slammed the window and screamed.

The next thing, there was a shotgun coming out the window, and her husband was behind it. I remember his asking me if I was English, I could understand that. And I said, "*Nein, nein,* Canadian." And I think he figured I was just a tourist or something. Anyway, they were very nice to me. They took me into the house, they offered me a little wizened apple which I didn't take. Then he gave me a pair of wooden clogs to walk in, and we walked over to a farmhouse nearby that had a phone. And they phoned the commandant of the military district, and he sent an *Unteroffizier* out to get me. And he took me to a jail at Templehof aerodrome. Put me in the same cell with my navigator, and right down the hall was the American, our bombardier.

Flying Officer John Achtim, 50 Squadron, RAF

We were shot down somewhere near Nancy. It was February 25, 1944.

I broke my foot when I hit the ground. And a day later, I think, I was crawling on my hands and knees and I was picked up by the French Underground. They took me into a farmhouse, where I stayed for approximately a week or two weeks. I had some medical attention there, too. There wasn't much they could do, just wrap up and bind up my foot.

Then we were taken by a series of couriers into the mountains near the Moselle, where I spent six weeks hiding in caves. There were about half a dozen of us. And then we were taken into Paris, France. Spent a week or so with members of the Underground there. Then we went by train to the foothills of the Pyrenees. From there, we marched through the snow trying to reach the Spanish border.

We were in civilian clothing, and the Underground had provided us with identity cards and some money. We reached a little place, a resort by the name of Luchon, right on the border between France and Spain. And as we were circumventing the village — the snow was quite deep, of course, and we weren't making very much progress — we were quite late in reaching our destination point, which was a cabin in the mountains. We were all dog tired and we flaked out about four o'clock that afternoon. We woke up to the sounds of gunfire and dogs. And we tried to race up the mountain, as it were, but we were too beat. So practically all of us were captured. I think there were thirty or thirty-five of us in my group.

The Germans managed to beat us up a bit. As I recall, they shot a few of the guides. Then they took us into Toulouse, and I spent about a month there in the prison.

Then I went to the Fresnes prison in Paris. They questioned me about the Underground, but the guides that we came in contact with, we didn't even know their names and we didn't inquire, in the event of this happening. Many times, they threatened to shoot me, and there was some rough stuff.

Eventually they believed me, and they moved us on to Dulag Luft in Frankfurt, and at that time I was recognized as a POW. So it was quite a relief once we were declared POWs.

IV/Escape From Italy

Italy's participation in the war was half-hearted at best. Benito Mussolini's bungled attempts to create a modern-day Roman Empire in North Africa dampened the ardour of the Italian people, especially after the colossal casualties suffered by Il Duce's legions in numerous defeats at the hands of the British in the North African desert. At no time was there any doubt about Italy's status as Germany's junior partner in the Axis Alliance.

As the war progressed, large numbers of Allied prisoners of war found their way into Italian prison camps. Most were captured, not by the Italians, but by the German Afrika Korps in the desert. The POWs were mostly British, Australians, New Zealanders, and Indians; there were also a few Canadians, most of them airmen. Although Italian prison camps were hardly pleasant, Allied officers were paid a small stipend with which to buy wine and various other items when they were available, and the POWs benefited from the generally slack attitude displayed by the Italians. Indeed, it seemed that the Italians were, if not awed, at least intimidated by their prisoners.

In 1943, with the final defeat of the Afrika Korps in May and the prospect of an invasion of Italy itself, morale among the Allied POWs in Italy rose steadily. The invasion took place in July, and in just over a month American, British and Canadian forces conquered Sicily. Then the Allies invaded the Italian mainland on September 3. On September 8, Italy surrendered.

Italy's decision to drop out of the war was hardly a surprise, especially to the Germans. Mussolini had resigned July 25 and was promptly arrested. Italy's new leader, Marshal Pietro Badoglio, declared martial law and quickly sought a peace agreement. Following the armistice announcement, the Germans reacted swiftly. On September 10 German troops occupied Rome and accepted the capitulation of Italian forces in northern Italy.

However, the Germans were not able to move fast enough to prevent mass breakouts from prison camps across Italy. Taking advantage of desultory Italian guards, thousands of Allied POWs seized the momentary lapse to head for the hills. With Germans hot on their heels, the POWs had two options open to them: they could try to work their way south to meet the advancing Allied armies, or they could hide in the mountains and await the arrival of the Allies. Most were recaptured by the Germans and shipped to prison camps in Germany.

Flight Sergeant Bill Oxendale, P.G. 59, Sevigliano

(Oxendale, as a member of Ferry Command, was flying a Wellington bomber from England to the Middle East when he was shot down February 25, 1942.)

We knew that the landings had taken place in Italy. We knew it was just a question of time. And then one afternoon the prisoners who had collected around the administration office started running down the camp road, yelling and screaming. And that was when Italy had capitulated.

Everyone was ecstatic. But some of us knew that the war wasn't going to be over, that the Germans would probably take over. And then we did learn that the Germans were coming, about twenty miles down the road from Ascoli, to take over our prison camp. Well, by this time the guards were terrified, too. They'd heard that the German officers were shooting the Italians on sight because of the double cross. They began deserting from their posts. And those that weren't deserting were coming on guard duty with a rifle in one hand and a suitcase in the other!

We were told that there might be a chance of release that night, if the Germans got too close. And it was kind of a mass break. But there was a lot of confusion because some of the guards were firing warning shots in the air. It was a bright moonlit night, and I remember when the mass break occurred, I could see all these streams of POWs in different groups making their way over the hills and generally in a southern direction.

I was in a group of twelve, with a British army sergeant-major. That first night we ended up in a farmer's house. And we just sat and stared at each other and grinned and laughed. What an exquisite feeling freedom was!

At dawn we heard the German military columns in the valley below coming in to take over our camp. So we stayed in a village near San Giovanni, probably about ten miles from the camp, for a week.

I decided to move south. I wanted to get as close to the Eighth Army as I could. We were saying our goodbyes all around when a woman came running down, screaming, "Tedeske! Tedeske!" which means German. And then shots started ringing out. And there were hundreds of prisoners of war in this ravine near San Giovanni, and the Germans had sent down a patrol to round up as many as they could. Just prior to this, the British sergeant-major was trying to talk me into staying, telling me how his sciatica was bothering him and he couldn't walk too well. Then the shots rang out and there was a stampede down the bottom of the ravine. Well, somebody shot by me in almost a blur, showing a pair of heels like you wouldn't believe. It was the sergeant-major! Not a trace of sciatica.

The group that had been in the ravine, they had all scattered. I chummed up with three others and we started moving in towards the mountains. We worked our way down to Ascoli and things were getting too dangerous. The Germans were on patrol all the time. So we split up our group of four. Two of them went on ahead of us, and we watched them walk way down in the valley and disappear around a corner in the road. And that's the last we saw of them because they walked right into a German patrol on the highway and were picked up and sent to Germany. We started to follow them, and an Italian woman told us all about it.

So we did thirty or forty miles. We were stumbling up streams, and I remember thinking, "This can't be happening to me!" I mean, I'd read innumerable stories where people run upstream just to throw the dogs off the scent. And here I was, doing it. I thought it was some kind of horror movie.

This fellow I was with was a British staff sergeant by the name of Claude Mee. We kept moving south, and that morning we could see transport on the road, and we knew we were awfully close to the Germans. But we were high up on this mountain path. We walked around this corner and walked right into the Germans, an emplacement for a 105-millimetre gun.

Of course, we were absolutely devastated, you know. Captured, after being free for two months. We were just so bloody depressed. They put us in what had been a monastery and we spent the day there. And then in the morning, they loaded us on open transport and we were part of a German convoy moving to Chieti. Chieti was a former British officers' camp.

We got there in the morning, and within hours I knew about an escape tunnel. A couple of fellas knew of this tunnel that these British army officers had built prior to the Italian capitulation and the Germans hadn't found the tunnel when they took over the camp. And they said there would be an escape attempt that night. So we met at the cookhouse — four of us — and a fellow showed us where the tunnel entrance was, behind the stove. The tunnel went down under the wall in the shape of a U, so that the lower part was filled with water. We had quite a time gaining a foothold and you could feel the ice particles on the water; this was late November. So we came out under the wall where a hole had been cut in the barbed wire.

It was a bright, moonlit night. So the four of us inched our way out across this cold, frosty grass, fifty yards or so, to get to tree cover. We decided to split up and keep to the low ground. And we realized that was the German strategy, always to hold the high ground when you get near the front lines. And we worked our way south again.

And finally, we got very close to the Sangro River. We stayed in the area for a couple of weeks. The activity on the front suddenly heated up, and we could see the American bombers every day bombing the German positions.

The next morning, the big attack came. So we decided to make a break for it. We were afraid of being caught by the Germans at any minute. So we just started out, and this Italian boy was shouting at us, "Come with me, come with me, British soldiers!" We didn't really believe him, but we went with him anyway. And in this house, if you please, were the advance scouts for the Second New Zealand Division.

We stayed with this New Zealand advance post during the day, and then we left that night on a jeep headed farther back. This was about four o'clock in the afternoon, and we understood later that we had no sooner left than the Germans had counterattacked and captured the advance post.

We hitchhiked to Bari, and we got on these troopships. We stopped off in a couple of places in Sicily, then across to Bizerte in North Africa. There was about a hundred of us, escapees, and we were headed for Algiers. And we left Algiers on the *Louis Pasteur*, the day after New Year's, 1944. And we landed in Greenock, in Scotland. Then they sent me down to Warrington, which was the Canadian "repat" station. And then I was interrogated in London for three or four days. We left England on my birthday, January 27, for Canada.

Pilot Officer Ed Patrick, P.G. 78, Sulmona

(Patrick was shot down in the North African desert October 19, 1942.)

We had heard, of course, that Italy had capitulated. Instructions from England were that all prisoners of war were to remain in the camps. I understand that some camps did just that, but they had forgotten there was a third party involved: the Germans. And the Germans were south of us. Our Senior British Officer disobeyed the instruction, thank God.

We managed to get up to the top of a hill, and we had made camp and found a water well. The Germans did come right up among us and captured a number of the boys. I hid under leaves and whatnot and you could see them as plain as day. But I wasn't recaptured. So anyway, when things died down a bit and the Germans moved away, there were six of us

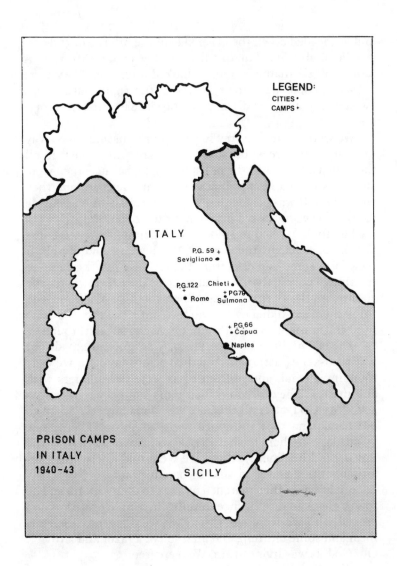

LEGEND:
CITIES •
CAMPS +

ITALY

P.G. 59 +
Sevigliano •

P.G.122 +   Chieti •
    • Rome   + PG79
         Sulmona

    + P.G.66
    • Capua

   ▪ Naples

PRISON CAMPS
IN ITALY
1940-43

SICILY

and we headed down the other side of the hill the next day.

We finally ended up in a little village of San Vittorino. A family by the name of Orsini looked after me. They were peasant people with their hearts in the right place. I had twisted my ankle and I had to stay in San Vittorino for a week.

We were warned to stay in the mountains and keep away from any large areas, because there were still Fascisti in all these areas. Stay with the peasant people, because they were anti-Mussolini and anti-Tedeske, or anti-German, and they would help.It was posted that if they were caught harbouring us, they'd be shot; we'd just go back to prison camp.

Finally I just had to go on. By this time, there were just two of us, a chap by the name of Middlemass[1] and myself. It took forty some-odd days from the time we left the camp to the time we were free. We had to cross over three rivers and go through the German lines. When you hear of a front, you think there's a soldier every two feet, but it isn't so. It's quite fluid and at night, when it's quiet, you can sneak through.

The last night, when everything was quiet, we made our way across the [last] river. And then before daylight, we were rounding a bend, and in front of us were two soldiers with automatics. They lifted up their guns and I thought to myself, "My God, after all this, are we gonna buy it?" So up go our hands and they motioned us to come on. Then I saw "Canada" on their flashes. They were two scouts for the Royal 22nd Regiment, whom we were told afterwards usually shoot first and then talk to you afterwards.

But anyway, they marched us back to their captain and he took us back to intelligence. Intelligence interrogated us and proved who we were. And then we were given a gorgeous meal and some clothing and an issue of a razor and a towel. Oh, God, it was living again! We were free.

Captain Henry "Barney" Byrnes, P.G. 122, Rome

(Byrnes was captured in Sicily July 24, 1943.)

This was a small interrogation camp just a mile or so north of Rome. There was only about three of us there at the time when I got there. Then we were joined by a British Seaforth

74

major. He had just spent three weeks loose in the hills, with a cast on his leg.

I think it was September 22, they were going to move us north. So they loaded us in a truck, under guard — the major, a sub-lieutenant, and myself — and moved us down to the station. But by this time, Italy had been knocked out of the war.

Well, the train didn't run and we were brought back to the camp. And the next day, the camp commandant said he was going to march us to the concentration point where we'd be shifted north.

So we were going down the road, and we passed a gate leading into a field. We broke off and started to go across the field. The guard behind me threw up his rifle, and I said, "Put down your goddam rifle." And he did! So we kept going, our idea being to circle around Rome, and we were sure we could cut through the lines and get to our own people.

We went through a small village. And in every village in Italy, there's always some guy called "Joe" who lived in Chicago or Toronto or somewhere like that, even Calgary. So Joe put us in the picture. He told us the Germans were all around and the best thing we could do was go into the Vatican. So we figured, okay, we'll go to the Vatican and stay in there for just a few days until Rome falls.

Finally a doctor came along in a small car, a little Fiat. He said, "What I'll do, I'll take you down to the Vatican and you can knock at the door and ask for sanctuary." So, okay, we got in. The major, his leg was still in a cast and he couldn't bend it, so it was sticking out the window.

So we tootled on down to the Vatican. And when we got there, the Santa Maria Gate was open so the doctor just whipped us inside quickly. And the secretary to the British Legation and the butler to the Ambassador both just happened to be down there at the time. So when the guard tried to toss us out, the secretary and the butler insisted that we had sanctuary.

They locked us up for about a month in the gendarmery barracks. We had good food, wine, and the British Embassy sent us down reading material. Then they gradually gave us more freedom, and they finally gave us the run of the whole

Vatican area. Except for the afternoons, when we had to clear the garden because His Holiness was out meditating and he wasn't supposed to see any of us rough characters.

So we were in the Vatican for a good nine months until Rome fell. Once I had a bit of freedom to go up to the [British] Legation, I became involved in the Rome Escape Line. The British Minister to the Holy See, Sir D'Arcy Osborne, and his most amazing butler, John May, were starting to get names of people who had got out of camps and were living somewhere around Rome. We were starting to support these characters.

First of all, we had contact with the Swiss who were running the Red Cross. We made arrangements for Red Cross parcels to be broken apart, the labels pulled off the tin cans so they could not be identified as Red Cross, and sent out with runners to these various people. We collected clothing and sent that out. And then we were able to raise money. Some of us wrote cheques on pieces of paper and the Italians took them, because they knew who was going to win the war. And we got a very good rate of exchange. We even raised loans from private Roman citizens and with that, of course, could buy supplies. Once we got the thing going, we were able to get money from the British Foreign Office.

The thing grew and grew, and more started coming into Rome. At one time, we had some three hundred living in Rome and about three thousand within fifty miles of Rome. And they were maintained by, principally, the Italians themselves, the country people.

Once Rome fell, strictly speaking, we should have been kept in the Vatican until the end of the war. But they just opened the gates and out we went. It's quite a sensation, sticking your foot out for the first time.

But we immediately started work on cleaning up the mess. We had, by this time, quite a military staff, all evaders. And one in particular, a British artillery major, was living under cover in the British Legation inside the Vatican, unknown to the Vatican authorities. And he was the military head of the organization. That was Sam Derry. Both he and the British minister felt that something should be done for the Italians who'd helped us. Some of them had suffered privation, and some, their families had been shot, their homes destroyed. So we were therefore requested to set up a thing called the Allied Screening Commission. And we had to seek out everybody who had helped the evaders. What we wanted to do was to repay them for the monies that they put out, for the losses they'd suffered. Some of it was in money, some of it was in kind. For example, a boys' school run by one of the Roman Catholic orders didn't want any money at all for the help they'd given to six or seven of our evaders. But they wanted a set of football gear, uniforms and several footballs. Everybody who helped also got a testimonial signed by the theatre commander, General Alexander.

Some ninety thousand cases were investigated by the Allied Screening Commission. It was headed, first of all, by Sam Derry. And he was then moved and promoted. And I was made CO of this organization. I was there, oh, for about a year and a half, working on this clean-up job. But by this time, the war was long over and I went home.

Footnotes

1. Flight Lieutenant Gilbert "Mickey" Middlemass, of Wainwright, Alberta. Middlemass was captured in rather a bizarre fashion. His aircraft was the Pathfinder for a bombing raid on Turin, in northern Italy, on the night of November 17, 1942. The plane dropped its flares to mark the target for the bombers following, but one flare lodged in the bomb bay. It appeared as though the aircraft was on fire, so the pilot gave the order to bail out. After the rest of the crew had done so, the pilot prepared to jump. But by that time, the flare had burned itself out. So the pilot returned to the cockpit and flew back to England, leaving his crew, including "Mickey" Middlemass, PWs in Italy!

V/The Kriegies

They called themselves Kriegies, from the German word for prisoners of war, *Kriegsgefangenen*. They lived in a barbed wire world, but since Germany generally kept within the bounds of the Geneva Convention, all things considered, the Kriegies were able to enjoy a reasonable lifestyle. Food was their foremost concern, but as long as Red Cross parcels arrived on a regular basis, along with mail from home, life in the prison camps was bearable. Nevertheless, they were prisoners; their world ended at the barbed wire fences surrounding the camps. Some Kriegies could not cope with that reality and committed suicide. Death was a constant companion; more than a few Kriegies were shot by their guards.

This was the world of the Kriegies: sometimes funny, sometimes sad, anything but ordinary.

Flight Sergeant Clem Hawkins, Stalag Luft VI, Heydekrug

My biggest concern was the constant hunger. You'd just nicely get started to eat, then you'd have to quit. You were hungry all the time, all the time. I suppose after the months went by your stomach shrunk up a little and you didn't require so much food perhaps. One of the main things that was talked about was: "When I get out of here, boy, what a feed I'm gonna have."

Flying Officer Pappy Plant, Stalag Luft I, Barth

According to the Geneva Convention, prisoners of war are supposed to be fed the rations of the garrison troops in that area. The Germans had a very complicated rationing system.

Their frontline troops got the best rations, and people in heavy industry got a higher ration scale. Clerical people would be entitled to less, and right down at the bottom of the scale were the old folks and the prisoners of war. The German mind was very methodical. They would feed the people that were the most important.

Flying Officer Arthur Low, Stalag Luft I, Barth

One of the first things I saw when I got into the camp was a cat hide hanging on the fence. Somebody'd made stew out of the cat. We were on as low as five hundred calories a day. They kept cutting the rations. Well, I went down to 120 pounds, from 170. And I was anaemic. To the point where, if I was sitting down and I stood up, I'd flake out. You stood up very slowly. If you were lying down, you sat up slowly.

Pilot Officer Don MacDonald, Stalag Luft III, Sagan

The food was the goddammedest garbage you ever saw in your life. We'd get up in the morning, and there'd be this ersatz coffee that was made out of God-knows-what, acorns and whatever else. Foul-tasting stuff. A lot of the boys used it for shaving in. Then at noon we'd get a bowl of barley soup — that was mostly liquid, there was damn little barley in it — or a so-called meat soup that had a few chunks of fat with pig's ears sticking out of it. And then sometimes we might get two, three potatoes that had been dug out of the ground, thrown in a bin, pitchforked into a big vat, boiled the hell out of — mud and all. It was a pretty grey-looking mess. You might get a dill pickle, or a combination of any of these things. And, sometimes, a pickled herring. A prize was one that you got with a roe in it.

And then there was the fishcheese. It was, without a doubt, the foulest-smelling thing anybody ever had. Outside of the dogfish. The dogfish was a fish that was caught in the Baltic. It smelled, and tasted, just like a ripe, wet collie. You took it back to your room — if you took it at all — and you'd boil the hell out of it and squeeze it in a rag and get some of the crap out of it. And eventually you'd dry it and then you could eat it. It had bones in it like — you could almost play a tune on them, they were so thick.

And fishcheese was a good companion to it. We had latrines that smelled better than that damn cheese. If we couldn't find somebody that wanted them, we'd bury them, because you couldn't leave them lying around — they'd stink you right out.

Corporal Earl Summerfield, Stalag VIII B, Lamsdorf

There were more fights about the bread ration. You get that black army bread, and they'd split it into five. That was for ten men. Well, naturally, the loaf slopes a bit at each end, and there's burnt pieces on it, and it's a year and half old, and it was harder'n hell. They wouldn't give us a [proper] knife. We only had one of those table knives. You'd take turns — today I pick first, tomorrow you pick first. And you'd see a guy looking at the bread, looking at the thickness of it and the crumbs laying beside it — 'cause they belonged to you too.

You got turnips every day. Turnip soup with horse heads — you got ears, you got teeth, you got the eyes. And you only got one tinful of it.

Then the Red Cross comes along and says, "They can't do that to you guys." So they told the Germans they had to give us cereal once a week. So they gave us "bedboard soup," we called it. It was like ground up wood chips. That was so bad we complained about it. So what did they do? They give us all the broken bread rations, and boiled it in sugar and water. You can imagine that sour German bread being boiled in water with a little bit of sugar. You couldn't eat it.

So we were waiting for the Red Cross guy to come back so we could kill him!

Sapper Wally Hair, Stalag VIII B, Lamsdorf

In the camps, you "mucked in" together. Maybe two, three, four, or five men would muck in together. We always felt that four muckers was the best. This way, you spun your food out.

Flying Officer Pappy Plant, Stalag Luft I, Barth

Inside the camp there was a kitchen of sorts. The Germans seemed to put everything in a bloody great boiler, soup by the gallon. Everything was in liquid form, it seemed. So we said, "Look, why don't you let us have the rations dry?" And this is what they did. They issued us the spuds and even the meat. So we decided to take the uncooked meat ration for the whole camp and give it to one hut, and the huts in turn would divide it again, so that when you got a meat ration, you got a decent chunk of meat, and then you forgot about it for a couple of months, until it was your turn again.

We found that by getting the German rations dry, and supplementing them with the Red Cross parcels, it wasn't too bad. What we did in our room, we pooled everything. We used to take turns cooking or looking after the food. You could maybe make one parcel feed three people with a little judicious juggling. Mind you, everything was rationed. You never put anything on the table such as a pot of jam. We tried that, but we found some guy would always take more than his share. When you're on tight rations, tempers do tend to get a little frayed. So the best way was, you'd have one guy do the spreading. If it was bread, he'd put the margarine on, he'd put the jam on.

One fellow was a dietician or a nutrition expert, and he cheered us by saying, "Well, if it comes to the German rations and you don't do a damn thing except lay in your bunks, you'll die, because there's not enough there to keep you going."

When the Red Cross parcels were coming in, morale was good, and you could see the whole tempo of the camp would change. There was more get-up-and-go. When the parcels were held up or they weren't coming in, the tempo slowed down. The Red Cross did try to provide one parcel per man per week, and it was quite a good collection. The idea of the Red Cross parcel was not to supply the main diet, it was supposed to be a supplement. But the Germans, of course, thought this was great, because it relieved them of having to provide the main ration.

Pilot Officer Don MacDonald, Stalag Luft III, Sagan

Once the Red Cross parcels started coming in, we were able to make up our own recipes. One was "prune glop." We used

81

to take these prunes, and we'd seed them, mash the prunes all to hell, boil them up until they were just like mush, then throw chocolate into it, and a little bit of sugar. We'd spoon this stuff out and when it hit the plate, "glop," that's exactly what it sounded like. That's not far off what it tasted like too! But we thought it was pretty good.

Tony Pengelly made this goddam Christmas pudding. This pudding weighed, oh, hell, three times the weight of a shot put. He made it out of mostly German bread. Tony was a damn good cook, actually, and he made this sauce to go with it. You'd eat a bowlful of that and, my God, you'd swear the thing had formed into a ball bearing down in your stomach. But it was tasty.

Lance-Corporal Don Craigie, Stalag VIII B, Lamsdorf

Everybody lost weight. I lost about thirty-five pounds over the period of time I spent in there. Thank goodness we used to get Red Cross parcels.

Sergeant George "Hayden" Auld, Stalag IV B, Mühlberg

Somebody should have had a medal of valour or honour for whoever designed the Canadian Red Cross parcel. I have never, never heard one criticism of it. The Canadian Red Cross parcel was so well-balanced and well thought-out. I don't know how you could have improved it.

You could make that parcel last for a week. When we got our first ones, I'm sure I could've sat right down and eaten the whole thing in one meal. And a lot of fellas did that. But you learned how to make a can of salmon go four meals. You could make a can of [luncheon meat] go four or five meals. Those big biscuits they put in them, you made pancakes out of them. I can think of a dozen different ways you could work those biscuits, they were wonderful things.

Sergeant Bert Gnam, Stalag IV B, Mühlberg

It was fantastic what the Red Cross got to us. If it hadn't been for them, I wouldn't be here today. We would have died of starvation, sooner or later. The British Red Cross parcels weren't near as good as ours; they had margarine in them. It would take two British Red Cross parcels to swap for a Canadian Red Cross parcel.[1]

Jerry didn't stick with the Geneva Convention by any stretch of the imagination. But in the end, he didn't have much either. I don't think his men were eating as well as we were with the Red Cross parcels.

Lieutenant Jack Dunlap, Oflag VII B, Eichstätt

In the fall of 1942, we had bulk fruits sent to us from the British citizens of Argentina. Raisins, peaches, prunes, and stuff like that, shipped in big wooden boxes. A lot of it was saved for escapers.

The Canadian [Red Cross] parcels were liked better than the British because of the meat content — real bully beef. And we had a pound of butter, which the British didn't have. But the British had a Christmas parcel that was real lovely. It had plum pudding in it. And you had condensed milk. As time went on, you got very hungry for sweets. The mess I was in, everybody saved condensed milk, and each of us had a can at Christmas. The first Christmas, we got sick because the condensed milk was too rich for us.

Flight Sergeant Doug Hawkes, Stalag IV B, Mühlberg

We used to heat our food on blowers. Blowers were little things you made: a fan, with a little shaft leading into a firebox, which we filled with clay. It would finally get like brick, and you'd put little bits of coal and chips of wood, and you'd get a very hot fire.

Pilot Officer Alden Magnus, Stalag VIII B, Lamsdorf

All we had issued was a bowl. Some of them, I think, had been to the Russian Front and back again two or three times, because they were the filthiest-looking things you ever saw. They were an aluminum pot about five inches in diameter and about four inches deep. That was your soup bowl, your tea pot — it had to serve as everything. But we made our own utensils out of butter cans or soup cans, whatever came in your Red Cross parcels. The handles were riveted on with aluminum wire we stole off the fence between the compounds.

When I was cutting the piece of metal to make the handle, a sliver of tin went in my eye. After I got back, cataracts formed, and I lost the sight of the eye. So I've got that to thank the Germans for.

Sergeant Bob Alldrick, Stalag Luft VI, Heydekrug

I only know for sure there was one case of theft. One case. And it was food. This one person who was doing the thieving had been guilty of raiding the lockers of seventy-five or eighty guys in this room, at night time. The strange thing is that there were about ten Canadians in this room, and none of the Canadians' food was ever touched. Now, that either meant that the guilty person was a Canadian, or for some reason he was being very selective.

So one Canadian issued a challenge in no uncertain terms: "That miserable so-and-so wouldn't dare touch my food." And he laid it on very loud and clear, to make sure everyone that was bunked in that room understood the situation.

Well, very shortly, one night, it happened. My friend got up the next morning and found that his locker had been raided, and he was mad! He put a guy on guard at that door and a guy on guard at that door, and said nobody was going out of that room until he found out who it was. And he started searching everybody's bunks and all their kit. And after he'd gone to everybody's belongings and searched them very carefully, he came back to one specific place — he'd already discovered it before — and he opened up the blankets, and there was bread and cheese and I don't know what all.

My friend Bill exacted his own punishment. He collected all of this fellow's belongings and threw them out into the compound. And then he frogmarched the guy out to the latrine, ripped off the covers, and threw him in. Head first. And then he got a pole and he pushed him down under, until he was good and soaked.

That was the only case of thieving I ever heard of. Now

you take a bunch of guys from all over the world and put them in a camp like that, that's something.

Private Bill Larin, Stalag VIII B, Lamsdorf

We were allowed to write, I think, two letters and four postcards a month. *Kriegsgefangenpost*, prisoner of war mail. The cards were sent through the Red Cross.

Lance-Corporal Don Craigie, Stalag VIII B, Lamsdorf

We used to get mail every four months, five months. We had a little type of postcard-letter. It opened up, so you actually had two postcards, and you could write in there. There was a lot of the fellows put stuff in there that the Germans would censor, black it right out. We were always happy when a mail day came. Particularly in our regiment, there were so many boys that were from the same general farming area. They passed word on what was happening in their part of the country. The Calgary Tanks, one squadron came from Stettler. "C" Squadron, the one I was in, most of them were from Red Deer and surrounding area. "A" Squadron was from Olds and Didsbury, and "Headquarters" was from Calgary. So it was good to hear how everyone was doing.

Flight Lieutenant Anthony Pengelly, Stalag Luft III, Sagan

And all the letters were censored, by the British government first, to stop the people in England or wherever from sending information to Germany; and then the German government, to prevent you from getting information they thought might be useful to you. So sometimes a letter would come looking like a paper doll, all cut out, you know, with just "ands" and "thes" left.

Chief Petty Officer Hec Cooper, Marlag und Milag Nord, Westertimke-Tarmstedt

Mail was scarce. I can remember my wife writing me, and she said she got a very nice letter from me. It said "Dear Una" at the top, and it was all cut out in the centre, and it was my name signed at the bottom.

Pilot Officer Harry Jay, Stalag Luft III, Sagan

We had what you would call a message board and a lot of people would put their letters, especially the Dear John letters, on the board. And you'd be surprised how many prisoners of war got Dear John letters.

This was to some poor British kid who was about nineteen when he was shot down: "Dear So-and-so: I've met this fabulous American soldier. I think he's wonderful and he's going to take me back to his ranch in Texas. Anyway, I'd rather marry a 1943 hero than a 1941 coward."

There was one fella in the camp, and his father was a very old British navy type. And when his son was shot down, his father — from out in the Far East, on whatever ship he was on — wrote him a letter disowning him for being a prisoner. And the funny thing was, his ship was sunk and he was taken prisoner very shortly after that. So his son spent a great deal of time in the prison camp gloating over this.

Flying Officer Pappy Plant, Stalag Luft I, Barth

There were means of writing coded letters back to England. The code was a fairly straight-forward one. People were picked at random by the RAF on the off-chance that they may become prisoners of war. Those who became prisoners were able to use this code, and it was surprising the amount of information that was passed back, and likewise came into the camp.

One of the bits that went back was in July 1940, when we were being moved from one camp to another. We were on a German train, and at one station, here were Germans in tropical kit. Fighting in the desert had started — we were fighting the Italians — but obviously the Germans were sending over observers, which would have been the forerunner of Rommel's Afrika Korps. Somebody passed this back to Air Ministry. This was the sort of thing that went through.

Sergeant Hayden Auld, Stalag IV B, Mühlberg

We as Canadians were very fortunate in that the Germans had a lot of prisoners in Canada, and they were very well treated. With the result that the mail, the shipments of Canadian parcels — they weren't great in arriving, but they were ten times better than anyone else's were.

Flying Officer Brian Filliter, Stalag Luft III, Sagan

I think we were allowed three clothing parcels a year. Well, the main thing that you wanted was blankets, because all they gave you was one blanket or maybe two. And you used to ask for chocolate. And you were very lucky if you ever got it, because almost every parcel was broken into before it ever got to you and the chocolate was gone. A lot of pilfering. Not by our people, by the Germans.

The people at home got taken by a lot of the stores. For example, my Mother and Father sent me a parcel of books, and the books turned out to be things like *Nancy So-and-So and Her School Girlfriends at Something-or-Other Tech*. I mean crap that you wouldn't ever read. Took them just terrible.[2]

But some of the stuff they sent was ridiculous. You write, and you don't want them to worry about you at home, so you say, "We're busy making a garden." Gardens! What a farce! Nothing grew, and people walked all over it. But the folks at home are sending you gardening books.

Flight Sergeant Soggy Norton, Stalag Luft VI, Heydekrug

One day this parcel arrived from my mother. We thought it was food. And everybody was hanging over my shoulder to see what was in it. And it was a pair of skates! I asked her to send me skates, you know, but I really hoped she'd send food.

Flying Officer Brian Filliter, Stalag Luft III, Sagan

After a while, the cigarette parcels started rolling in. You were allowed as many cigarettes as you could handle. And the Canadians, in this area, were way ahead of their poor English counterparts. Cigarettes were gold, you see, they were the barter exchange. Canadians were flooded with cigarettes from home. Your parents, your friends, sent all kinds of cigarettes over. And we were, perhaps, able to live a little better than some of our counterparts from other countries, because of the cigarettes.

Sergeant Bert Gnam, Stalag IV B, Mühlberg

Cigarettes were money. We could swap or barter anything. You could get a gun. I'm not lying! You could get a gun from a German guard. He'd steal it from his buddy for twenty cigarettes. For a while there, you could get a woman too.

Private Bill Douglas, Stalag VIII B, Lamsdorf

We made up trading stores. It got to the point where there was guitars, all kinds of things that came into these trading stores. If you had cigarettes, you could buy anything.

Sergeant Sam Ebsary, Stalag VIII B, Lamsdorf

I didn't smoke, and that was a blessing. I know I came through better than a lot of guys. Some guys were smoking pretty heavy there and didn't get any food and got sick, and very likely, if they didn't die there, they're dead today, because they went two or three years with eating minimum rations. Whatever good food they got, they would sell for cigarettes, you see. Well, I used to buy, and I sometimes used to feel sorry, but I had to do it because I was hungry and would willingly give up my cigarettes 'cause I didn't smoke.

Flight Sergeant Arnold "Skid" Hanes, Stalag Luft VI, Heydekrug

I started smoking when I was a kid, when I was eleven years of age. We were starving to death at different places. But I've seen myself trade a piece of bread for cigarettes. Sure. A cigarette was more of a pacifier than a piece of bread, mentally.

Flight Lieutenant Art Crighton, Stalag Luft III, Sagan

I don't smoke, I never did smoke. Of course, these were the days before the campaign against smoking. I mean, smoking was a person's right. It wasn't a privilege, it was a right. You were expected to smoke. And cigarettes were the most important thing in the world. Well, they certainly were not to me, because I didn't smoke, and I didn't care if cigarettes never came to the camp. But this was the most important thing in some people's lives, the cigarettes. And, you know, living in a room with eight Kriegies there, with the shutters closed at night, it got so smoky you couldn't see across the room. And for a non-smoker, of course, you never dared complain, and you just had to put up with it.

Sergeant Hayden Auld, Stalag IV B, Mühlberg

Once the cigarettes started rolling in, then of course the poker games would get going. I never realized before — a man will play poker with his last cigarette, and he will throw his last cigarette into a damn poker game.

We got into some wild games. I had just got twenty-five hundred cigarettes in, and we used to value the cigarettes on the basis of our dollar. That's what one cigarette was worth, a buck, in our Canadian money at that time, not like it is today. Well, after dinner this day, they decided they were going to have a game, and the minimum you could get into the game was a thousand. I had a thousand, so I got into it.

The game was so big, well, you had to have a handler behind you to handle your cigarettes. You couldn't put all the cigarettes on the table. So, I had fifteen thousand in the game. I had fifteen thousand cigarettes, and there was only one guy with as many cigarettes as I had, a fellow from Sudbury. And I had five kings — we're playing a wild-card game — and I had seen three aces discarded. There was only one ace out against me, and the only thing that could beat me was the ace and four wild cards. And we threw every cigarette we had in. And he come up with that ace and he had four wild cards. I lost every single cigarette I had. I had to bum a smoke when the darn game was over!

Warrant Officer Harold White, Stalag Luft VI, Heydekrug

We had a radio in the camp. Three men knew where the radio was: the man who took care of the radio, our senior officer, and a man that could take shorthand. And they used to tune into the BBC from London at eleven o'clock at night. It used to be taken down in shorthand, and then it was written out longhand, and certain men that had the privilege of moving from one compound to the other used to come in with this news report. And they'd come into the barracks, and one of our men would be at one end of the barracks and another at the other end looking for the goons. Then this man would get on the table and he'd read the BBC news out to us.

Pilot Officer Russ Rogers, Stalag Luft III, Sagan

We used to get the BBC news every night. In each room there'd be twelve or fourteen fellas, and eight or ten rooms to a hut. And around midnight they would have two or three fellas set up the equipment. If there were guards around — we used to take turns watching different windows and doors — if these guys got too close, we'd say, "Goon up." And they'd have the radio put away and be playing cards in about twenty seconds.

Flight Sergeant Steve Putnam, Stalag IV B, Mühlberg

We were always being pulled out of our beds in the middle of the night, the lights would be on, and the guards were shouting, "We're going to have an inspection." They knew that there was a radio somewhere in the camp and they were looking for that. And if we could get any prior knowledge of that by bribing a guard with a few cigarettes, then we would play our little tricks.

We would get a wire, and I remember we ran the wire from a very obvious place right near the door up the side of the wall and along the ceiling and down into one of the bricks on the floor. So some guy would be clumsy enough to sort of point the wire out. And the guards would pounce on that wire and they would follow it all the way along and open the brick up on the other end. And there'd be a note under there: "Not here!" And it got the guards pretty annoyed.

Pilot Officer Don MacDonald, Stalag Luft I, Barth

"Goon-baiting" was one of the best pastimes that we had.

And that consisted of almost anything. We could bait the Germans until the cows came home.

Warrant Officer Harold White, Stalag Luft VI, Heydekrug

The German authorities used to parade us twice a day on a head count, in the morning and then again around four-thirty in the afternoon. One day about eight Canadians decided to have a little fun, and they formed up a little bit of a band. They had combs with toilet paper. They had one man as a bass drummer and his drum was a metal wash container.

On this particular roll call this one afternoon, they kept out of sight. The prisoners were all formed up in a three-sided square, in threes, and they were all counted. And the Germans find they're eight men short. So the German officer had them recounted and they still came out eight short. So now he's getting a little bit excited. And by this time he's calling for the full complement of guards to find these eight bodies.

Then, all of a sudden, this terrible noise came from behind this particular barracks, and these eight Canadians come marching out in the form of a band. And the big bass drummer's banging away on this tin tub he's got roped around him to hold it up. And they marched up to the square. And just about this time, the bass drummer stepped into a bit of a hole in the sand and he lost his balance, and he fell forward on this drum. And he can't get up because it's too heavy.

Of course, everybody started laughing and they all started to whistle and howl. And even the German officer kinda broke out in a little smile. I remember this because the man on the bass drum was me.

We kind of expected to get charged for that, but we didn't.

Pilot Officer Harold Garland, Stalag Luft III, Sagan

A general came down from Luftwaffe in a car one day. He seemed to be quite flattered that the guys would like to be shown around this car, under the hood and whatnot. And somebody stripped out of his car a set of orders marked "For Senior Staff Purposes Only," which was very secret. And when he got back in the car he found he was missing something that he should have kept in his pocket. They begged our people to return them. This went on for a day or two, until they finally gave back the orders. And I'm told they marked every page — somebody had made a big rubber stamp — "Inspected by the Officers of Luft III".

Trooper Cliff Hooey, Stalag II D, Stargard

A good incident was when the V-1s came along, the "buzz bombs." Then they made a tremendous advancement which they called the V-2. This one guard liked to tell us the V-2 would win the war for Germany. Then one day I told him, "The V-2 is nothing. We've had the V-8 in Canada since 1932!" He just walked away, muttering to himself.

Trooper Dick Clark, Stalag VIII B, Lamsdorf

Sometimes the guards would keep their guns cocked. And we'd sneak up behind 'em and pull the trigger. There'd be so many prisoners around, they could never tell who the hell done it!

Corporal Al Comfort, Stalag IX C, Molsdorf

The Germans had guard dogs who were trained by two different systems. They would stuff a British uniform with straw and set the dogs on it where we could see it getting torn to bits. Or a German would put the uniform on and pad himself so he couldn't get hurt, and the dogs would be set on him. Vicious dogs.

But in one of the stone quarries, they weren't so strict. At night, the boys were feeding these two dogs chocolate through the wire and got very friendly. And when they were ready to escape, they went — and they took the dogs with them!

Sergeant Bert Gnam, Stalag IV B, Mühlberg

One thing I could not understand about the Germans was their searching. We would get wind from our grapevine that we were going to be searched, and we knew every time the day before what we were going to be searched for.

One time the Germans would be looking for coal. So we

would take everything else out that you weren't supposed to have, like knives, forks, salt, and pepper, and you would bring it out. But the Germans would be looking for coal, and that's all they'd look for. They'd make a little note that Hut 15 had knives and forks. Then, sure enough, three days later the word would come around they'd be looking for knives and forks. So then you'd bring the coal out, and hide the knives and forks! This kept going on, just as regular as clockwork. It was ridiculous, but that's what the Germans were like.

Pilot Officer Don MacDonald, Stalag Luft III, Sagan

We used to train goons. Not too many of them would turn against their own country unless they had a purpose. So we had to blackmail them. You'd get a guy in for coffee. Because at that time, they didn't know what real coffee was and this was like nectar to them. And we'd give him a little chunk of chocolate and a few cigarettes. And then we'd ask him for something. And if he said "No," we'd threaten to hand him over to the Gestapo. These guys could be sent to the Russian Front for taking bribes. So we got most of our supplies by blackmailing a German.

Flight Sergeant Bill Rowbotham, Stalag IV B, Mühlberg

When we first got to the camp, the guards were quite tough. I know one of them was a young fellow, a very smart man, and every time he went home on leave, in Leipzig, they'd bomb Leipzig. And he'd come back just fit to be tied. Just a terrible temper. It gradually demoralized that guy. As the war went on, and the bombing raids continued, most of the guards finally got demoralized too.

Trooper Cliff Hooey, Stalag II D, Stargard

The German attitude changed as the war progressed. The process of getting you up to be counted in the morning went on just as if you were in the military. You got up at six o'clock. Then you lined up in fives, so that the guard went along and counted you. And they'd think nothing of pistol-whipping you in 1942. Come 1943, after the fall of Stalingrad and things don't look so good, they didn't pistol-whip you anymore — they just threatened to. Come along 1944, they'd step into your hut, "Gentlemen, it's time to be counted." Then in 1945, "Gentlemen, just stay in your beds. We'll count you there!"

Flight Sergeant Doug Hawkes, Stalag IV B, Mühlberg

We had this guard, an older fella, that would come in for coffee every now and again. We proposed giving him a pound of butter, some sugar and some this, that, and the other thing that we'd saved, and we asked him if he'd take it home to his wife and have her bake us a Christmas cake. He said, "Sure," and sneaked the stuff out of the camp in his respirator. And he brought the cake in to us by hanging it, somehow, under his greatcoat. We got one of the fellows, a baker from London, to decorate the cake for us. Then we decided to pool all our food and the twelve of us would sit down to Christmas dinner. There were some Red Cross parcels with turkey in them. And we also decided we'd have white table cloths. So we grabbed the sheets off our beds, got the water out and the blowers going, and boiled the bloody sheets. Then we spread out the table and sat down to Christmas dinner.

Private Lou Pantaleo, Stalag VIII B, Lamsdorf

Most of the guards we had were the older people, the old "Kaiser men" we called them. We had a few of the proper Nazis though. I remember we had one young fellow, a real Nazi. I guess he was wounded and couldn't go back to the front. So they gave him a job as a guard. We would have to salute him. We taught him to say, "I am a dirty German bastard." And we would salute back and say, "We know you are!"

So one day one of the generals or something came to the camp. And very proudly [our guard] called us to attention and saluted us and hollered out, "I am a dirty German bastard." Well, the shit flew that day!

Corporal Bill Dignam, Stalag VIII B, Lamsdorf

I honestly never ran across a good German over there. I ran

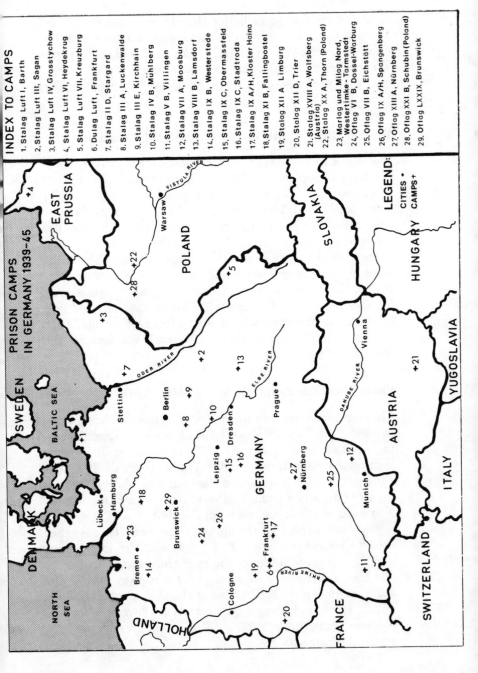

PRISON CAMPS IN GERMANY 1939-45

INDEX TO CAMPS

1. Stalag Luft I, Barth
2. Stalag Luft III, Sagan
3. Stalag Luft IV, Grosstychow
4. Stalag Luft VI, Heydekrug
5. Stalag Luft VII, Kreuzburg
6. Dulag Luft, Frankfurt
7. Stalag II D, Stargard
8. Stalag III A, Luckenwalde
9. Stalag III E, Kirchhain
10. Stalag IV B, Mühlberg
11. Stalag V B, Villingen
12. Stalag VII A, Moosburg
13. Stalag VIII B, Lamsdorf
14. Stalag IX B, Westerstede
15. Stalag IX C, Obermassfeld
16. Stalag IX C, Stadtroda
17. Stalag IX A/H, Kloster Haina
18. Stalag XI B, Fallingbostel
19. Stalag XII A, Limburg
20. Stalag XII D, Trier
21. Stalag XVIII A, Wolfsberg (Austria)
22. Stalag XX A, Thorn (Poland)
23. Marlag und Milag Nord, Westertimke - Tarmstedt
24. Oflag VI B, Dossel-Warburg
25. Oflag VII B, Eichstätt
26. Oflag IX A/H, Spangenberg
27. Oflag XIII A, Nürnberg
28. Oflag XXI B, Schubin (Poland)
29. Oflag LXXIX, Brunswick

LEGEND:
CITIES •
CAMPS †

95

across some that were better than others, and by far and away, ninety-nine percent of them were old guys with ribbons up for the First War. The ones that scared the supreme shit out of me were the Hitler Jugend, that's Hitler Youth. I always figured they'd get trigger-happy, so they were buggers to watch for.

Warrant Officer Keith Tate, Stalag Luft VII, Kreuzburg

It was one or two days after Christmas [1944] that my rear gunner, Les Stevenson — he was from Dawson Creek, B.C. — Les got shot. Les was nineteen years old, and I guess he was a daydreamer kind of a kid. And an air raid had been on this particular day, and our orders were to stay inside. Les had got up and walked down the hallway and stepped out. He was going to the lavatory. One of the guards shot him. The bullet went in his right side and came out the left. We hauled him inside. He was on the bed there, and he was very conscious. He asked me to say goodbye to his Mom and Dad. And then he started to make remarks about his feet getting cold. Then he just closed his eyes and passed away. It was just out and out murder, really.

Pilot Officer Jim McIntosh, Stalag Luft I, Barth

The Germans were very strict. They had rules which you had to adhere to. They did shoot some of us for obvious disobeying. I got a crease across the ass. There was air raids going on continuously and during the daylight hours the [U.S.] Eighth Air Force would fly over, and they put a regulation through for all of us, when an air raid went, to get back in our huts. And if we were outside, we would be shot.

I wasn't aware that the air raid siren went, because they used to go continuously. And I was outside, just poking around, within four feet of the hut. And I sort of looked up and here was a guard about, oh, fifty feet away with a rifle aimed at me. I just dove from where I was through a window, which, fortunately, was open. And just as I dove, he shot, and as I was going through the air, that bullet creased me right across the buttocks.

Flying Officer Pappy Plant, Stalag Luft III, Sagan

The main barrier around each compound was a double fence about eight feet high, about six or seven feet apart, with barbed wire entanglements or concertina wire inside. Then inside the main fence about forty or fifty feet, there was a low wire, a single strand on stakes, known as the warning wire. And anyone caught between the warning wire and the main fence would be shot without warning.

We had one fellow, he was laying on the grass, and he put his arms back and one of them went under the warning wire. A guard shot him.

Lieutenant Howard Paillefer, Oflag LXXIX, Brunswick

I can't complain of any bad treatment in the camp, unless we broke the rules. Now, one day, I did note that a group of the fellas were playing quoits. That was a game not unlike volleyball. You had a string attached between two poles, and you'd throw this piece of rope that was tied together back and forth like a volleyball.

Once the quoit was thrown beyond the barbed wire restraining line that was about ten feet inside the main barbed wire fence. Admittedly, there were signs saying, "*Achtung*. Warning. Do not cross the restraining line." And one fellow stepped over it to get the quoit, and he was shot and killed on the spot. But, admittedly, he had done something they told us not to do.

Warrant Officer Ed Houston, Stalag Luft VI, Heydekrug

Germans are, technically, a very clever race. But I always thought they were so goddam stupid about some things. They'd bayonet you and then take you to a doctor to fix you up. They really were hard to read. They were a bunch of bastards, you know.

Pilot Officer Jim Davies, Oflag VI B, Dossel-Warburg

You had in the camp the Senior British Officer, and he would be the senior guy shot down at that time. And every officers' camp had a Senior British Officer, it didn't matter whether he was air force or whatever. There were no perks, but he was the guy that had to pound the Germans' door and say, "You're not feeding us enough," or "There's no coal," "We've got some sick people here." That type of thing. And he would be the contact for the Germans, the Germans would hold him responsible for the camp.

He'd have an adjutant and a couple of officers as administrative people, just to help with the daily running of the camp.

You lived in huts, and you'd have a hut leader. And that person would usually have a small room at the end, and there might be two of them in there, instead of anywhere from eight to twenty in the other rooms. You were counted by huts, and drew rations by huts, and things like that. Later in the war, we didn't have that setup because we were being moved around. But most of the camps worked like this.

Pilot Officer Harold Garland, Stalag Luft III, Sagan

In the camp, I recall, was a Canadian, Larry Wray. He became the Senior British Officer. He called all the Canadians together and said that the Germans had come to him and said that because of the fine treatment of the prisoners of war in Canada, they were prepared to build a separate camp for Canadians, and they would give it a few more amenities. And then, after a pause, he said, "I told them we would accept it. Provided they do the same for the rest of the prisoners." Which got him a big cheer. And, of course, we never got the special camp.

Warrant Officer Ross Elford, Stalag Luft VI, Heydekrug

That was at a time, I think in 1944, when repatriation went on between prisoners of war — amputees, health problems. When they got back, the Germans that had been in Canada, they were quite pleased with the way they had been treated. So the Jerries said, "We'll give the Canadians preferential treatment, for treating our people that well." We all refused. We said, "No. We're Allied prisoners of war."

And they couldn't understand why we wouldn't take preferential treatment.

Flight Sergeant Doug Hawkes, Stalag IV B, Mühlberg

"Snowshoe" Meyers was a Canadian, a great fellow. He was our Man of Confidence[3]; in other words, he was the man who was elected by our group to talk to the Germans on our behalf. Not everybody could get in to see the CO. We lodged our complaints through Snowshoe Meyers.

We had elections for the Man of Confidence. The British wanted to do it by seniority. They had a regimental sergeant-major and, anyway, they figured [that since] the army is the senior service, this fellow should be our Man of Confidence. And besides, they pointed out there were more Englishmen than Canadians there. So we agreed to have an election. When the votes were counted, it was no contest. Snowshoe Meyers went back in with a great majority. So he was our only Man of Confidence the whole time we were there.

Flight Lieutenant Dallas Laskey, Stalag Luft III, Sagan

Stalag Luft III had quite a large proportion of Canadians. And the Canadians had a vitality and an openness, I think, and a kind of exploratory attitude.

I think that they did a lot to keep spirits up. Their enthusiasm, and their know-how, too. And, certainly, Canadians had an identity. Anyone who was there would realize that they were Canadians. It wasn't just a matter of accent or grammar. We weren't burdened with the heavy hand of tradition. This is one of the things that always sort of puzzled us in England; at four o'clock, every damn thing stopped for tea, war or no war. We had a kind of refreshing ignorance, although it must have been awfully offensive to other people. A kind of brashness and confidence that really wasn't based on much that I could see! But I think we did contribute to the liveliness of the place.

Trooper Forbes Morton, Stalag VIII B, Lamsdorf

There was a bunch of British prisoners that had been captured at Dunkirk, so they were well-established in the camp. We heard of this Scotch gang from Glasgow. They decided that they were going to rule the roost, so they had a "razor gang," all armed with straight razors. This one night, they happened to cut up a Canadian. Not seriously, but we took it upon ourselves to arm ourselves with whatever we could — bedboards and you name it — and we went down to their barracks. And we had a battle royal. The Germans didn't step in either. There was nobody killed or anything [but] that was the end of the gang.

Flight Lieutenant Al Aldridge, Stalag Luft III, Sagan

One Canadian tried to commit suicide while I was there. Tried to slash his wrists, but he didn't do a very good job of it. A lot of those chaps were very despondent. And I have a feeling that some of them — I don't know whether I should say this — some of them may have thought that they hadn't performed well, you know, in their operation, and felt guilty about being there. But some of them, at any rate, were very despondent. Of course, nobody was too happy. But you just tried to make the best of it. And they were a great bunch of chaps in there.

Sergeant Gordon Harrison, Stalag Luft VI, Heydekrug

This is one of the hardest things in prison camp — you never know when you were gonna get out. If ever. And I often think about when, you know, you hear about a guy getting a couple of years in the pen up here. At least he knows he's going to get out in a couple of years or, if he behaves himself, it could be earlier than that. But there, we just never knew. The uncertainty, if you really wanted to sit down and think about it, could get to you. Some of the guys obviously did think about it, because they had problems. We had fellas run at the wire. Just give up and actually commit suicide by climbing the barbed wire, and the guards would shoot them. Some people couldn't take it. A lot of the fellas that couldn't take it weren't the active types, they just sat and brooded and thought about these things, and finally they just gave up.

Flight Sergeant George Thom, Stalag VIII B, Lamsdorf

It was a boring bloody existence. You'd see people going crazy — it just shocks you, too — almost drift away, and there's nothing you can do about it. And then one day you'd see 'em sawing at their wrists. It scares you.

Sergeant Gordon Harrison, Stalag Luft VI, Heydekrug

You've probably been at the zoo and seen these animals walking around along the fence. That's exactly what we did. Circuit bashing.

Sergeant Bert Gnam, Stalag IV B, Mühlberg

You'd go out there and look for cigarette butts, or see if you could see somebody that you hadn't seen for five minutes. If you hadn't seen him for fifteen minutes, he was a long lost buddy!

Pilot Officer Harold Garland, Stalag Luft III, Sagan

After they'd been there for a while, the Americans got permission to come over and have a softball game with the Canadians. All these Americans had baseball uniforms, all these lovely, white, fitting baseball uniforms. And the Canadians, we were in the clothes we'd slept in for two or three years. And there were some professional American baseball players in there, too.

The Canadian pitcher was Bill Paton, and he had pitched in the Beaches League in Toronto. And the umpire was Larry Wray, our Senior British Officer. And Larry Wray had to go to Bill about inning number five or six and say, "Please let them hit, Bill." They hadn't touched the ball all that game!

Flight Lieutenant Art Deacon, Stalag Luft I, Barth

The first skates we had, we made when we were up at Barth. We took the angle irons off the benches, metal angle irons. We took them off and then you could screw them onto your boots and then you could skate on the other edge of the angle iron. But things got better as the war went on, we had actual skates and actual hockey sticks. Had some good games too.

Flight Lieutenant Barry Davidson, Stalag Luft III, Sagan

Later, there was another fellow in camp who knew Connie

Smythe, and I knew Don MacKay in Calgary. And we [decided to] see if they could send equipment to us through the Red Cross. And I wrote to Don and someone else wrote to Connie Smythe. We got enough equipment to make up two pretty good hockey teams. We had guys in there who had played with some of the top pro teams, so we had some real good hockey games. The Germans loved to watch.

Flight Lieutenant Cliff Irwin, Stalag Luft III, Sagan

We had a a nine-hole golf course. It was all sand, we had sand greens. There were balls whizzing all over the place. I remember there was a fellow sitting on his bunk strumming a guitar and, Jesus, a ball came through the window and right through his strings. God, was he mad!

We made our own golf balls. We took the rubber soles from the old running shoes, we'd take a razor blade and cut them into strips. Then we took a marble and we wound and wound and wound. And then when we got it the same size as a golf ball, we took some tongues out of old shoes and cut them in the shape of a baseball cover, then we sewed them all together. They'd go about a hundred yards, these balls. If you hooked a shot, and it went outside the fence, that was another week's work.

I had a hole-in-one one day. The only time I ever did.

Flight Lieutenant Anthony Pengelly, Stalag Luft III, Sagan

I was very involved in the theatre. I was in the cast of some shows, and I was working backstage. At one point, I produced a couple of shows myself. I was a stage manager for a long time.

A whole group of us built the theatre. It was made out of brick debris from Dresden. The seats were all made of the boxes that the Red Cross parcels came in. The theatre seated 360 with tip-up seats.

Flight Sergeant John Cox, Stalag IV B, Mühlberg

They made all the sets out of Red Cross packing cases and old Italian blankets. And from here to there, you couldn't tell they hadn't got them out of a furniture store. One chap made

102

a suit of armour for this one particular play out of tin cans, and it was fabulous.

Pilot Officer Gord King, Stalag Luft III, Sagan

The Germans would rent us costumes. I was, at that time, small and slight, I weighed about 112 pounds. And I was young, I was twenty-one. And I made up into a girl very easily, so I was in *The Man Who Came to Dinner* as the daughter. I had falsies, a wig — they really looked after you, they had real professional people doing everything.

In one scene, I had to show this fella some pictures of my "boyfriend's" photography. But on the last night of the show, some wag in the prop room had got some filthy postcards and just handed them to me as I was going out. And I showed him these pictures and he just about fell out of his chair. And he was saying, "Well, how interesting" — he was ad libbing — "My, this is a good one," and we were just killing ourselves!

Flight Lieutenant Barry Davidson, Stalag Luft III, Sagan

When a new prisoner came in, we'd find out what the latest shows in London were at that time. We saw *Arsenic and Old Lace*, *Macbeth*, pretty top-notch entertainment.

We tried to encourage everybody to get dressed up as best they could and come pretending it's a night out. But you couldn't get that into the heads of those damn Americans. They used to come in in their sloppy, dirty clothes. But I sure take my hat off to the guys who organized that.

Flight Lieutenant Art Crighton, Stalag Luft III, Sagan

I started right out in Stalag Luft III, teaching some guy to play saxophone. I bought a trumpet for two thousand cigarettes. I used to teach boys' bands down in Cornwall, Ontario. And the music helped me make the adjustment to POW life.

Entertainment, of course, was the second-biggest activity in the camp. The first was escape, naturally, that took precedence over everything. And then entertainment came next, which had to do with camp morale. It was encouraged by the Germans too.

When I got to Stalag Luft III, the East Compound, a fellow by the name of Roy Wilkins was in charge of the music. He had a sort of a stage band. I eventually took over this band and then naturally formed an orchestra, and we had chamber music groups. Everything was on a primitive level at that time, because we had very poor instruments. But when the Americans started coming, the American Red Cross sent fine instruments over. The best trumpet I ever owned was in Germany. The music progressed in stages, and eventually it became very good quality.

Corporal Al Comfort, Stalag IX C, Molsdorf

Many of the men had instruments. You could get almost anything you wanted, but you had to pay *Lagergeld*, the camp money. And men at the stone quarries were paid this *Lagergeld*. And so men could accumulate this money. You could ask for a hundred marks and you could send it to Geneva and get a banjo or guitar, ukeleles. There were Scotties there that had their bagpipes, but they were restricted in their practising because it'd drive you crazy! The Germans called the bagpipes "doodle sacks."

Lieutenant Jack Dunlap, Oflag VII B, Eichstätt

We also put on a music festival. Each nationality in the camp had to produce something for the music festival. We had Maoris there, captured in Crete and Greece, and they dressed in their native costumes. They put on a war dance that was absolutely amazing. The Australians sang "Waltzing Matilda." And the English and the Welsh and the Irish and the Scots all did their particular thing.

And for Canada, it was the members of the FMR from Montreal. I often look back on it. To think that when it came to cultural representation for Canada, it was the French Canadians that did it. We were from the Calgary Tanks. There was the South Saskatchewan Regiment, the Cameron Highlanders from Winnipeg, the Royal Regiment from Toronto, the Hamilton Light Infantry, the Essex Scottish. As much as there's antipathy between the West and the East today, it was the French Canadians that had to represent Canada at that music festival.

Sergeant Tommy Cunningham, Stalag VIII B, Lamsdorf

Boredom, boredom, boredom. That was the big thing. We had two guys, the best of buddies. Oh, they used to argue! They were two Americans in the Essex Scottish. The Essex Scottish was from Windsor, and a lot of these guys came up from Detroit and joined the Canadian Army. But, oh, these two used to argue! One time they got into, "Could you eat a Red Cross parcel?" One says, "Sure, I could." And then the inevitable argument would break out. So the big bet was on, and they got a Red Cross parcel. This guy starts in on it, and he ate, and he ate, and he ate, and he couldn't quite make it. I swear the guy's complexion was purple. I'll bet there were two hundred guys crowded around, watching this thing. Any diversion, any little thing became a big thing, blown out of proportion. Anything different was a big thing.

Trooper Fred Tanner, Stalag VIII B, Lamsdorf

It was a well-established camp, and they had a fairly good library and a good school. That's where I studied to be a diesel mechanic. I studied the theory of it. We had several good teachers there.

Sergeant Tommy Cunningham, Stalag VIII B, Lamsdorf

We had a number of books. There was a Prisoners of War Relatives Association, which was across Canada, and we could get books from them. We had a librarian, and he catalogued the books: Classics, Detective, Fiction. And for westerns, he had them catalogued under "S-H-I-T"!

Flight Lieutenant Dallas Laskey, Stalag Luft III, Sagan

And I remember when *Lady Chatterley's Lover* came into our room, it came in units of ten pages, and you'd read ten and pass them along.

Flight Sergeant Bill Rowbotham, Stalag IV B, Mühlberg

There was just about every occupation represented in the camp. Artists, painters, teachers, lawyers. In fact, there was one lawyer who was busy all the time doing legal work and sending it back to England. He was handling cases right there in the camp, divorces and separations. There was a lot of that.

I remember one guy slapped a picture of a woman on his bunk bed. A second guy came along and asked, "Where did you get that picture?" The first fella said, "Well, that's my wife." And the other guy says, "Well, it's mine, too!" It is a fact that some of these girls in Halifax married more than one fellow. They'd marry half a dozen, or a dozen, and while all these guys were overseas or in a prison camp, these women would be drawing marriage allowance from twelve people.

Pilot Officer Harry Jay, Stalag Luft III, Sagan

I had a fight or two. But, you know, it was a test of strength. People would get nasty with one another and then snap out of it. Occasionally, somebody would have to move from a room because they just couldn't cope anymore. And the teasing was just terrible. If you were engaged to a girl, as I was, everybody'd tell you that was ridiculous. They'd bet you six months' pay that the girl wouldn't be there when you got there. And this would get to you a bit. And they were usually right.

Flight Sergeant Skid Hanes, Stalag IV B, Mühlberg

You had to have a sense of humour in prison camp. You get fifty people in one room, night after night after night, in three-tier bunks. People farting, going for a piss and coming back, and various things like this. It could drive you crazy.

Corporal Alex Masterton, Stalag XX A, Thorn (Poland)

Most of us were very young when we were captured. I was nineteen. If we were starving, the subject was food. If a Red Cross parcel came through, it was amazing — within about three minutes, sex was the subject, until we were hungry again. And of course most of us were inexperienced people. There was the odd married man that would sort of tell us the secrets of married life. We'd lay in our bloody bunks at night with our ears wide open, drinking it all in!

Sergeant Bert Gnam, Stalag IV B, Mühlberg

Every so often we'd have a party. I would donate, say, a tin of Prem and someone else would donate a tin of sardines and so on. And we would invite, through permission of the Germans, the next hut to come to our hut after dark, when nobody was supposed to be wandering around. So I'd go to you and say, "Okay, you be the girl tonight, I'll be the boy." And we'd have this party. We even had records. And we danced. Then the next time, I'd be the girl and you'd be the boy. All I'm referring to in this is dancing. Who would lead who. Never had any of that other stuff that I know about.

Private Geoffrey Ellwood, Stalag VIII B, Lamsdorf

This is where you'd see the odd queer show up. I mean, it was one thing for guys to dance together because there's nobody else to dance with. But when they start dancing together and likin' it, and start snugglin' up, it became very, very obvious, you know. This went on, but nobody seemed to take it as serious, you know. They'd look at it, and discuss it amongst themselves, and that was it. It was accepted that some people are that way.

Warrant Officer Arnold Dawkins, Stalag VIII B, Lamsdorf

We used to make our own booze there. Some of the stuff they brought up was a bit unpalatable, some of the German jam. And if you worked it right, you could steal a barrel from one of their canteens. And you'd knock the top out of it and then you'd put this German jam in. You put in some water with it, and if you could get hold of some yeast, eventually it would bubble. And then if you drank it, it just cleaned out your innards.

So somebody figured it would be better if it was distilled. I don't think, really, in the Geneva Convention, we were supposed to do any distilling at all. You could get a bunch of dried apricots, and you'd put those into a vessel and pour water on. You didn't need yeast, because they had yeast on their skin, we discovered. And when you distilled that, you had a very potent brandy. It burned all the way down. It was somewhat stronger than the stuff the Liquor Board sells you.

107

Sergeant Tommy Cunningham, Stalag VIII B, Lamsdorf

We had the option of joining the German army. We woke up one day, and here's this poster: "The Legion of St. George. Any volunteers will be accepted into the German army. You will not go to the Western Front. You will go to the Russian Front, to help stop the Bolshevik hordes." Of course, with us it was a big joke. But I'm sure I later saw a German soldier walking down the road outside our camp with a Union Jack on his sleeve.

Sergeant Gordon Harrison, Stalag Luft VI, Heydekrug

My first impression when I got there? "My God, everybody's crazy!" Guys were running around, hiding behind telephone poles, around corners: "Bang, bang you're dead!" And I thought, "Holy Jesus, I've dropped into an insane asylum here." Six months later I was the same way.

Sergeant George Sendall, Stalag Luft I, Barth

When people are first shot down, or however they become a prisoner, they talk a blue streak, and this seemed to be a common pattern. And they were friends with everyone! After three or four weeks, they would get over that talking craze and draw more and more into themselves. And they would have to make an adjustment. What happened, so far as I could see, was that those fellows who tried to maintain their sanity on the level of the sanity of the outside world really went round the bend. They weren't making the kind of adjustment to the crazy, topsy-turvy world in which they were living. And the fellows who did, who said, "Well, this isn't like life at home, this is camp life," they became like ten-year-old kids. Laughed, played, talked, what have you. They kept their sanity. Those who thought of only one thing, and that is to get out of that barbed wire fence and get back to sanity, were the ones who very often went against the barbed wire fence, and had it.

The Kriegie was reacting to what was, not what should be. This was a crazy, upside-down existence, and one adjusted as best they could to it.

Footnotes

1. The Canadian Red Cross food parcel was designed by Dr. F.F. Tisdall of the University of Toronto. The late Dr. Tisdall was an internationally recognized nutrition expert. The Canadian parcel contained 2070 calories, more than any other food parcel prepared by branches of the International Red Cross. The food therein was intended to supplement the rations provided by the enemy; one parcel was to last one man one week, but they rarely arrived that often. The popularity of the Canadian food parcel cannot be denied. A post-war survey indicated more than eighty percent of Canadian POWs preferred it to parcels from the British, American, and New Zealand Red Cross; seventy percent of British POWs surveyed also preferred the Canadian parcel.

2. Families of POWs were given a list of government-authorized firms through which they could order books, games, playing cards, and other articles. The families would never see these items. They would send in an order, and the articles would be sent by these firms directly to the POWs. So the families had to rely on the integrity of the businessmen with whom they were dealing.

3. The Man of Confidence was the NCO counterpart of the Senior British Officer in POW camps.

VI/Escape — Great, and Not So Great

Today it is almost a cliché: "It is the duty of every prisoner of war to try to escape." But in those days most, if not all, POWs really believed that. The creed was even written into the 1929 Geneva Convention. Article 51 of the Convention stated that attempted escape, even when performed repeatedly, was not to be considered an "aggravating circumstance" and imposed limits on the disciplinary action that could be taken against would-be escapers. For the most part, the Germans went along with it until 1944, when, preoccupied with the impending invasion of France by the Allies, they tried to put a stop to the practice; they simply could not afford to tie up valuable troops chasing POWs around the countryside. But until that point in the war, escaping was a cat-and-mouse game between the prisoners and the Germans, with each side becoming progressively more sophisticated in its methods of escape and detection, respectively.

Canadian POWs in Europe took part in escape attempts of every description, although few were successful. The Canadians proved themselves most adept at tunnelling, which turned out to be the most popular form of escape from prison camps, and Canadians participated in two of the most famous tunnelling episodes, the Wooden Horse and the Great Escape.

Warrant Officer Harold White, Stalag Luft I, Barth

Even if you were taken prisoner of war, you know, the war wasn't over. Your job, as a prisoner of war, was to create as many problems as you possibly could for the enemy. Because the more problems that you could create for the enemy, the

110

more men it takes to guard you to keep you in your place, and consequently, the less men they have for the front. So there was always something going on re escaping.

Sapper Wally Hair, Stalag VIII B, Lamsdorf

Unless you were put through the proper escape channels, [escape] was almost a useless thing. And they wouldn't risk an escape route just for any Tom, Dick, or Harry. We only ever knew of a couple of fellas that actually made it back. Everybody else got caught, because I think every twenty or thirty miles or so, you had to have a different pass. Let's face it, you got an area, Germany, that you could put into Ontario four times. And look how many millions were under arms. And this included the Home Guard, their Hitler Youth, who were little bearcats — they spent their weekends looking for escaped prisoners. So your chances of getting through were almost nil.

Pilot Officer Jim Davies, Oflag XXI B, Schubin (Poland)

Most of the camps had a "Mr. X" and he was responsible for coordinating escapes, everything. In other words, you had to go to him, explain your proposition to him, and then he'd give you the okay or not. As a result, you didn't have one plan interfering with another.

Flying Officer Pappy Plant, Stalag Luft I, Barth

The set-up was called the "X committee," the Escape Committee. This in turn was broken down into intelligence and security. Intelligence was people who could talk to Germans and get little bits of information, or bribing them for maps and railway timetables or passes. Security was concerned with security of the camp. Back in England, on an aerodrome, there was always a duty pilot, whose job it was to keep tabs on aircraft taking off and landing. In other words, he kept a log. So we just followed the same procedure in the camp, only he sat up near the main gate and he had a log there, and whichever German came into the camp, the officer had a name, a time in, and a time out. And certain people came under different classifications. For instance, the guy who brought the mail in was innocent enough. But if a security officer came in, there would be a real red warning on. The Germans realized this was going on and tried to put a stop to it. But it was impossible because they would take one list away, and five minutes later there would be another list.

Warrant Officer Harold White, Stalag Luft I, Barth

I was on the security end. I had washed a pair of socks and a pair of underwear, and I went just inside the front gate, and I had a piece of string tied on two nails and I hung up my washing there. And I sat there waiting for it to dry. My purpose was to watch the front gate. As soon as anything suspicious was to arrive, like a covered truck or a squad of Germans that was gonna be marched in, then I immediately got up to take off my washing. And in the barracks where the tunnel was going on was stationed a man watching me. And as soon as he saw me start taking down my washing, he knew the alarm was on and he notified them inside the tunnel.

Trooper Cliff Hooey, Stalag VIII B, Lamsdorf

And while the tunnel's being dug, the clothes and passports and money were being prepared, so that the minute it was fully dug and operational, those people could be gone. A camp of eighteen, twenty thousand men has every manner of criminal. The best thieves in the world are right there. The finest forgers are right there for your use when you want to make a passport. There was an Irishman there that was so good, he had to be careful that he didn't do it too well! Everything that was official was stamped with a swastika with an eagle sitting on it. He carved that out of a potato. Stamped it, then ate the potato. Didn't waste anything.

Pilot Officer Don MacDonald, Stalag Luft III, Sagan

A bigger bunch of shysters and crooks and con men you'd never find anywhere in the world, than in a prison camp. They could steal, they could draw, they could make anything. They could forge stuff that you wouldn't believe was

112

forged, including a typewritten page that had never seen a typewriter. Some of the passes that they forged were really better-looking passes than the originals. We had forgers, we had tailors, we had artists.

Flight Lieutenant Cliff Irwin, Stalag Luft III, Sagan

It's easy to make a camera. We made uniforms, German uniforms. Dummy guns. And we weren't supposed to have any tools, the people in the workshop were supposed to turn everything in again, but they smuggled them in.

They had our room loaded with escape stuff. It was just panelled, about four inches wide, with pine. You know, you'd take it out and there was insulation in there, fibreglass stuff. And then they'd load in all this escape stuff.

And one day, the Germans were searching, and they went in and called everybody out. Some guy had left this piece of paper sticking out between the rafters. Well, you should have seen our room. They smashed the hell out of it and they got all this escape stuff. We had passports with pictures, and uniforms and money, and train schedules. I didn't know a lot of that stuff was there till they piled it up outside.

Flying Officer Pappy Plant, Stalag Luft I, Barth

This is where we dug our first tunnel. It was sand, very easy to dig in but also treacherous because the stuff kept falling. The water table at Barth was only six or seven feet, and it's pretty hard to keep a tunnel level, so you'd leave the thing and come back the next day, and if there had been a dip, it was usually full of water. So we used to work down there practically naked, because you didn't dare get your clothes all dirty.

We found you could dig less than twenty feet and you had to have air. So we made up the first air pump, an old Jerry jam can, and we made a plunger with a flop valve and a bicycle pump handle.

The Germans were learning as well. They found our first tunnel when it collapsed. Then they started looking under the huts. They developed a team called Abwehr, the German word for defence. We called them ferrets. They dressed in

113

coveralls and they used to have these long steel probers. They would dive under a hut and start probing around. You see, this first tunnel was just open. The huts were about two feet off the ground, and we'd just crawl under and start digging. It became a game of wits about hiding the entrance to the tunnel.

We got very cagey. One of the most common ways was to make small sandbags. You sank your shaft, then you cribbed it in with wood. When you were closing it down, you put your boards over, then you piled these sandbags around it, then brushed the earth on top. So the ferrets would have to probe down quite a ways. But it meant it took time to uncover and cover up. This was the danger. If there was a roll call, you had to get the guys out of the hole in a hurry and get the thing covered up.

Warrant Officer Al Hayward, Stalag Luft I, Barth

There was one funny incident I'll never forget. A couple of Australian boys and I were down in this tunnel, and the Jerries pulled a surprise raid. While we're lying there in the tunnel, one of the chaps decided he has to relieve himself. Well, all of a sudden there's a roar of water. And one of my Australian buddies was terrified. He thought they put a hose down the tunnel, which they did sometimes when they found one. He says, "I'm not gonna drown like a rat. Let me outta here!" But we finally cooled him off and let him know what really happened.

Actually, I hated working in those tunnels. I hated it every time I went down.

Flight Lieutenant Barry Davidson, Stalag Luft III, Sagan

The bunks had slats of wood, bedboards, and with the big tunnels going, the Escape Committee would come and say, "We need six more pieces of wood from your bunk." Actually, it got so bad that some of the boys got rope from the Red Cross parcels, bound it together, and weaved a sort of hammock and put it across the bunks.

And, of course, the Germans knew the goddam wood was gone, and why, but they didn't know where. And they wouldn't supply us with more wood, because it would just go to shoring up more tunnels!

Pilot Officer Gord King, Stalag Luft III, Sagan

I started out as a "penguin," which was sand dispersal. In the legs of our pants, we had long canvas bags filled with sand and there was a peg holding the bottom together and a string in our pockets. And we'd walk out to the playing field and pull the pin, and the sand would dribble out and then we'd kick it around so it wouldn't show fresh sand. We picked up tons and tons of that. We must have raised the level of that playing field about six inches.

Flight Lieutenant Anthony Pengelly, Stalag Luft III, Sagan

There was an awful lot of non-productive but diversive tunnelling that was never intended to go anywhere, just to be a nuisance. They were intended to be caught, because the Germans just had no concept of how fast one could make a tunnel. Therefore, if they caught one, they were relaxed for quite a time. The good ones were the ones that were kept secure.

Flying Officer Pappy Plant, Stalag Luft I, Barth

We used to lay out and sunbathe. Four or five of us got together and said, "Why don't we start a tunnel right out in the open?"

The Germans had very kindly provided us with one of these old-fashioned washtubs. My part of this project was to turn this thing upside down, and with a makeshift saw, cut a square out of the bottom of this thing, enough for a guy to get in. Then we put hinges on this so it could be flopped up.

When we figured the coast was clear, we dug a hole and put a blanket over it. We got the okay when the guard had gone by, and we pushed this tub out the washroom window. A couple of guys grabbed it, rushed it over to the hole, turned it upsidedown, and just plopped it in. The smallest guy in camp was a little wee Australian named Mulligan. We lifted the hatch and pushed him in. He cleaned out around it and

115

cut it so the tub would settle level. Then we had almost like a small working chamber, and we put sandbags on top to cover it. We worked on it all summer.

You could go out there in the morning, stretch your blankets out. When the guards weren't looking, the guys would peel off the sand, lift out the sandbags, and down would go the crew. We would have had to dig some hundred-odd feet, and we got about thirty or forty feet. Somebody in the German security must have got smart and figured there was something going on, because sometimes there'd be sunbathing going on when there wasn't much sun out.

One day there was a roll call, and we were all moved out of the compound. When we came back, some German with a sense of humour had stuck a big cross over the entrance to the tunnel: "Here lies your last hope!"

Trooper Cliff Hooey, Stalag VIII B, Lamsdorf

The first person out of that tunnel at Stalag VIII B was a Canadian of Swedish descent. He looked like a Swede and spoke perfect Swedish. He went out the tunnel, walked to the train, got his ticket, and went to the nearest port. When he boarded the Swedish ship, clothes were hanging on the clothesline. If the clothes hadn't been there, he was not to board or he would be turned in to the German authorities. But he got on board, hid till they cleared port, and he was in Stockholm in a matter of hours.

Warrant Officer Ross Elford, Stalag Luft VI, Heydekrug

We had a tunnel going, and the Germans had an idea it was going, but they couldn't find it. One morning we woke up and, Christ, through the gate comes this huge great steamroller. So they started that thing around and, sure enough, we weren't down that deep. When she hit that tunnel, down went the back end. Then they couldn't get it out!

Sergeant Donald Macdonald, Stalag Luft I, Barth

We tried to outfox them, digging three tunnels all at once. And finally, we did get one through. I think there were six or seven fellas who were supposed to escape. I'll be doggoned if a *Posten*, guard, with his dog walking around the yard stepped on the damn thing and went right through it!

Flight Lieutenant Anthony Pengelly, Stalag Luft III, Sagan

There were a lot of people who went out "on the ground" as opposed to "under the ground." They'd go out in the garbage trucks, or just a number of different ways.

We also had a shower parade outside in the administration area of the camp. There were buildings with hot showers, and you could go out with your towel and soap, and you could have a shower and come back into the camp. And by phonying the counts which were continually being taken, you could find ways of disappearing and fooling the Germans. Very rarely did those attempts work though.

Warrant Officer Don Campbell, Marlag und Milag Nord, Westertimke-Tarmstedt

Albert was one way to get out of the camp. Albert was made out of tin cans and various other things. Everyone helped create this "man." Made a face, arms, legs, out of papier-mâché. We had to go out of the camp to a shower, and everybody carried a little bit of Albert to the shower. After we had this shower, we'd start back to camp. But a real man would remain in the shower, and that night he'd escape. So then Albert was assembled — they put a hat on him, cigarette in his mouth, great coat — and he'd "walk" between two other men. And as we came into the camp we were counted, and everybody was accounted for.

The Germans couldn't figure out how these men were getting out of the camp. One day we were coming back with Albert and there were, oh, about twenty Germans standing at the gate waiting for us. And they just went up to every man and looked right at him. And finally they discovered Albert. They just took Albert and kicked him and beat him and tore him to pieces. The two people beside him got solitary confinement.

Major Allan Glenn, Oflag VII B, Eichstätt

We had one escape from our camp that was absolutely fabulous. I was walking down the *Lagerstrasse*, and I met this party going out the gate. There was a little fat general, and a guy in civvies with a briefcase, and about four or five soldiers. They marched right out and started downtown. Hell, they're all our guys! They'd made all those uniforms and civilian clothing. And their high-top black boots, they were cardboard, polished black. And they made these damn uniforms and dyed them the proper colour. And these "leather" briefcases, they were all paper.

They were only two or three blocks away from the camp, and there was an *Unteroffizier* coming back from downtown. And he recognized the "general" as an Englishman. So the gag was up. But the Germans thought that was a good deal too. They took pictures of it. And they got more laughs out of that themselves.

Pilot Officer Harold Garland, Stalag Luft III, Sagan

There was another escape that I must admire. A man had worked out how he could climb the wire in broad daylight. The wire was a good ten to twelve feet high, two fences perhaps twelve feet apart, with a bramble in between. The fence not only had vertical wire, but a forty-five degree inward-sloping chunk on the inside and the outside. And the wire was surmounted by goonboxes which were raised above the wire with people with machine guns. And there was a trip wire, perhaps thirty feet inside the wire. It was agreed that you could be shot by stepping over the trip wire. So he had to traverse this thirty feet and then climb the fence.

And this fellow had worked out that if he could distract the attention of the guards in the goonboxes, plus the guard who walked on the outside of the fence, if he could attract their attention to one spot, then he could climb over that fence.

A man set up the habit of throwing a bucket of dishwater every day over the trip wire. And this particular day, he came out carrying the bucket like a waiter. And another person knocked the bucket from his hand, so the water drenched him, and they fell into an altercation with a great amount of noise. And this playacting was the distraction while the other fellow climbed the fence. And he did make it over the fence!

It was the usual thing. He was out for one or two or three weeks, and then they caught him, and then he had his cooler time.

Captain Barney Byrnes, P.G. 66, Capua (Italy)

This was a transit camp, and nobody was there, really, long enough to formulate real escapes. There was an Escape Committee and there were attempts made. As a matter of fact, there was a sewer with a manhole that led to the city of Capua two miles away. One chap going past this manhole lifted it up, had a look down, and figured it was big enough to get through. Good idea! So he goes back and gets his great-coat and his Red Cross parcel, and then he goes dashing down this manhole and starts away along the sewer. Somebody saw him go down. So that fellow dashed into his hut, got his Red Cross parcel and his greatcoat, and he went down too. He was seen by another PW. And before you could say Jack Robinson, there's a queue of would-be escapers lined up with their Red Cross parcels and their greatcoats over their arm, disappearing down the manhole. Well, the Italian guards thought this was a little strange, and they went to the exit of the sewer and picked them up as they came up!

Corporal Alex Masterton, Stalag XX A, Thorn (Poland)

At the beginning of 1944, I was moved to a small farm camp [in Poland]. There were only nine of us. One chap died, so that left eight. We were all in the British army, but we were all Canadians. We all worked on a separate farm, and the guard would patrol the area on his bicycle.

It was obvious there was going to be a landing in France soon. We could see by the number of American bombers coming over in the daytime, and we could hear the British at night, that they were pasting the hell out of Germany. And I thought the time was coming when we should take off.

So, I think it was either August or September — by then, D-Day had taken place — I discussed an escape with some of the boys in the camp. Five of us decided to go. We decided we'd go in uniform and hide.

119

It was nothing to cut the wire, and we went through the wire. The prison camp was just a little stone house and in front of this house, a road ran. Well, just as we were cutting the wire, a battalion of bloody German tanks came down the road. And by the time the tanks had gone, dawn was breaking. Over the highway, we split up. When it was known that the five of us had gone, the whole area was teeming with police and soldiers. The two boys went to the left to a huge wood — we found out later the Germans recaptured them and shot them — and we went to a big house, a very rich farm.

Well, you knew that any rich farm belonged to a German. But most of the workers were Poles. I was the best German-speaker, so I was delegated to go into the barn and see if there was anybody that could help us, while the other two chaps hid behind the manure pile. I went into the barn and I met the groom. I told him we were British on the run. He said, "Sure, I'll help you."

We stayed there three days. He brought us food, and told us where to go when we left there. We had to get back to Thorn, because we had to cross the Vistula River. When we got to Thorn, travelling at night of course, we came to a little Polish house. I rapped on the door, and a fellow came to the door, and by great good luck he was a railway worker. We told him that we were on the run. He told us to meet him by a certain spot down by the tracks, and he'd put us on the right train. By God, he did. He put us on a train that took us a hundred and fifty kilometres east, in a boxcar. We thought, "This'll run right into the Russians if we're lucky!" But it didn't.

We got off the train and we eventually found a large house. Again, a farm. We figured it was owned by Germans, but Poles would be working for them. Again we approached a Pole, absolutely no problem. To cut a long story short, we could hear the gunfire coming closer and closer. So the next thing we knew, a bloody battle raged all round us. Suddenly there was quite a lull, and we could hear voices outside this window. And here we were, looking right into the muzzles of three bloody Russian tommy guns. And we yelled up, "English prisoners!" They weren't too friendly. They ordered us

out and they searched us and took us back to Russian headquarters.

It took us, from the time we met the Russian army, exactly three months to reach Odessa, where we were put in a sort of semi-jail thing. There were two B-17 crews who had been over Ploesti bombing oilfields, and the Russians had confiscated their aircraft and torn out their wireless. They were pretty cheesed off about being there.

But I got out of this jail, and I went down to the docks. And here's a ship flying the Stars and Stripes. She was in with ammunition from the United States for the Russians. I had a little card in my pocket that said, "Gift of the Canadian Red Cross," and I showed it to the Russian guard on the gang-plank, and he just waved me aboard!

So I went on board the bloody ship, and I got a crewman and I said, "Listen, I'm an escaped prisoner of war. I want to get out of here." So he called over four or five of his pals, and they sat me down at a table and said, "You gotta hear this." They had a bloody gramophone, and they played a record by Frank Sinatra. "It's the hottest thing in the States!" So after about fifteen minutes of this, one of them asked me if I was hungry. And I said, "Listen, I'm starving to death." So they opened a great big walk-in fridge, you know, there was cold chicken and ham and oranges.

Well, I loaded up on chicken and ham and oranges. And I ate about four mouthfuls and I threw up over the side. But I did enjoy their coffee.

They told the captain I was there, and the captain said, "Well, look, I'm sailing tomorrow morning for Key West, Florida." I said, "Fine." So he put me in an empty cabin.

The bloody Russians came on the next morning with dogs. And of course, the dogs scratched at my door. So I got marched back to the jail. Then about two weeks later, a British ship came in with a great big crane for their docks. Somehow the captain knew that we were in this jail. He came up to the jail and he said, "Listen. You guys are coming with me." So we sailed from Odessa, and he wirelessed Istanbul. And the [British] Consul said, "Drop them off here, but they've got to put on civilian clothes before they land." Because Turkey was neutral.

So we stayed in Istanbul for two weeks, and then we got a British ship again. And she was heading for Italy. We were dropped off at Naples and we stayed there for maybe a week. And then a British troopship was leaving Naples, and we got home to England that way. Just after Christmas, 1944.

Flight Sergeant Doug Hawkes, Stalag IV B, Mühlberg

Most of the escapes that were made in our camp involved changing identity with a Russian, then going out to live like a bloody Russian. I thought to myself, "There's a better way of getting home that that," so I didn't transfer with any Russian. A lot of fellows thought the great dramatic thing to do was to escape. I didn't and I make no apology for it. I think I went through enough getting there.

(October 29, 1943, was the date of one of the most sensational escapes of the war. It happened at Stalag Luft III, where three British officers, Oliver Philpot, Michael Codner, and the mastermind, Eric Williams, escaped and made their way to Sweden. This was the famous Wooden Horse.)

Flight Lieutenant Dallas Laskey

I don't suppose I was in Luft III more than a couple of days before I got involved in the Wooden Horse. I felt sick and I had this swelling on the back of my head, and it was suggested I better go into the hospital to get checked out. The fellow in the next bed was Eric Williams. We struck up a friendship, and he asked me if I was interested in escaping and I said, "Yes, you bet."

And he told me about the Wooden Horse and what they were doing. The idea was that each day you'd take a vaulting horse, which is a wooden box with a padded top, a box about seven feet long and pyramid-shaped. You actually have a person inside the box! And you'd take it out each day to the exact same spot. So the fellow inside, all he had to do was scoop out the sand, lift up the trap which he'd made — and he'd shored up a little entrance, you see — and jump in and go to work.[1]

I had been a gymnast and had a lot of experience in university gymnastics, so this is where I came in. I conducted the gymnastics on top. My job was to go through all the manoeuvres, the vaulting manoeuvres; the hand springs and the hand stands and head stands and all that kind of thing. And there were always ten, fifteen, twenty people involved in this.

There was an Englishman who was especially clumsy. He got the nickname of "Harry the Horse." And he always fell. Come to think of it, one day he went to do one of his manoeuvres and in actual fact knocked the horse over. Luckily the guards were looking the other way and we were able to get the damn thing back up. Then another day, he did a vault and he landed so damn hard on the other side there was a cave-in. That's when I fell down and pretended to be hurt, and everyone gathered round and we were able to cover it up.

Flight Lieutenant Cliff Irwin

I watched them carry that thing in every day. When they brought it back, there'd be probably a hundred pounds of sand in it, or more. And it looked like they were carrying a baby grand piano! And it was supposed to be a light thing to jump on. And I'd watch the guards sitting on the step watching them go in with that, and think, "Holy doodle! Don't they notice how heavy it is? God, how dumb can they be?"

Pilot Officer Harry Jay

And they had to stage-manage it to get the three people into the tunnel who'd been accepted by the Escape Committee as being entitled to try this. One of them was Ollie Philpot — who's written two books since, very fine escape stories — a British airman. There was a Michael Codner, who was really an army ack-ack type. And there was a third one [Eric Williams].

Flight Lieutenant Dallas Laskey

Three fellows got out. They made their way down to the railway station, bought their tickets. Actually, Williams and

Codner went together, and Philpot went on his own. And I think they ended up at Stettin, and eventually they got a ship to Sweden.

I was scheduled to go out on that tunnel. The chief of security and the second-in-charge, Crawley and Lubbock, and myself, we were the three that were scheduled to go the next morning. But that didn't come about because the tunnel was discovered about nine-thirty that night. I must admit I wasn't too upset. I couldn't speak any German, so my plan was to hoof it through the sixty miles of woods to Czechoslovakia and try, eventually, to get to Yugoslavia, hook up with the guerrillas down there. That was my plan but, of course, it was sheer balderdash.

Pilot Officer Harry Jay

The lights went out and everybody was going to bed. And suddenly the doors were swung open and the lights all came on, and the screaming and shouting and stamping started. They had the commandant and all his officers and troops, and they started trying to get a roll call to find out how many people had escaped. They tried all night long to get this roll call, but they never succeeded. Because people would wander from room to room, and leave the barracks, and people were fusing the lights. So they gave it up for that night.

The next morning, we were called out earlier than usual to roll call. They brought out tables with our actual photographs and our cards, and they started to go methodically through the whole camp to try to establish how many and which ones had got loose. They went on all morning at that and still didn't succeed, because somebody had a soccer ball and kicked it from one side of the square to the other, and others would chase it.

So we went to lunch, proud that we'd bought this much time for the escapers. And a bugle went for another *Appell*. So I sauntered out of my room and went out and loitered around enjoying the sun. I wasn't going to hurry over to the parade ground. But something prompted me to look back around the end of the building, towards the entrance. And there were the Germans, and they looked quite different to the way they'd looked in the morning. Because they had

124

helmets on, they had fixed bayonets, some of them had automatic weapons. And they had several very tall men in very long leather coats, obviously Gestapo people. So I hurried back to my room and I said, "You guys had better stop horsing around, I think they're not kidding anymore."

Anyway, they got their roll call in.

Flight Lieutenant Dallas Laskey

The Germans were quick with the reprisals. The water went off, and I think the lights went off. But the biggest one was, "The wheel of the wagon [is] broken." This was a reference to the little carts that brought in the Red Cross parcels. It stayed broken for a long time. If I recall, I think we were nearly six months on less than half rations. And of course, all privileges were out, like walks and visits to the other camps. And there were five parades a day. And you had to stay in at night, you couldn't open your windows.

Flight Lieutenant Art Crighton

The tragedy of that, as far as we were concerned, is that we lost our golf course! I guess we had nine holes and the bunkers, naturally, were made of sand. And the Germans accused us of using the bunkers to disperse sand from the tunnels. We hadn't done that, but that's what they accused us of doing. And that was like taking candy from a baby, because right from the [SBO] down, golf was the most important thing in that camp. That really broke our hearts.

Flight Lieutenant Dallas Laskey

It wasn't that pleasant but we didn't care. Because we knew the three got out and got all the way back.

(If the Wooden Horse was among the most sensational escapes of World War II, the best known — and most tragic — was the Great Escape. It too happened at Stalag Luft III. Seventy-six Allied officers broke out of a 350-foot tunnel, perhaps the most sophisticated tunnel built by any POWs during the war. Three of the escapees eventually reached freedom, but their success was overshadowed by the fate of the officers who were recaptured by the Germans.)

Pilot Officer Gord King

The man in charge of all this was Mr. X, Roger Bushell, an English squadron leader. He was the brains and the co-ordinator of the Great Escape. A brilliant, brilliant man. Fluent German-speaker.

Pilot Officer Wally Floody

I was in charge of all the tunnelling in the Great Escape. I had been a hard rock miner before the war in Kirkland Lake, and the British figured if I had been a miner, I'd know a lot about tunnelling in sand. But there was absolutely no similarity between tunnelling on your stomach through a two-by-two tunnel in sand and a seven-foot-by-seven-foot tunnel in rock, I'll tell you! But anyway, that's how I got started. And I was a member of the Escape Committee.

Flying Officer Pappy Plant

We had three tunnels underway, and they were code-named "Tom", "Dick," and "Harry." We had one tunnel from the Polish hut, and it was a dandy. The Poles had made the hatch for it: they had a cement floor in the kitchen and bathroom, and they had chipped a very irregular-shaped hole that they could lift out of the concrete, and they started the tunnel there. The other tunnel was started from a washroom, in a floor drain.

The remaining tunnel started in my hut, 104. These stoves sat on a cement slab. We swung a stove out of the way, chipped the cement slab right off, and put it on hinges so it could be lifted. This shaft went straight down about twenty-odd feet. From there, the tunnel went out under the wire. It was that deep because we had heard the Germans were using sound detectors in the wire. There were three chambers in the shaft. One was a pump chamber, and by this time we were into very sophisticated pumping. There also a storage chamber, then the other was the main shaft itself.

After a while, this tunnel was getting to be more than a hundred feet long. It's a long haul to try and bring the earth back. So they started to lay down little tracks made out of wood. And where did the wood come from? The huts. It's a wonder these huts even stood up after a while, because they were stripped! We figured a good wind and the things would collapse. So we found these battens in the partitions, about an inch and a half wide, just right for the track. Somebody'd make wheels for a trolley. Part way along the tunnel, there was what they called "a half-way house." This was an indent where a person could lie, because it got to be too much to haul that cart all the way back full of dirt. So this person could lay at the side of the tunnel and pull the cart back when it got to him. Then the earth was hauled up and went to the dispersers.

The tunnel had electric lights. We had pinched some wiring from a German workman.

Pilot Officer Gord King

I was small and muscular, in good shape from athletics. I got a job at manning the pump, the air bellows. We had a pump made of kit bags, a concertina kind of arrangement that you pushed in and out. That would shove air down an air line made of Klim tins joined together for the fellas that were working on the face of the tunnel chopping the sand. We went down in shifts of about four hours.

We had a food department, where they gathered up food from parcels and made condensed cakes, or something like fudge, from brown sugar and raisins, something you could nibble on that was full of calories. Everyone going out got these rations. So the whole thing was just fantastically well-organized.

Flight Lieutenant Anthony Pengelly

We had two functions. One was documents, and the other was civilian clothes, which had to be made out of blankets and that kind of thing, out of uniforms. A chap who went out as a civilian didn't look like he'd just stepped out of a tailor's shop, but he was quite presentable, based upon the rôle that he was supposed to be assuming. And most good tailoring is done by hand, isn't it?

I had a small group of experts who made maps, made compasses. They forged documents, letters of commendation, letters of transfer, just a myriad of things which were required by people who spoke German who escaped with the idea of travelling openly, disguised, perhaps as a technical foreign worker being transferred to some other city.

We had to get original documents, but that was no problem. We had a lot of contacts with the Germans. You've watched the series, *Hogan's Heroes*? That's an extremely good series, and a lot of things in it were true. We had access through the character in *Hogan's Heroes* called Schultz, but in our camp, his name was Glemnitz. Now Glemnitz was just like Schultz, and a very nice guy. Not dumb, but not empathetic to the Nazis and somewhat sympathetic to our plight. He was in the Luftwaffe in the First World War and was a great friend of a lot of us after the war. In fact, in our reunion in 1965, we brought him over here by Air Canada and he was our guest of honour.

So we got original documents, Glemnitz would provide them. And one of the guards, his girlfriend worked in the commandant's office, and she was plied with chocolates and soap and stuff from our Red Cross parcels, in return for which she made documents available to us.

Now, our penmen could reproduce notepaper with an authentic signature from Göring. We never used Hitler's, but we used Göring's signature frequently. We had banks of names that we took from the newspapers — because we had access to all the German newspapers in the camp — and we could, by studying the newspapers, find out most of the key people in the civil service in Germany; who might, for instance, be responsible for transport, responsible for supplying bodies for factories, consultants.

We also had to invent documents, the ones we didn't have. The Germans, just like a lot of people in Ottawa, are very big on rubber stamps. So the more rubber stamps you had on a document, the more authentic it was. Particularly if you changed the colour of the ink.

Initially, using India ink and a pen, we had [what] looked

like typewritten letters. Eventually we got a typewriter. After the Great Escape, the Germans told us the documents we used were too good. Secretaries make mistakes. We didn't make mistakes.

All the barrack blocks were wood, double-walled, so we had wall safes all over the place where we kept all our stuff: inks, pens, paper.

We would "borrow" cameras from the Germans, and "borrow" film. And the Germans took a lot of pictures for us. In the early part of the war, birthdays for instance, they'd come in and take your picture.

Flight Lieutenant Barry Davidson

Pieber was a hell of a nice person. He's Austrian. There was no way you could turn him to do anything against his people. He was great on the camera. Part of my job was to get him to take pictures. We'd always try and arrange it so when he took a picture, it was something that could be used in a passport. I had to put them in albums so he didn't think they were being used otherwise. There was a lot of this cloak-and-dagger type of thing going on. It doesn't seem important but you gotta know it was.

Flying Officer Keith Ogilvie

I had a job as the Parcels Officer. The Germans used to take a party outside the gates, into a working area, and the Red Cross parcels would come in. And so we couldn't accumulate any food for escape purposes, we had to puncture all the cans. And when parcels came from home, we'd open them up, and the Germans would inspect them there. And there were also some parcels, through our intelligence inside the camp who had contacts from outside — not through the Red Cross, but private parcels, mostly through France — and we would look after these parcels. They would contain, oh, maybe bits of radio sets or fountain pens or photographic material, anything that could be used for escape purposes. When we saw one of these parcels, you'd one way or another distract the guard and get the parcel, and then get them back into camp.

So, because of my job out there, I had a free pass out onto the tunnel break. There were about twenty-five chaps who were highly-organized — they probably spoke German and had passes made up and clothing and all this sort of thing. They had the best chance of getting home. The rest of us were just what we called "hardassing" it. We wore whatever clothes we wanted to, and I went out in my uniform. Our object was to make our way through the woods into Czechoslovakia, and if we were lucky, we'd meet up with the Resistance people there, and maybe get home that way. But it was more of a distraction, really, to cause the Germans the most discomfort possible.

I was number seventy-four to go out.

Pilot Officer Wally Floody

I was moved out of the camp at the beginning of March, before the break. I guess they suspected something.

Flying Officer Keith Ogilvie

It was getting into March, and the Germans knew there was a tunnel, they just couldn't find it. And they were forever in the camp, probing under the huts and that.

The tunnel was all sealed, the work was finished on it. We were just waiting until the weather improved. You see, it was March and their temperatures are much like Canada, it was really cold and frosty. They hoped for the sake of the fellas like myself, going hardass, that if the weather was better, our chances of hiding out in the woods or getting something to eat would be a little better.

But the German activity got a little more fierce, and the Escape Committee decided they would open the tunnel.

Flying Officer Pappy Plant

Since the tunnel was in our hut, I had to exchange rooms with one of those going out. They completed this changeover before the lockup, when the Germans came around and locked the doors of the huts. This was the night of March 25, 1944.

Pilot Officer Harold Garland

It was quite an eyesight. A man appeared dressed in complete evening dress, beautifully done. He was going to catch the train. He could speak the language. There was another chap had a priest's robe outfit that they'd concocted. There were infinite variations. But, as I say, most of us were going to hardass it.

Flying Officer Keith Ogilvie

It started, and it was slow going. We'd been hoping to get out, oh, a maximum of two hundred and fifty people out of the thing. The tunnel was very, very small, and several chaps had bundles that were too big to take in it. One chap had a small valise he was carrying and it was so large they had a cave-in that had to be shored up and fixed up.

When we broke the surface, the tunnel was supposed to come out in trees. Instead [it] broke through short.

The search lights used to swing around and that area would be illuminated. And so we had to wait till the searchlight went back, and they'd pop out two or three guys. So that changed the whole system. They had a guy on the surface behind a tree, and he'd signal the next guy who was waiting at the face to come up — he'd jerk a rope and the guy would pop up and scatter off into the trees, and he'd get on his way.

Flying Officer Pappy Plant

They had other problems, too. Some people had never been down the tunnel before and claustrophobia got to them. And in the midst of all this, there was a bloody air raid. All the lights went out, including the lights in the tunnel. All this slowed things down.

The hut I'd been moved to, we could look out the window and see what was happening. This was about five o'clock in the morning now. You couldn't see much activity, except you could see this damn hole. And by that time, it was like a volcano, with all the steam from the bodies lined up in the tunnel. I don't know how the Germans ever missed it. And it was starting to get a bit light by this time.

Flying Officer Keith Ogilvie

It was just about dawn when I got out. I was number seventy-four. The chap behind me was called Revell-Carter, who was an English Olympic discus thrower, I think. Anyway, there was a German guard walking along the outside of the camp. And he apparently stopped to relieve himself and he practically stepped on the next guys coming out of the tunnel! He saw this guy and unslung his rifle. And Revell-Carter got up and yelled, "Don't shoot, don't shoot!"

The guard fired his gun off. I just took off through the trees, and Revell-Carter stayed there because he was caught by the guard. So I guess I was actually the last chap to get clear of the tunnel. I was by myself, so I just took off through the forest.

Pilot Officer Gord King

I was one of the hardassers, but I was well down the list. After they discovered the tunnel, they surrounded all the huts and we were stuck there until they decided what they were going to do with us. So we had all these rations to eat. And we had a great big party, eating all this stuff that we'd made in the previous days. And it was very rich and full of vitamins and, of course, we all got sick.

They called us out in front of the hut. It was cold, there was snow on the ground, and they made us strip right down, stark bollix naked. We stood there for some time while they made up their mind whether they were going to shoot us. They were absolutely just livid. Finally, they let us get our clothes and go back to our huts, after they had taken all our names. That was a bit scary.

Flying Officer Pappy Plant

We had been told that when the balloon went up, cooperate with the Germans. Because, normally, we'd play around and be awkward about getting on parade. But we were warned they'd be bloody-minded about this.

And this is one time I really had doubts. I thought we'd

had it. The Germans came in and they all had these potato-masher hand grenades stuck in their belts, and their NCOs all had submachine guns. Then they lined us up and set up a heavy machine gun on a tripod. The commandant, he was just white. I guess he figured this would be the end of his career.[2] They knew something big had happened, but at this point they had no idea how many were out.

The thing just overwhelmed them. They brought in the Gestapo, which was quite unusual, because there was no love between the German armed forces and the Gestapo. It was unbelievable to see the lack of cooperation the Luftwaffe would give the Gestapo. And the Gestapo didn't really know what to look for, or where to start.

Flying Officer Keith Ogilvie

I was out for just two days and two nights. I got as far as the big autobahn from Leipzig to Berlin.

I ran out of food, and it was still wet in the trees and the snow. And you couldn't sleep. You were cold and wet and really bloody miserable, and scared kinda poopless. I gather this is what happened to most of the others, too. It was just too wet to be in the forest, so I did what most of the other chaps did, got out onto a little road. Well, the Germans didn't bother looking for us in the trees, they just patrolled the roads, and I walked right into a patrol.

They took me back to Sagan and stuck us in the city jail there. There were a bunch of air force people there, and we were all speculating on what was going to happen to us. We figured we'd go back to the camp. And after a couple of days, we were told we were going back to the camp, so we figured we were going to what they called the *Straflager*, a punishment camp. But this was just speculation, we really didn't know where we were going.

One night, these Sicherheitsdienst chaps — these were sort of German security guards, with the skull and cross-bones on their helmets, they were supposed to be real tough babies — they took us to different places. I think there were twenty-four in our group. We travelled all night and a day. We ended up in a Gestapo prison in Czechoslovakia.

I think there were three of us in a cell, and you could just about stand up and all lie down together. And we were in there for three or four days. There was no rough stuff at all. They'd just take us and ask about the escape and the organization behind it. My story was quite simple: "I'm a British officer and it's my duty to escape."

They must have gone along with that, because they interrogated all twenty-four of us in there. After a week or so, one day they just opened the cell and there were some Luftwaffe guards. One was a corporal that I knew from Luft III. So I yelled at him, "Say, Horst, when are you gonna get me out of this place?" And he said, "Oh, Mr. Ogilvie, tomorrow morning, you'll go."

So the air force guards came and took eight of us back to Sagan. And the other sixteen were just shot.

Flying Officer Pappy Plant

A few days later, we had a few people come back to the camp, people who'd escaped and been picked up. They were thrown in the cooler, and we had communication with them. And they described others who'd been recaptured. Pretty soon we were able to establish a list of those people known to have been recaptured.

Then the German commandant, von Lindeiner, asked to see the Senior British Officer. He said forty-one British or Allied officers had been shot while trying to escape or evade arrest.

Morale really took a beating. You knew that if you were caught climbing over the wire, or running away after a guard had warned you, that you could be shot. Fine, that's fair game. But you sure didn't expect to be picked up, taken to jail, then taken out and shot.

Then a few days later, another nine names came out. It came to fifty that were shot.[3]

Flying Officer Keith Ogilvie

[I] didn't know anything about it, of course. I got back to the camp at Sagan, and I got two weeks in the cooler. And one day, "Red" Noble came by and said, "Jeez, did you hear what happened? They shot all those guys, trying to escape."

I said, "That's not so, Red. These guys were fine. I saw them. There's no way they could re-escape." Some of them had frostbitten feet. Like myself, you know, they had their little fling and all they wanted to do was get back in the air force camp again and wait for the end of the war. But, as it turned out, they shot fifty of them.

It was just luck of the draw, as far as I can gather, that I wasn't one of the ones that were shot. I don't know. I'll never know.

Pilot Officer Wally Floody

They murdered fifty of my close friends. It's a little different than losing a friend in combat, because it's sort of impersonal. You don't know the other guy that shoots him down. But these people were hired, paid, bloody murderers. The Gestapo were murderers and the Gestapo ran Germany.

Flight Lieutenant Anthony Pengelly

After the Great Escape, of course, the invasion followed and the war was at a kind of fever pitch. One of the reasons the German government were so anxious — to the point of shooting the fifty you've heard about — was because they believed that the officers who were prisoners of war in Germany were probably going to be a kind of a fifth column who would organize the millions of foreign labourers who were in Germany. And they wanted, at all costs, to keep the officer contingents inside barbed wire. So it's my understanding that the reason they shot the guys that got out of our place was to make sure that there was gonna be no more escapes.

While we had all kinds of diversionary tactics and did all sorts of shit-disturbing in the camp, there were no actual escapes took place after that. It wasn't really practical to do so because they'd posted notices, if we escaped, we'd be shot out of hand. We kept up tunnelling, we kept up all the preparations, we did all the things that were intended to show that we were going to try to escape. From the German

135

point of view there were lots of attempts, but they weren't serious.

Flying Officer Keith Ogilvie

The Germans gave us permission to build a memorial to the fifty.[4] They had some Czech stonemasons, and they did build a memorial outside the camp somewhere. They deposited the chaps' ashes there.

Footnotes

1. The project started with one man being carried in the horse to do the daily digging. Later, in a bid to speed up the tunnelling, two men did the digging.
2. The commandant, an officer by the name of von Lindeiner, was later arrested and court-martialled.
3. Of the fifty officers executed — murdered — by the Germans, six were Canadians: Henry Birkland, Patrick Watson, James Wernham, George Wiley, George McGill, Gordon Kidder.
4. Despite the terrible tragedy of the Great Escape, three of the seventy-six officers did in fact get away. They included a Belgian, Bob Van Der Stok, and two Norwegians, Jens Muller and Rocky Rockland.

VII/The Repats

Escape may have been the best-known way for a prisoner of war to come home early, but it was not the only way. It has become an accepted rule of "civilized warfare" to exchange prisoners who are no longer fit for combat. These are men who may be missing one or more limbs, or in some other way crippled; they may be partially or totally blind or paralyzed; they might even be mentally unstable. Whatever the case, they must be deemed unlikely to take part in their country's war effort.

During World War II, the repatriation process was relatively simple. A medical team from the International Red Cross would examine candidates and decide whether or not these individuals qualified. If a doctor appointed by the protecting power (the nation holding the prisoners) concurred with the Red Cross ruling, these candidates would then be eligible for repatriation.

With the Red Cross acting as intermediary, the Allies and Germans agreed to several prisoner exchanges during the war. These men were called "repats," and no POW begrudged them their early ticket home. However, it was not until the latter part of 1943 that the first Canadian repats were on their way back to Canada.

Flight Lieutenant Don Morrison

It was November 8, 1942. We were flying Spitfires. Just at the end of my tour as fighter escort to a bunch of American Fortresses, on a bombing raid to the steel works just outside Lyon — we were headed back, and somewhere in the neighbourhood of Saint Omer, my oxygen gave out, and I really

137

don't remember anything that happened from there on. The only information I have, I was able to get later.

I really don't remember anything much after turning around and heading back toward the coast. I had two very, very brief flashes. One was falling through the air and the second was being jostled or being put on a stretcher. Other than that, I didn't know anything for ten days.

What actually happened, when I was shot down, I got hit in the leg with a cannon shell which blew it off. And I left the leg in the aircraft when I bailed out. I found out — matter of fact, only a couple of years ago, when I went back and found some of the people who had actually picked me up when I landed in France — that as I was coming down in the 'chute, some Germans were standing and shooting at me with rifles. The German doctor told me later he figured that, because we were so high and it was so cool, the blood had congealed and therefore I hadn't bled to death.

I woke up in hospital in Saint Omer ten days later. As a matter of fact, when I came to, there was a German guard standing by my bed and the first thing he said, in German, was "Your leg is gone."

They sewed up my leg, did some cleaning up on it. My other leg was burned and they looked after that, dressed it. And they patched up a couple of small assorted holes in my arm. So they really brought me around after ten days, which indicates that they really must have looked after me. It would have been pretty easy to let me go if they wanted to.

So they basically got me into shape until I was ready to be moved into the interrogation camp, which was in Frankfurt. That would have been in the middle of January 1943. I think I was there perhaps two weeks, and then I was moved on to a hospital in Obermassfeld, which was staffed by British doctors. At that time, it was pretty full of Canadians from the Dieppe raid. You know, it's a fairly large hospital with a lot of people in it, and almost everybody there was pretty seriously wounded. So you didn't have much chance to feel sorry for yourself, because you didn't have to look very far to see somebody that was a lot worse off.

Then I moved on to a convalescent hospital at Kloster Haina. I was there for another couple of months, and then moved from there on into Stalag Luft III. I was on crutches, but other than that, I was fine.

I was only in Luft III for three months, because I was repatriated on the first repatriation. We left the camp on October 25, 1943, and headed for home. When we were in Kloster Haina, actually, a Swiss medical commission came around and examined some of the more seriously wounded people, and they simply gave the opinion that the people were no longer fit for combat duties and we were given a little pass which said we were to be repatriated, if and when it came about. There had been one attempted repatriation, I guess it would be in the summer of 1942, and in actual fact the people involved got to the docks when the thing fell through and they had to turn around and go back to the prison camps. I remember seeing newsreels of it in England.

I found out about the repatriation, I think, a week or ten days before it happened. We gathered up on very short notice all the things we could carry. I think, as I recall, there were only about ten of us left Stalag Luft III. We were taken to the train station.

We gradually made our way up to the German naval camp just on the Baltic and took the ferry across to Sweden. Of course, people were being fed into that area from the different camps all across the country. It was a funny feeling going across on the ferry because, having seen the newsreels, you were wondering if the thing would turn around and head back to Germany. And I think it got to the point when it got close to Sweden that some people were ready to jump overboard if it started to turn around.

We crossed with the German prisoners in the centre of Sweden. We landed at the bottom of Sweden and went across, and we passed the trains carrying the German prisoners.

We got [to Edinburgh] and we were hustled right off to a Canadian army hospital. Then we were brought home. We came back on the *Lady Nelson*, which was a hospital ship at that time. We arrived in Halifax and we were really there only a matter of hours before we were on the trains to head home. Toronto was home for me.

We were the first ones to be repatriated, and there was quite a lot of publicity. I got a great deal of mail from people all across the country who were looking for news of next-of-kin who might have turned up in prison camp. It was the Prisoners of War Relatives Association which coordinated the efforts of the prisoners' relatives, gave them information on sending parcels and mail and so on. They did a great job for the POWs. There were lots of interviews too and actually I did quite a bit of work with the Red Cross and the bond drives and so on.

Captain Fred Woodcock[1]

There were twenty-seven of us [at Kloster Haina], blind. Now this was a fourteen-block, or building, German insane asylum. We were in Block Seven. The rest were all empty. They died like flies that winter, 1942.

It was touch and go whether I lived or died, for a long while. I got down to ninety-eight pounds. There were no nurses or orderlies there, except one Australian orderly. You depended on the walking wounded to carry out the doctor's instructions.

I was at Kloster Haina for fourteen months. I made one trip, as a holiday trip, back to Obermassfeld, to see about my ears. We knew there was nothing they could do, but it was just a break. I made one other trip out of there, to Kassel, for an artificial eye.

But then the Gestapo intervened — we were being treated too kindly! The village doctor was a Doctor Jung. If your recording will stand it, I'll say the son of a bitch should have been where I was and I'd have castrated him. He was vicious. Here we are, a three-storey, red-brick building, a toilet on each floor, and close to a hundred and fifty patients. Three flush toilets, and he shut off the water. In the wintertime, he shut off the heat. And he'd make you put up the blackout boards in the middle of the afternoon.

Eventually, it ended up that I was the only one left there. They moved most of them to the *Oflag*, the officers.

I was exchanged in the first exchange of prisoners, in October 1943. Went to St. Dunstan's in England. This is a training centre. I trained at St. Dunstan's until the end of February 1944, and came back to Canada.

Until I got a little bit of my hearing back — months and months — the only communication with the outside world was one tap on the forehead for "no" and two taps for "yes." I had a responsibility at home, and I used to worry myself sick. What am I gonna do? The only blind person I knew at that stage of the game was Old Blind Charlie. He sat outside a restaurant on King Street in Hamilton, sawing away on his violin and selling pencils. I didn't want to end up like that.

This stone wall was ahead of me at all times. Well, what the hell can I do in life? Did I want to be a mattress maker? Did I want to be a shoemaker? Did I want to be a telephone operator? Good God, surely, no. And when I got back home, I had had enough of this training. Colonel Baker came down and talked me into going down to CNIB.

Then, one day in the cafeteria, old Dave Lawley came up and said, "How would you like to be a field secretary?" What's a field secretary? A field secretary goes out and does all he can for the other blind people. That's for me! And it just opened the door. Eventually, they called on me to do the liaison job with all the war-blinded who were starting to come home from overseas.

Private Gren Juniper

I was repatriated in May 1944. I had been wounded at Dieppe. First of all, I was shot in the side, the right side. The bullet went in just above the waist and came out in the middle of my chest. Then I had three machine gun bullets in my left ankle.

I passed the Repat Board. That's three Swiss doctors from the Red Cross who come around and examine you. They just look you over, and then there's a file on you and they look that over, and they look at the X-rays. They make the decision right there.

Now, I was classified as a 2B. 1A goes home. 2B, you go to a neutral country. And then the stories start. We heard nobody wanted us. Switzerland didn't want us. Sweden didn't want us. Spain didn't want us. So what the heck are we gonna do?

They were making preparations for the second exchange,

and we heard the 2Bs were gonna be left behind. We couldn't go to a neutral country because they didn't want us. And yet our case wasn't severe enough to be sent directly home. You almost had to be a stretcher case. Anyway, about two or three days before the exchange was gonna take place, they finally consented to send the 2Bs home as well.

Around the middle of May '44, we walked out of camp. I was on crutches. And I remember we got on a train. They had music piped through all the cars. At the end of each carriage there was an open observation platform. We had to go down to Spain. There were several hundred of us. There were Palestinian Jews, there were Australians, a few Arabs. British. American. And there were about a dozen Canadians. All Dieppe fellas, except one sailor.

We were put on a boat, the *Gradiska*. We were on that for three days, until we got to Barcelona. And all they served us was mainly soup. And the last day we were on, the last meal that we had, it was either a steak or a chop, I can't remember which — there was no dining room or anything like that, we had to eat at our beds — and a bottle of Pilsner beer.

Then the exchange took place at the dock in Barcelona. It was a complicated one-for-one exchange. So then we got on the *Gripsholm*. Now we're not just in a great big ward, we're in staterooms. The ship was painted white and had the Red Cross on it. It was an ocean liner.

Then we had to go up and eat. Ohhh! White table cloths, flowers in the centre. Hors d'oeuvres: celery, olives, pickles. Holy Christmas, we were in seventh heaven! For dessert, baked Alaska in the form of a small ship!

Well, the Germans had the same treatment going over. The German prisoners, I guess, had been in Canada, and the *Gripsholm* took them over to Spain. We found out later, when they got on the *Gradiska* and saw what accommodations were available for them, the *Gradiska* left early because they were having a riot on the ship. These guys didn't want to go back to Germany.

We went up to Belfast and let off the British guys. After we left Belfast, we came across the ocean. I think it was six days. Fifty of us, twelve Canadians and the rest Americans, on board this luxury liner. With a bar.

Then we landed in New Jersey. We got on a train and headed for Toronto. I think the train took us to the Exhibition Grounds. The Royal Regiment of Canada had a band there, and we were supposed to walk in behind it. This was June 7, the day after D-Day. My sister finally found me, and the rest of the family was there, and neighbours.

So then they took me to my home. And there was a welcoming committee. The front of the house was all decorated, "Welcome Home." It was the funniest feeling. Here I can walk out on the street all by myself, with nobody around! It was hard to get over.

As soon as I was able to, I was going around visiting the families of some of the guys left in the camp. Those that I couldn't visit, I wrote letters.

At first, it was a novelty being a celebrity. It didn't take me long to get tired of it. Reporters. Photographers. I remember a reporter from the Peterborough *Examiner*, a young fellow. I told him, "Okay, I'll tell you my story, but I want you to print it the way I tell it." He didn't. So I was a hero again, and the phone started ringing again. But he phoned me up and thanked me for the interview, and told me that he got a bonus of fifty dollars for that interview. All I got was a bunch of phone calls![2]

Footnotes

1. Woodcock was blinded and partially paralyzed during the Dieppe raid.
2. There were at least two more prisoner exchanges involving Canadians, in September 1944 and January 1945.

VIII/HMCS Athabaskan

Some considered HMCS *Athabaskan* an unlucky ship. The "Tribal" Class destroyer was hit by a bomb while under construction in England. She was badly damaged in a storm in the North Sea, and later she collided with a small vessel outside Scapa Flow, the big naval base in the Orkney Islands north of Scotland. In August 1943, she became one of the first victims of a new German weapon, the glider bomb, a radio-controlled mini-airplane carried by a bomber. Five crewmen died and twelve were injured when one of these glider bombs hit *Athabaskan* while on duty in the Bay of Biscay; the incident put her out of commission for three months. Not long after the big destroyer returned to duty she encountered still more ill-fortune.

Athabaskan was one of four "Tribals" in the RCN. Her sister ships were *Iroquois*, *Haida*, and *Huron*. Big and fast, this class of destroyer boasted the firepower of a small cruiser. Unlike most Canadian destroyers, which were used mainly for escorting convoys in the North Atlantic to protect them from German U-boats, the "Tribals" had an offensive role. They were used primarily in search-and-destroy missions in the English Channel and the Bay of Biscay, often teamed with British destroyers and cruisers.

In February 1944, *Athabaskan*, along with *Huron* and *Haida*, joined the newly-formed 10th Destroyer Flotilla at Plymouth. With British forces, the three Canadian destroyers launched a series of operations in preparation for D-Day, clearing the Channel of German shipping, harrassing enemy convoys, and screening minelaying operations. On April 26, *Athabaskan* and *Haida* teamed up to sink a German "Elbing" Class destroyer, or E-boat. That was to be *Athabaskan*'s last hurrah.

144

Chief Petty Officer Hec Cooper

We had previously been operating out of Plymouth, on a nightly basis, disrupting all types of shipping along the English Channel. This particular night, we — the *Athabaskan* and the *Haida* — ran into a flotilla of German E-boats and coastal vessels. One of them hit us with a torpedo. It was sufficient to cut off our stern and make us a sitting duck. That was about four, four-thirty in the morning of April 29.

Able Seaman Roy Westaway

My job was to pipe hands to abandon ship stations. Then we got torpedoed again[1], amidships, which blew her in half as far as I can recall. Then I started running around like a hen with its head off. And one chap who was older than I was — I was pretty young at the time — grabbed hold of me and settled me down and said, "You'd better get over the side." So we jumped over the side.

We swam around for a while, watched the ship go down. She went down stern first.[2] Swam into a lot of heavy oil. We gradually formed a group in the water. There'd be maybe fifteen, sixteen of us. We found a carley float. We had just been issued new life jackets from the Canadian navy about two weeks prior to this. They were a vest type, far superior to the old style you had to blow up. And I think possibly they saved a lot of lives. They had a cord attached to them with a snap hook on the end. We all couldn't get in this carley float because there was so many of us, so we all hooked onto it. But the thing was apparently full of holes. It started to sink, and there were some hectic moments trying to get these snap hooks off, because our hands were cold.

Haida came back in the meantime, after she'd run one of the German ships aground. *Haida* fired some star shells to light up the scene and started to take on a few guys. I guess I was maybe a hundred yards from her when she had to leave. Of course, she could only stop for a few minutes and even then she was taking a big risk.

Leading Seaman Jim L'Esperance

So eventually, the *Haida* came alongside our boat. I grabbed

145

with one arm through the scramble-net, and with the other arm I was holding onto the float. In the meantime, one of the fellas who'd already been rescued came down to help me, because I kept drifting away from the ship. So he sat on one end and I was hanging onto the other end while the chaps are going up the scramble-net. Just then the ship started to move, and being hooked onto the bloody float, it pulled me away from the scramble-net. So I unhooked the thing and swam after the scramble-net. And I was just one hand's-length away, and there was a guy on the scramble-net trying to reach me, and I couldn't make it. I touched his fingers.

Eventually, I got to another float and got into it. It was pitch black. We could hear people, you know, and I could hear one fella yelling, "Help, help, help." So I left the float and I swam out and grabbed him and pulled him back to the float. He'd injured his back, he was paralyzed. And he was burnt. The skin was hanging from his face, and his hands were like gloves hanging from his fingernails, the skin. I got him into the float and got him as comfortable as he could get. We sat in the float until daylight, maybe six-thirty, and a German minesweeper came and picked us up.

So I got the rest of the guys up on the ship. Then they stripped all our clothes off. We were covered in fuel oil. They took us two at a time into this showerroom and they gave us a detergent soap to try to get this oil off us. It worked partially, but it took weeks to get rid of all the oil. They gave us a bit of breakfast after that. About four prunes and a bowl of macaroni.

Chief Petty Officer Hec Cooper

We were kept very comfortable in the aft part of the ship. In the run from our pickup point to Brest, we were bombed twice by our own planes. We were afraid that the bombs we had helped pay for at that particular time by Canada War Bonds were going to fall on us! But we landed safely in Brest. I was interned, along with eighty-four others.[3]

Leading Seaman Jim L'Esperance

They landed alongside the jetty in Brest and unloaded us,

still naked, into trucks. They drove us through the town, out to a naval barracks. They marched a guard of about twelve or fifteen men in, with rifles. They told us to stand up. The officer stood there with his sword out and went through some instructions in German. They ended up aiming at us. And the officer said, "If you escape, you shall be shot."

They issued us French naval clothing. And they took us into these barracks. We were instructed to lay on the floor, and anybody caught talking got a rifle butt across the side of the head. These were naval guards we had during the afternoon, and in the evening they brought in German army soldiers. And the whole routine changed. We could talk to one another, they gave us cigarettes.

Now we were only there four or five days. Any time there was an air raid, we were taken from that room on the second floor and put up in the attic.

Chief Petty Officer Hec Cooper

The Geneva Convention says you only give your name, rank, and number. The Germans figured they should be entitled to more, and they used to try and get information from us. The things that they wanted to know were wartime bits and pieces of information as to what ships were around. They were worried about the invasion at this time. Naturally, being a storeman, I used to tell them, "If you want to know the price of peas in Australia, I can tell you that, but don't ask me about ships. I don't know anything about them."

Leading Seaman Jim L'Esperance

Then they came along and said, "All right, you're going to Germany." So they took us to the railroad yard and put us on a train. It was crowded, so at all times there had to be somebody standing. Even when you went to the washroom — you went individually — a guard took you down, you went into the washroom, and he brought you back. The windows were barred, and the doors. And no food, no water.

Chief Petty Officer Hec Cooper

The morale was pretty good, there's no question about that,

although there's fear because you don't know what's going to happen next. We spent five days on the train. The five days on the train were rather horrendous because, my God, we were bombed I don't know how many times. It took five days to go a route that would ordinarily take just a few hours.

Leading Seaman Jim L'Esperance

We got into Bremen, and they took us by a smaller railroad to the prison camp, which was between Bremen and Hamburg, a place called Westertimke. Marlag [und] Milag Nord.

We were marched into this barracks, and as you went by a door, they pushed you in. In the room, there was a folding table against the wall, a bed, and a stove, and a little frosted glass window about eight feet from the floor. So they left us there all night. No heat. And in the morning, they woke you up individually and took you to the washroom. You had to shave in cold water. Ersatz soap, and everybody used the same razor. And then they served you breakfast. Usually, it was a piece of bread and jam. And then for dinner, as far as I can remember, it was prunes and macaroni. Saw nobody for four days. If you had to use the toilet facilities, they had a plug in the wall with a flag on it. You pushed the plug and the flag came up. And the guard would wait till nobody else was in the lavatory, then he'd take you into the lavatory.

A fellow came in to interrogate me. It wasn't too harsh. They were more interested in radar and stuff like that, you know, which I knew nothing about, being a gunnery rating. They questioned me for two or three days. He brought me a book about the First World War, how the British abused the Germans. And he brought me a sandwich. Every day, he'd come in for about two hours and ask me different questions. They went through the whole block like this. We were there two weeks, or something.

Chief Petty Officer Hec Cooper

I spent over thirty days in this solitary confinement. And I never figured out why.

Next, I got into this interrogation camp, where one of the interrogators I met knew my part of Alberta very well. In fact, this was one of the tricks they pulled. Try to find interrogators that were familiar with the area that you were from. However, I was quite amazed at the time that this German civilian was one of the engineers that helped build Highway 13 from Wetaskiwin up to Hardisty. He told me they used to use wooden piles to cover some of the bogs. And he told me he had travelled south to pick up railway ties from my own father, who was section foreman with the Canadian National in Kelsey, Alberta. He seemed to know so much about the area that I had to feel that at least he'd been there.

Leading Seaman Jim L'Esperance

While we were in there we were interrogated again. It was the same routine. And they wanted to know if we had gas shells on board the *Athabaskan* and all this stuff.

We hadn't had a cigarette, either, for all this time. We were standing in the compound one day, and over the fence came a parcel. We ran and picked it up. It was cartons of cigarettes. The prisoners in the main compound had collected them for us. So at least we had a smoke for a while.

We were there about two weeks, and then they took us out and put us in the main compound.

Able Seaman Roy Westaway

They put us in solitary confinement in a transit camp. It was just a little cell with a wooden bunk and a folding table and a stool. Every third or fourth day, a German officer would come in and interrogate us. They had an aerial photograph of Plymouth Harbour, which was our home base, taken the day before we were sunk. They asked the names of all the ships and the size. So I just made up things. After the interrogation, he turned the photograph over, and they had [already] identified everything and all the sizes anyway.

Seems to me I was in there twenty-one days. They didn't let us speak to anyone and we never saw anyone. At eight o'clock, we got two slices of black bread with margarine. At 12:30, we got three boiled potatoes or a type of tasteless porridge, with no milk or sugar. At 5:00 P.M., we got two slices of bread and jam, with no margarine. We had herb tea with the first and last meals.

Then they took us into the main camp. Seems to me there were about ten thousand prisoners there, but most of them were civilian — political internees from practically every country you could think of. There was a few Americans there, off an American navy ship, and a lot of English naval fellas there. I think, altogether, there was about seven or eight hundred naval personnel, and the rest were made up of civilians and merchant seamen.

Leading Seaman Jim L'Esperance

We were in wooden huts with French windows that opened up. And we had double bunks and straw palliasses. We were issued two blankets. One, we laid over the straw palliasse and the other we folded — at least, in the room I was in — and we got newspaper and stuff like that and sewed it in between. In the wintertime, we slept with everything on but our boots. They issued us with British overcoats and uniforms, with a big "KGF" stamped on the back in red — *Kriegsgefangener*. There was no heat, no hot water. In the wintertime, they'd leave the taps running so they wouldn't freeze. If you wanted to have a sponge bath, you stood there and stripped off and washed yourself down. They did have shower facilities there, but they were about a mile down the road. We used to march there, but that wasn't too often. And like I say, the soap was ersatz. It was clay or something.

Able Seaman Roy Westaway

They allowed the English prisoners to go out on working parties around the farms, but they wouldn't let us go out because we were Canadians. Apparently the German prisoners in Canada didn't have to work, so they said, "Well, you guys don't have to work too." But we would have sooner gone out to work, because you could scrounge a turnip or something. We were allowed once every two weeks, it seems to me, to go on a walking party, picking up dead branches for firewood.

If it was left to the rations that we got from the Germans, I'm sure none of us would have made it. But the Canadian and International Red Cross supplied food parcels which

150

were supposed to be supplied once a week, but the most we ever got was once every two weeks. They gave us some kind of goat's milk cheese now and again, and turnip soup. I used to get up early and root through the garbage cans looking for potato peels.

Chief Petty Officer Hec Cooper

About Christmas of '44, a lot of people were starting to be marched in. There was a whole group of French internees that were in bad shape. They were moved into a camp right next to us. I have to admit, the Germans always respected a prisoner of war. This is an odd thing about their thinking. They respected what they called "the fighting man," but they wouldn't respect the civilian that refused to become a loyal German.

Footnotes

1. A board of inquiry later concluded that one of the *Athabaskan's* magazines exploded. However, at the time, many members of the crew believed the stricken ship had been hit by another torpedo.
2. One hundred and twenty-seven members of *Athabaskan's* crew perished that night, including the skipper, Lieutenant-Commander J.H. Stubbs.
3. Of the eighty-five prisoners of war produced by the sinking of HMCS *Athabaskan*, eighty-three were Canadians; the other two were British. Only ninety-eight RCN personnel became POWs during the entire war.

IX/The Latecomers

D-Day: June 6, 1944. The Normandy Invasion. It was not only the biggest amphibious landing in military history, it was also the beginning of the end of Hitler's Germany. By that point, the Reich that Hitler promised would last a thousand years was a little more than eleven years old; in less than a year, it would be dead.

Once Allied forces gained their foothold in France, Germany's defeat was just a matter of time. The Germans simply did not have the resources to fight a war on three fronts. Besides being tied down in France, the Germans had their hands full with a bloody war of attrition in Italy, and in the east the Russian steamroller was picking up momentum. The Germans were suffering catastrophic and irreplaceable losses. On top of that, the strategic bomber offensive was about to resume. After a year of pounding Germany's industrial heartland between March 1943 and March 1944, much of the air power of the western Allies was diverted to support the D-Day invasion. But once the Allied ground forces broke out of Normandy and started sweeping across France, the air forces returned their undivided attention to Germany in September, and German targets were subjected to even more furious and devastating attacks from the air.

For the prisoners of war in Germany, all this was a combination of good news and bad news. The good news was that Germany's collapse was imminent and the POWs could look forward to liberation. The bad news was that conditions in the prison camps began to deteriorate. The already poor rations given the POWs would be cut back even further because Germany was, in effect, being strangled by the Allies.

The only food available was that which the Germans produced themselves, including synthetic concoctions of every description. Even worse from the POWs' point of view, the destruction of Germany's transportation system made it that much harder, and sometimes impossible, to deliver Red Cross food parcels to the prisoners. It was a grim situation, not only for the longtime POWs, but also for the latecomers, the soldiers and airmen captured after D-Day.

Corporal Phil Mechlair, 1st Canadian Parachute Battalion

At 10:30 P.M. on June 5, '44, we left Farnborough, England, and we bailed out on the Orne River approximately 11:15, 11:30. The winds were so high, we were eighteen kilometres from where we were supposed to land. I guess I would have been one of the first ones to land in Normandy.

We went back, looking for this bridge we were supposed to blow up. There were six sentries when we got there. And then, I guess, there weren't six sentries. Then it started to become daylight and the Germans realized what was going on. They opened up on us with everything they had. We managed to blow up the bridge. But I got hit. I got one [bullet] in the shoulder and two in my stomach. A fella named Greg Pidluberg says, "I'm gonna drag you out." But I told him, "I'll be honest with you, I've had it." I was going conscious and unconscious.

The next thing I knew, this German soldier put me on a boxcar, and I was taken to Ghent, Belgium. I spent three months in the hospital at Ghent.

Private Simon Avery, North Nova Scotia Highlanders

We went in on D-Day. We rode tanks inland, and they left us to dig in while the tanks went back. We'd dig in, and then we'd get out of there and move a little further and dig in again. I guess in the forty-eight hours I was there, I must've dug in a dozen times or more.

So it was June 8. And the Germans counterattacked, and we were pinned down and surrounded. There was a lot of casualties. I don't know where the order came from, but it came from somewhere, to surrender.

They lined everybody up and took all possessions. Even wallets and pictures, your watch, rings, everything. Pencils, pens, anything you had. I recall a fellow wouldn't [give] them his mother's picture. They shot him. A few fellas they took out for interrogation. Their bodies were found later. They were reported killed in action, but they weren't. The Germans killed them after they were captured.[1]

I expected to be shot, too. Hitler Youth, that's what they called that outfit. They were only college kids, and they were devils. They looked like they were doped up.

We marched quite a ways, and we were strafed on the road. They couldn't get us to move fast enough, so that's when they slapped us in boxcars. It was desperate on those boxcars. I think they let us out a couple of times at some kind of a trough, and we washed ourselves. It was over thirty days we had in the boxcars, the whole month of June.

We ended up at Stalag IV A.

Flight Lieutenant George Gardiner, 429 Squadron, RCAF

(Gardiner was the pilot of the Halifax bomber pictured in a photograph in this book.)

I was well under a thousand feet by the time I got out. And I landed on top of a German dugout and knocked myself out. Obviously, I was pulled inside the dugout by the German crew. And we were on the receiving end of an artillery barrage from our Canadian army.

From about 6:30 to around eight o'clock, there was heavy artillery fire and explosions around the area. But at around eight o'clock, a staff car came up and removed me from the gun emplacement and moved me back into secondary lines.

We got out of the staff car and there were two German guards with me. We were walking up a hill, and I looked up, and the American air force was bombing. So the two Germans jumped for protection, but I beat them to it. And we were on the receiving end of a heavy barrage of bombs from the U.S. Eighth Army Air Force.

After that was over, they moved me up the hill. A building had been flattened by the bombing, and a German officer came out of the basement, knocking plaster and what have you off him. He was quite angry. I wouldn't give him anything more than my rank and number, and he wanted to know what other activities would be happening the rest of the day. And since his headquarters had been bombed out, I was in the wrong place at the wrong time, I guess. Because he spit in my face and manhandled me a bit, you know, worked me over.

After that, these two guards were told to take me further back. We ended up in a farmhouse. They took me downstairs and they paraded Phil Brunet in front of me. Phil Brunet was my navigator. His face was black and blue and his nose was broken. He was the most pitiful sight that you could ever see.

They put us in this staff car and started moving Phil and I farther back. And on the way to Alençon, a Typhoon spotted the German staff car. I had to tell Phil to stand up and I hit him as hard as I could, into the ditch. So he and I ended up in the ditch, and the two German guards were on top of us as well. But then our car was destroyed by the Typhoon.

So we walked into Alençon, which was a gathering place for prisoners. They took Phil away to a doctor, and I was transferred, along with some other army boys that had been picked up, to the city of Chartres. There must have been twenty-seven or thirty prisoners: American army, Canadian army, paratroopers, and stuff like that. I was segregated from them. One German explained that pilots were a different breed, they were murderers of women and children, and we wouldn't be treated as POWs, as the army people would be.

We were only in Chartres for two or three days. We were put on a train to be moved back into Germany. We finally got into Frankfurt, which was the interrogation centre. We had one Jewish lad that was in the American army. The guards pushed him onto the station platform and told the people what he was. I had to keep control of the prisoners while the civilians worked over the Jewish lad.

I was in the interrogation centre for about three weeks. They took different approaches in the interrogation. It was easy sometimes, hard other times — offering cigarettes, offering food. It amazed me how much they knew about us. Also, they'd ask if we, in turn, would join them eventually and go against the common foe, the Russians. They spent one whole day on that.

They gave up on me after about three weeks. And I ended up at Stalag Luft I. It was an all-officers' camp. Roughly about five thousand American airmen and one thousand or fifteen hundred British Commonwealth airmen.

By this time, the war was going our way. I thought at the time, "If I can survive a while, it's going to be over before too long." I was actually more concerned that messages could be gotten back to Canada for my wife and family.

Private Ronald Barton, Lincoln and Welland Regiment

We were part of the Fourth Armoured Division, infantry support for the armour. We went to France in July '44. We had been in some secondary positions. Around July 26 or 27, we relieved the Queen's Own Rifles. We were in a little town called Bourguébus and this was in a salient.

On the night of August 1, I had a nice hot meal around midnight. The scouts came back and said, "There's nothing out there." Off we went across a wheatfield. In single file, five or ten yards apart. I was in the first section of the first platoon of the first company, which meant I was maybe eighth or ninth from the head of the line. This is about two o'clock in the morning. The wheat had been cut, there was stubble that was probably about four inches high.

And one of our corporals who was walking off to the right of us fell into a German slit trench. And they were set in their slit trenches, with their machine guns sited to cover the field. They fired a star shell, and all hell broke loose. Of course, we started to fire back, and somebody yelled, "Down!" We laid there for a few minutes. Their machine guns were sited to fire maybe six inches off the ground.

The next thing I knew, they came around behind us, and everybody who was left, they just scooped up and took along with them. I am aware of only four or five that survived.

The next day, they took us to a little French house on a road — there were four of us there — and we were there for about four days. I remember thinking, "What in hell is my wife gonna think?" That came to me so often: she's not gonna know where I am, she's not gonna know what's going on. They fed us nothing for those four days.

Then one morning, they loaded us into army trucks, German army trucks displaying the Red Cross. That highway to Paris, nothing moved on it. That was the highway that the Allied air forces completely controlled, and there were trucks and ambulances just littered in all the ditches along the way. The Germans had us sitting up on top of the truck, and when this P-38 came down to have a look, they jumped out of the truck and ran into the ditch, and told us to stay there! In any case, this P-38 came down and made one pass over us and swung around, and he came back over once more. I'm sitting in the back of this truck, and I'm watching him swoop across the field and thinking, "What's his decision?" He waggled his wings and went back up. Those planes were in the air the whole time we were on the road, but they never bothered us after that.

And we went through Paris about three days before the Americans and French got there. The Free French were in Paris, fighting, as we went through. I saw the Eiffel Tower. I took a good look at it because I thought I may never get another chance to see it.

We got into a place called Châlons-sur-Marne, which was a big old army barracks. There I was interrogated by a chap who went to the University of Toronto and knew Eaton's and Simpson's, et cetera. Most of it was nostalgia time. Whether he got anything out of me, I don't know.

Then I had my first experience in a boxcar. We left Châlons in a boxcar, five or six days, no food, no sanitary facilities. There was one window in the car, and one of the fellas had a tin can, and we used to line up and urinate in the tin can and throw it out through the barbed wire. That was a pretty bad scene.

We stopped at a place called Limburg, which was Stalag XII A. At Stalag XII A, we met the Red Cross. They photographed us and gave us a serial number. Now we have to be accounted for, so it was a little better after that.

It was an established camp. I think, in many ways, the crowd that came from Normandy was a bit of an embarrassment to everybody, because these chaps were very well-organized. They had little gardens. They were prisoners, but things were not too bad. Then all of a sudden, there's a flood of new prisoners and they didn't know what to do with them all.

We were at XII A for a while, then back on the boxcars, to Mühlberg, on the Elbe. This was Stalag IV B and that was a British NCO camp. It was very well-organized.

And because I was under the rank of corporal, I was required to work. So they made up a group of about a hundred and twenty of us, twenty Canadians and about a hundred Englishmen, and we were sent to Leipzig, again by boxcar. Again no food. It was frosty that morning, October 5. We marched through into the gasworks, and we were introduced to our barracks, which was on the second floor. They had built three-tier bunks, floor to ceiling, with straw in them. No blankets. Two rooms had beds, and one room had long benches and tables.

I got on a job that required us to go all over the city and dig holes in the road so they could service these gas connections. We dug holes all over Leipzig. We had some German civilians we worked with who were terrific. I had a German share his lunch with me one day. But we had other ones who were Nazis, who were real bastards.

Flight Lieutenant Al Aldridge
Flying Officer Ray Epstein, 115 Squadron, RAF

Aldridge: On the night of August 25, 1944, we were detailed to bomb a target at a place called Rüsselsheim, in Germany, which is near Frankfurt and which, we were told, manufactured parts for the German V-weapons. The bombing run was uneventful. We were flying straight and level out of the target when suddenly I noticed another aircraft to my left and below and coming straight up at me. So I turned my Lancaster to the right and pulled the nose back. But the other aircraft just touched my left wing. The engines of the other Lancaster chewed off part of my port wing tip. And apparently my propellers tore his wing off. That plane went straight in and all the crewmembers were killed.

It was very difficult to handle the airplane. I had both feet on the right rudder. After a time, I had the flight engineer lie down and brace himself on the rudder too. We were losing height. And the aircraft would stall, as I recall, at about a hundred and thirty-five miles an hour. We flew for about twenty minutes. I think about six thousand feet, I ordered the crew to bail out.

Epstein: And we bailed out. I landed in a nice little clearing in the woods, just off of a road. Didn't even sink to my knees. And I pulled the 'chute down, hid it.

Aldridge: I landed on the ground, and it was a very soft, easy landing. I only fell to my knees on a plowed field.

That was a Friday night and I was on the loose till Monday noon. I was caught by a patrol of some sort, somewhere near Trier. Then a couple of German soldiers came into the station with their cocked Lugers and they took me outside. And outside was a four-wheeled wagon, and attached to the front of the wagon were five or six ropes, and manning each of these ropes were five or six people. Fifteen or twenty men pulling this wagon, which was piled high with tree stumps. Obviously, it was a working party of Dutchmen, and they were in sad shape. All young. No hair on their heads at all, all shaved. And sort of grey in pallor. Some of them had shoes, some of them didn't. Some of them had feet with bandages, with blood seeping through them.

So anyway, I got stationed behind the wagon and off we went. Our little procession went on for four or five miles till we came to this camp.[2] We went into this camp, and the prisoners went their way, and I was stood on the parade square.

[After interrogation] they put me in a cell. I was in there for the day, in handcuffs, behind my back. I wasn't allowed to sit down. Late in the day, an officer came in and took my handcuffs off, and he rubbed my wrists, they were all swollen. And he brought me a piece of bread and some soup.

Epstein: I must describe the escape kit that we were equipped with. These were two plastic bottles that fitted in your front pockets. And one had European currencies of every type. And

159

little cards, how to ask questions in various languages. They didn't tell you how to understand the answer, just how to ask the questions! And it had heavily concentrated milk tablets and Horlick's tablets and benzedrine tablets and water purifying tablets and a little nylon fishing line and a little razor. The map, which was an absolutely superb map of Europe, was on pure silk with a paisley pattern imprinted over the map so that it didn't look like a map of Europe at all. You kept it tied around your neck. And all the buttons on our clothes were compasses, so that if you tied a string with a knot, a little dot on the bottom of the button would point north. And any of the brass buttons that you had, you could unscrew the top and you'd have a little glass-covered compass inside. And in our flying boots, our sheepskin-lined flying boots, there were secret little pockets with a file for cutting steel bars. A real marvellous little escape package.

I walked for two or three nights in Germany. I'd take half a benzedrine tablet at dark and half of a tablet at midnight, and I'd just walk all night, nonstop. I think I put in — I'm guessing — thirty miles a night. I was finally captured near Trier, very close to the French border.

They tied my hands behind my back and marched me a few miles back to this village and took me to the little local Gestapo office. And I was lucky as hell to be caught near a little village, because the local Gestapo were two big fat farmers. One reached in, pulled out my dog tags, and he said, "Epstein. Jude?" I said, "I'm sorry. I don't speak German."

Then they brought in this very pretty girl who was in her twenties and she said, "I speak English, and they want me to translate. They want to know if you're a Jew."

And I said, "Well, will you please tell them that according to international law, I'm only allowed to give my name, rank, and number."

So she told them, and one of these guys turned to the other and he said, "*Ja, er habe recht.* He is right." And I was lucky that they took that attitude, because they just could have hauled off and kicked the shit out of me. They took me across the street to the local army establishment, with instructions to take me to the nearest Luftwaffe.

They had a soldier with a rifle and a bayonet and a

corporal with a holster and a pistol, and these two were going to escort me to this air force base. So as they marched me down the street, everybody in the village was lined up on both sides of the street to see this captured flier. And a girl — oh, I guess she'd be about twelve or thirteen years old — jumped off the curb and came up towards me. And she spit at me, got me right in the cheek. And if you've never had that done to you — it's the most demeaning feeling.

Aldridge: Then the next morning, I went by truck with two or three guards into Trier. They drove me to this building, and it was Gestapo headquarters and I thought, "I'm done." They took me upstairs, and they put me into a room and turned the light off. Eventually, I was taken out to be interviewed by a Gestapo man in civilian clothes. He tried to impress upon me the fact that London was in ruins because of the V-weapons, the V-1s and V-2s. The only thing I said to him was, "Very strange. I was in London last weekend on leave, and I had a terrific time."

I went back into my cell, and eventually a Luftwaffe sergeant-major came and took me out of the building. We actually went on a streetcar. I had my tunic folded over my arm so the insignia wouldn't show. We got on a tram and went to the end of the line. We walked a ways and there was a Messerschmitt, Me 109, airfield. We went to the guardhouse. And in the guardhouse was Ray Epstein.

From there we were taken by train to Frankfurt, the interrogation centre. And we went right through Rüsselsheim, the place we had bombed four nights before. We knew we hit our target, the factories were just in ruins, blown to hell.

I think I was only in Frankfurt for a day, overnight. The interrogation officer pushed a folder over to me. On the top was "115 Squadron, RAF." There was a complete battle order for that night, August 25, for our squadron. And I mean complete: pilot, navigator, bomb aimer, everybody on the squadron, just as though it had been mimeographed at the squadron and sent over. He said the only thing he didn't know about us or our aircraft was the number of gallons of gas we had on board.

161

Epstein: By this time it was dusk, and they announced that trains would be leaving for permanent prisoner of war camps the following day. And there were Americans in the lineup and RAF and Australians and New Zealanders. We were all taken over to the next building, full of these wooden doubledecker beds scattered all through it. No lights.

Fellas started to talk. "Well, where were you captured? What happened to you?" "Well, I was flying a Typhoon with these new damn dive brakes that aren't worth a shit." And, all of a sudden, it occurred to somebody that the place might have been bugged and we started a search. And we found microphones all over the place. And people started yelling, "Stop talking about anything military!"

This, I thought, was extremely clever. The tension of being isolated, going through a formal interrogation where you're on your guard not to say anything — and how many of these guys were English-speaking Germans in uniform, mixing in with the group to pick up little bits of information?

Being a Jew never caused me any problems. The interrogator never mentioned it, I was assigned a prisoner of war number and the matter was never brought up again. Now, I didn't do anything to stand out in a crowd either. No goddam way! I think there were only two or three Jewish fellas in that camp.

I think the Germans had a benign attitude toward Canadians. I think they were a little less anti-Canadian probably than they would be anything else.

But the Germans had quite a propaganda effect of what they called *Terrorangreifen*, "terror attacks," and they treated all air raids as a terror attack. And I think after the war, when they did careful analysis and studies of what had actually been bombed versus what was supposed to have been bombed, they really were terror attacks! On some of the raids, there'd be three waves, there could be nine hundred bombers going in on a city. And they would pinpoint the factory that you were supposed to bomb, and these Pathfinders would go in first — and they were superb — and there'd be all these flares lighting the targets you were supposed to bomb. But then you'd hear the makeup of the three waves of bombers. How the first ones would be a mixture of high explosives and incendiaries. This would smash the buildings apart and the incendiaries would then start the fires going. And the second one would be additional incendiaries plus timebombs, and those would be going off for hours after the attack, and that would keep the fire department away. And then the third wave was more high explosives, to shake up the fire a little bit, and some more incendiaries to keep it going. It was like stoking a fire: very planned, very cold, calculating. I'm sure bombs went off all over the place, and I don't think I ever was curious enough to go see my photographs that were automatically taken when you pressed the button to release the bombs.

Aldridge: From the Dulag we went to Stalag Luft III in Sagan. We got into Luft III on Labour Day. The American band in the middle of the compound was playing.

I suppose there was a little bit of apprehension. You're naturally apprehensive going into these compounds, with all the barbed wire and the guard towers and the Germans and the dogs. I don't know how they stood it, some of those guys had been there four years.

Private Dennis Richard, Black Watch of Canada

It was October 13, 1944. It was a place called Bergen op Zoom, in Holland. Our objective was a railroad crossing. We were supposed to be covered by a smokescreen. When it cleared off, we were in a sugar beet field, and the Germans were dug in on both sides. They were well camouflaged, you couldn't see them. And they had us in a crossfire.

We had no place to hide, so we just ducked down amongst the sugar beets and they just plastered the whole outfit with rifles and machine guns. We had no chance whatever. So, after two or three hours, nobody was moving because you didn't dare show your head.

Then the shooting stopped. We had no choice but to surrender. I heard afterwards they took twenty-five of us prisoner out of a hundred and thirty [in my company].

Then they gathered us up and took us to a house — maybe half a mile or a mile — and put us there for the night. They were friendly enough, there was nothing rough. They put us in this big white house, it was almost like a big mansion. Then the Canadian air force came and bombed around the place. Jesus, you could feel that house shiverin' and shakin', but we never got a direct hit.

The next day, we started on a route march. We walked almost twenty miles that first day, and they put us in a barn. Then the next day, we walked quite a bit again, and they put us in a big building. It was marked "POW." We stayed there a few days, and they filled it up with prisoners, British, Canadians. The worst part was that we were only getting one small bowl of soup and two slices of bread.

Then they walked us to the railroad station and we were packed fifty to a boxcar, a very small boxcar. Then after dark the train took off. They gave us two buckets of water and, I would say, five or six loaves of bread. And we were only moving at night. In the daytime, you could hear them banging on the cars, tacking down trees and bushes to camouflage the train.

Finally they opened the doors, and they took us to the camp, Stalag XI B. But even though we were starved, it was great to get out and stretch our legs, because we were packed just like sardines. That was the worst of my experience as a prisoner of war. I got claustrophobia from that.

Flying Officer Joseph St. Arnaud, 425 Squadron, RCAF

I had just about completed a tour. It was November 1, '44. We were flying a Halifax named D for Dog and it had about ninety-some trips on it. It was considered a very lucky aircraft because it had never been shot down. We had nine people on board that night. I was the navigator.

By the time we hit the Dutch coast, it was about seven o'clock at night. We were flying about twenty-two thousand feet, and it was bright moonlight. We went in and bombed Oberhausen. We were just coming out, and there was a tremendous noise all over the airplane. I think a fighter got us. Sounded like a bunch of rocks hitting the airplane. We went on for about two or three minutes and then one of the gas tanks blew up and we were on fire.

164

The navigator's on the hatch, so I guess I was the first one out. I was at twenty-two thousand feet and it was forty below! Oh, it was cold! And there were eight hundred planes on the raid that night and we were in the lead. I went right down through the middle of all these airplanes. And I was hitting slipstreams, and it was swinging me so high I could look down into my parachute! Did that for three or four minutes, and I'd just get straightened out and another airplane would come along and blow my 'chute again. It must have taken me twenty minutes to come down in that parachute.

I just saw the earth rushing up at me and I hit. About forty people came rushing at me with pitchforks and shovels and hoes and sticks and bricks. So I decided discretion was the better part of valour, and I just held up my hands.

There were two soldiers there and they took me to the farmhouse. I was sitting in the kitchen and there was a young girl there who spoke just a little bit of English. And she said, "Do you want something to eat?" I said, "Yes." And she brought me a glass of milk.

These two soldiers got two bicycles and I rode the crossbar of one of them and they pedalled me about five miles into the nearest town. I was thrown in a stone cell, and there were two of my crew there. Next morning, three guards came in and they were Luftwaffe guards. We walked, I guess, seven or eight miles, right into this military camp.

We were there for about three days. We were issued with a loaf of black bread, a chunk of margarine, and some cheese, and that was to do our trip. We were told that we were going to Frankfurt am Main, the interrogation centre.

Well, it took us four days to do that trip. We were locked in this compartment. We went about fifty, sixty miles and then we found ourselves right in the middle of an air raid. The guards went to an air raid shelter and just locked us in and left us there. The station was shaking, and the track was shaking, and everything was blowing up around us. It took us two or three days to get through the Ruhr. And the devastation, oh, the devastation!

One place we stopped to change trains. And I was terrified, I really was terrified. We were on the platform and this old man and old woman saw us. They saw our "Canada" badges and they saw our wings, and they came after us! They were shoving and hitting us with their umbrellas and they were drooling at the mouth. The guards were very good. They pushed the old people away — they were calling us *Terrorfliegers* and whatnot — and the guards brought us down into the basement of this station. They took us out of sight of all the other passengers. The civilians really wanted to do us physical harm and it was the guards that saved us.

At the interrogation centre, we were searched and stripped. And then I was put in a cell, in solitary. I just slept the first three days. They started to feed me — two slices of bread and coffee in the morning, a little thin soup at noon, and a slice at night, with this ersatz coffee which, actually, you get to like after a while.

I stayed there nineteen days in solitary confinement. And I think the reason was I spoke French, and we were quite close to Belgium when we were shot down. We had four commissioned officers on the airplane that night, and we had extra numbers, so they thought we were being dropped. And they kept harping on this, saying, "You're saboteurs."

It was very, very trying, that nineteen days. They turned the lights on for twenty-four hours, then shut them off for twenty-four hours. Put the heat up for twenty-four hours, put the heat down for twenty-four hours. It's a very mild form of torture to break you down. They handed me a pamphlet about communism. And I read it about ten times, because there was nothing else to read. Finally, I got tired of reading about communism, so I cut it up and made a pack of playing cards. And I played solitaire all day long. Solitaire in solitary!

Sergeant John Nicolaiff, 619 Squadron, RAF

We were shot down December 4, 1944, and we were on Heidelberg. It was a marshalling yard. Just as we were coming up on the target, we got hit and the starboard rudder was shot off. I was the tail gunner, and I noticed it going off. We got about sixty miles away from the target to where we crashed.

Now, I'm not sure what happened, whether we got hit by a fighter or what. It's very vague to me. We all went down with the aircraft. I was unconscious. My leg was broken and my foot was crushed, and I had these severe head injuries. The mid-upper gunner, Ross Keilty, ended up in the ditch on the side of a road. From what we found out afterwards, they picked us up and took us into the hospital in Freudenstadt. At first, they thought I was dead. But this other doctor, Meltzer, he came in and apparently he started working on the both of us. He gave us a shot in the heart, to stimulate the heart. I remember waking up once, in the operating room, but things after that are very vague till about the day before Christmas.

Private Cecil Cook, Princess Louise Dragoon Guards

I was captured in Italy, on the Po River. It was in December '44. We had to go through this canal, waded through it. And first thing we know, the Germans opened up. We kept going until we hit the trenches that the Germans had built, eight-foot trenches.

Then we moved over to a house where the Germans were supposed to be. We went in and set up a Bren gun upstairs. As fast as we put this Bren gun up, they'd knock him down. One of our officers just about had his stomach blown out, but he was still alive. And then we ran out of ammunition.

So the officer said to the sergeant, "Holler 'surrender.'" The sergeant wouldn't give up. He said, "You're still in command, you do the hollering." So the officer — his stomach was hanging out — he hollered. Then we went out with our hands over our heads and lined up outside.

They marched us to this holding unit. We stayed there until there was about seven hundred of us, English, Canadians, Americans. When they got the amount they wanted to take to Germany, they took us down and put us on a train, around fifty to a boxcar.

We finally got to Munich on Christmas Eve. Our idea was that they'd keep us there to keep the Allies from bombing it. So then the next day, we moved into Moosburg. I think it's thirty miles from Munich to Moosburg. Stalag VII A. And our

167

Canadians, they got together and they took their Red Cross parcels and they sent what they could over to us.

Flying Officer Pappy Plant, Stalag Luft III, Sagan

We had a real good do our last Christmas, in '44. As I say, if you got near the wire, you were shot without warning. And some of the fellas got this home brew in them. They walked right up to the wire and started throwing cigarettes to the guards. People were climbing over the wire, from one compound into the next, and the guards were putting their searchlights down so the fellas could find their way to the wire! One guy even walked up to the main gate, which was unheard of — he was a Canadian, too — and he told the guard he wanted to go home. So the guard opened the gate for him and off he went down the road! They picked him up later, out in the bush someplace.

Sergeant Bob Charman, Stalag IV B, Mühlberg

As the Allies pushed further and further into Germany, we saw more bomber raids. We were right on the track into Berlin, and a lot of times there'd be fierce dogfights very close to the camp. You've probably read about the raid on Dresden[3]. We were only twenty kilometres from Dresden. It was almost completely levelled. Flying Fortresses would hit it in the daytime and the RAF would hit it at night. We could see the red glow in the sky.

We were shot up by our own fighters one time. As the pincer movement pushed Germany into a narrow neck of land, columns started moving along the roads linking the two areas. Fighters would come in and attack these columns. And one column, moving right close to the camp, was hit by a Mustang fighter, American air force. He overshot the column and hit the camp. Three or four prisoners were killed by machine gun fire. It was just an unfortunate accident.

Warrant Officer John MacMullin, Stalag IV B, Mühlberg

One of these Junkers 88s was flying just a few feet above the ground. And all of a sudden we seen this dust over in the middle of the compound. He took the head off of this fella from Woodstock, New Brunswick, took the head right off him. There was an Australian walking with him, broke his leg. He was flying so low, he pulled down the telegraph wires too. So the Red Cross officials and the German authorities investigated. I don't know what happened after that.

Flying Officer Allister McDiarmid, 415 Squadron, RCAF

The target we were on was Hamburg, and it was March 8, 1945. We were over the target when we were hit on the starboard wing and the rear of the fuselage. It was evident there was no way of continuing, so I ordered the crew to bail out. I was on the ground in seconds.

I travelled the whole night without stopping, the idea being just to get as far away as I could. And then the following day, I just laid low in the bush. I travelled the next night. And towards evening, I was on top of a small hill looking down on a town. And I saw a bicycle. So I went down and got the bicycle all right, and I pedalled through the town.

I was doing great when, at the edge of town, there were four or five farmers standing there, and one of them had a pitchfork. And talking to him later, he said that he recognized my flying boots. They stopped me and took me to the house of the mayor of the town. And of course they phoned the Luftwaffe. Which is very fortunate, I might add, to be picked up by the Luftwaffe rather than the SS.

Sergeant Hayden Auld, Stalag IV B, Mühlberg

Then came Christmas of '44, when the Germans made their big push, the Battle of the Bulge. And they captured thousands of Americans. We got them after Christmas, we got all those guys in this camp. We all volunteered to take one of these Americans each, to make sure they got something to eat. You see, they had no Red Cross parcels, nothing. We had them for a good week or ten days. We had to sleep with one of them and share our food. Then all of a sudden one day they came in and took the Americans out to a separate camp a few miles away.

Corporal Phil Mechlair, Stalag IX B, Westerstede

Half the camp was Russians. There were three thousand

Russians in the camp. And there were a few Poles, a few English. No Americans. And the rest were Canadians, there were about eighty Canadians in that camp.

The Russians were treated really rough, like dogs. If they stepped outta line, they got a butt in the head or a butt in the stomach. We tried to give them food from our parcels, but if we were caught we were beaten.

Sergeant Bert Gnam, Stalag IV B, Mühlberg

The Russian POWs were slowly starving to death. They got German rations, which consisted of one mess tin full of soup, one or two pieces of bread, one or two potatoes, and ersatz coffee. The Russians had no Red Cross. They were just locked up and that was it. They'd go around to our garbage cans. If you ever saw a dog in that camp, and one would come around every so often, he didn't last long if he got into that Russian compound. We watched one go in there once, and we never saw it come out. But you know what came out? A hat made out of its fur.

The German Luftwaffe station where I was taken was a night fighter aerodrome. And I stayed there for some four or five days, until they rounded up a few more airmen. And seven or eight of us were bundled into a train and taken to Frankfurt, the "sweat box," where you get your initial interrogation. At the Frankfurt [train] station the German guards actually had to use their guns to keep the people away from us. It appeared they were ready to take us apart.

We were a week or two at Frankfurt. The initial questioning was from a "Red Cross man." He came in and wanted information so that he could write to my mother. He wore a Red Cross armband. Of course, it was the old name, rank, and number game, and after two or three days they gave that up.

Then the serious interrogation started. It was questioning over a period of several days, I guess. And one of the things I remember was the Gee box which was on the desk of the German interrogator. A Gee box is a navigational device which the bomb aimer and/or the navigator used and, indeed, was an excellent navigational aid. It crossed my mind that I would slip or give something away. This was seven

170

weeks before the end of the war and the interrogators were not that tough or threatening.

. We got into cattlecars and headed for Nürnberg, and the camp there was situated right beside the Olympic Stadium[4]. And we stayed there, I think, for about a month.

Pilot Officer Jim McIntosh, Stalag Luft I, Barth

We'd heard rumours, especially after the Great Escape attempt, that the Gestapo — Himmler — was going to have us all shot. Especially towards the end of the war, the last six months, there were all these rumours around, that as a last resort he was going to shoot all the Allied prisoners, destroy them.

Footnotes

1. Between June 7 and June 17, 1944, as many as 134 Canadians died in this manner after being captured by the 12th SS Panzer Division. After the war, the commander of the 12th SS, Kurt Meyer, stood trial for war crimes. He was found responsible for eighteen of the Canadian deaths and sentenced to be hanged. That was later commuted to life imprisonment and Meyer was released from prison in 1954.
2. Stalag XII D.
3. The bombing of Dresden was one of the most controversial incidents of the war. Ostensibly chosen as a target because it was one of the few remaining transportation centres in Germany, the Allies opened with a night raid on Dresden on February 13, 1945. American bombers hit the city during the next two days. It's believed as many as a hundred and thirty-five thousand people died in the attack, compared to the estimated seventy to one hundred thousand who died when the atomic bomb was dropped on Hiroshima, Japan, on August 6 of that year.
4. Oflag XIII A.

X/The Run Up the Road

Air force prisoners of war were not very popular in Germany. The Germans had a name for Allied airmen: *Terrorfleigers*, literally "terror flyers." They were considered to be nothing more than terrorists because of the destruction they were inflicting on German cities and their civilian populations.

Despite these strong feelings, air force POWs were, as a rule, well-treated once they were in the hands of the German armed forces. There were exceptions, however, and one of the most notable exceptions occurred in July 1944, when the Germans decided to abandon Stalag Luft VI. This camp, primarily an NCO camp, was located in East Prussia and was in the path of advancing Soviet forces; therefore the Germans moved the POWs further west in two groups. One group entrained for Stalag XX A in Thorn, Poland, and was later shifted to Stalag XI B in Fallingbostel in northern Germany. The other group, which contained a large contingent of Canadians, was taken to Stalag Luft IV in northeastern Germany. Theirs was a most memorable trip.

Warrant Officer Harold White

We were up there until July '44. The war in the east was getting a little too close to us, and the Germans figured they'd transport us back into Germany itself.

Sergeant Stan Bryant

We were taken out of our camp. We carried as much stuff as we could but we tried to destroy everything we couldn't carry so the Germans couldn't use it — canned goods and things like that. Even rolls of toilet tissue, we just threw them all over the compound and let the paper drift.

Warrant Officer Harold White

We ended up in the port of Memel, which is right on the eastern end of the Baltic Sea, not too far away from where we were. They had cleaned out the hold of this freighter. I was about the middle of the column and by the time I got on deck and looked down the hold, all I could see down there was a mass of faces. It looked like the place was jammed. So there were some objections to the German authorities that they were jamming too many of us in this ship. But it didn't do any good. They just used their rifle butts and we were all forced down into the hold of this ship.

There was only, if I remember correctly, three steel ladders that went vertically from the bottom of this ship up to the deck. If we had ever been torpedoed, I don't think more than ten of us would've got out of that ship.

Sergeant Stan Bryant

And there was so little room that we couldn't even stretch out and lay. If we wanted to lay, we had to take turns. We could sort of squat but there was no room for everybody to lay down at night.

Warrant Officer Keith Pettigrew

We were down in the hold, pissing in one bucket and drinking out of the other, and then drinking out of the piss bucket and pissing in the drinking bucket. Because they wouldn't let us up on deck.

Warrant Officer Harold White

That only lasted for a night and about midway through the next day, and then we ended up in Stettin. And when they were bringing us out of the hold of the ship, as soon as we would get up on the deck, we were chained together in pairs. Then we were marched off the ship and we were put in boxcars again. While we were on the siding, there was an air raid. When the air raid was over, the train started to move out. And we weren't on the train too long this time, only about a day. And this was in the middle of July '44. The weather was very, very warm and a lot of us had been prisoners for — well, we had one fella who was a prisoner in '39. The first day of the war he was shot down over the North Sea.

They unloaded us off the cars about mid-day in this little village.[1] We were still handcuffed together in pairs, and they lined us up four across, and the Germans came down and counted us.

And then we noticed there was a contingent of very young German soldiers being marched into our area, under charge of a red-headed *Hauptmann*. These were young men — they appeared to be around eighteen to twenty-four years of age — and they replaced our regular, older guards.

Warrant Officer Ross Elford

They had what they called *Kriegsmarines* escort us for the three-kilometre move from the railway up to this camp. The *Kriegsmarines* were all navy, all young guys, and they had the big long bayonets on their rifles. They weren't going to march us, they were going to run us. And if you didn't run, they'd run the bayonets at you.

Warrant Officer Harold White

It wasn't very long before we noticed the speed of the column was increasing, and the next thing you know, we're on the run. And there was shouting going on, and there was some dogs there. There was an odd shot or two from a rifle. And it went down through the column, what the Germans were doing, they wanted us to throw away our stuff, all our equipment. And we were being driven on a road that seemed to be going into a forest, so some of us thought, "Well, this is it. They're just driving us up into the forest, and then they're going to mow us down."

Warrant Officer Ross Elford

They'd set this whole thing up. Along the way, they'd tell us in German, "Go ahead, make an escape, we'll let you go." But in the trees were machine guns. They were just waiting to get rid of us. We were smart enough and we wouldn't break

174

for it. We just ran up the road and got many stab wounds and rifle butt smacks.

The German that was in charge of moving us, his family came from one of the towns in the Ruhr, and his family had been wiped out three or four nights before, in a raid.

Flight Sergeant Soggy Norton

They handcuffed us all together, and they ran us up this road. It seemed like thirty miles but they tell me it's about three kilometres. They ran us up the road, chained together. They stabbed us and chased dogs at us and hit us on the heads with rifle butts.

I was hooked onto a Polish guy, and he was about five-foot-six, a real good athlete. And I had made my pack with a tote line over the head, and I was hooked onto him, and I couldn't get it off. I wanted to get rid of the goddam thing. Most of the guys got rid of their packs on the way up the road. But I couldn't get rid of mine. And this little Polish guy still had his. When we got to the end of the goddam road, I guess it really upset them that we still had our packs. So they cut them off and they beat us over the head, flat on our arse, with rifle butts.

Warrant Officer Keith Pettigrew

I got three bayonet wounds in the ass. I got one right at the base of the spine and one right in the cheek of the ass and the other one in the thigh. And I don't even remember getting them.

Sergeant Stan Bryant

As an example of what happened that day, one man was jabbed fifty times in the back and rear end before we finished that run up the road. At one point, we even passed a dog that was chewing a German.

Warrant Officer Harold White

Actually, nobody was killed. Nobody died on this. There was about fifty of us, I think, lined up for medical attention when we got to this camp.

Sergeant Stan Bryant

We lost our kits, and so did most of the other people. And we feel that the Germans managed to get about a million and a half cigarettes that day. Which they didn't have. [In] the camp at Heydekrug, we got quite friendly with the guard in the cookhouse, and he told us that the front line soldiers in Russia — and he was a wounded veteran — only got three cigarettes a day. So nobody else in Germany was getting any rations at all. And goodness knows what else they picked up, because we had nothing when we got into the compound.

Flight Sergeant Soggy Norton

They put us in a compound, wouldn't give us any goddam water. They made us sit in this open compound. Oh, Christ, it was hot! It was July, really hot, and no shade.

And they were screaming at us. It was right at the height of the big air raids where they were really doing damage in Germany. And they kept on screaming, "Murderers" and all this bullshit, in German, you know.

Pilot Officer Daniel Almon

Another thing. They cut all our hair off, too. So we were a baldheaded crowd in the camp.

Warrant Officer Harold White

This was our reception at Stalag Luft IV. When we arrived there, it was mostly American airmen in there. But they had no accommodations for us. So they had built what we called "doghouses." You got down on your hands and knees and crawled in the opening. And there was just enough room in there that six men could lay side by side on the wooden floor. That was our accommodations until such time as they got the barracks ready for us so that we could move in. And then we were right back into the normal type of prison life.

Footnotes

1. Grosstychow, in northeastern Germany.

Left: Identification photo for George "Hayden" Auld of Winnipeg, taken shortly after his arrival at Stalag IV B, Mühlberg, in September 1943. Because the camp was infested with lice, the Germans shaved the heads of incoming POWS.

Below: Each prisoner of war was entitled to fill out a capture card to inform his next-of-kin of his whereabouts. The card would be sent postage-free and processed by the International Red Cross.

Below: A typical identification card for prisoners of war held in Germany. The reverse side would contain medical history and other relevant data. This card is from the records at Stalag Luft III, Sagan.

To all Prisoners of War!

The escape from prison camps is no longer a sport!

Germany has always kept to the Hague Convention and only punished recaptured prisoners of war with minor disciplinary punishment.

Germany will still maintain these principles of international law.

But England has besides fighting at the front in an honest manner instituted an illegal warfare in non combat zones in the form of gangster commandos, terror bandits and sabotage troops even up to the frontiers of Germany.

They say in a captured secret and confidential English military pamphlet.

THE HANDBOOK OF MODERN IRREGULAR WARFARE:

"... the days when we could practise the rules of sportsmanship are over. For the time being, every soldier must be a potential gangster and must be prepared to adopt their methods whenever necessary."

"The sphere of operations should always include the enemy's own country, any occupied territory, and in certain circumstances, such neutral countries as he is using as a source of supply."

England has with these instructions opened up a non military form of gangster war!

Germany is determined to safeguard her homeland, and especially her war industry and provisional centres for the fighting fronts. Therefore it has become necessary to create strictly forbidden zones, called death zones, in which all unauthorised trespassers will be immediately shot on sight.

Escaping prisoners of war, entering such death zones, will certainly lose their lives. They are therefore in constant danger of being mistaken for enemy agents or sabotage groups.

Urgent warning is given against making future escapes!

In plain English: Stay in the camp where you will be safe! Breaking out of it is now a damned dangerous act.

The chances of preserving your life are almost nil!

All police and military guards have been given the most strict orders to shoot on sight all suspected persons.

Escaping from prison camps has ceased to be a sport!

Left: A poster issued by the Germans in the fall of 1943 in an effort to discourage escape attempts. The POWs ignored its advice.

Below: Some of the first Canadian POWs in World War II. Back row, left to right: R. H. Barlett, Jim "Pappy" Plant, C. D. Clancy, Barry Davidson. Front row, left to right: Don MacDonald, R. A. Willis, L. Chambers, L. S. Adams. Stalag Luft I, Barth, 1940.

Above: Four of the early arrivals at Stalag Luft I, Barth, 1940. All are Canadians. Left to right: Bert Clark, Art Deacon, J. B. Smiley, J. B. Hanlon.

Below: Appell at Stalag Luft I, Barth. This camp was located right on the Baltic Sea, and on a clear day the prisoners could see Sweden on the horizon.

Above: The memorial outside Stalag Luft III, Sagan, commemorating the fifty Allied POWs executed by the Germans following the Great Escape in March 1944. Six of the fifty were Canadians.

Right: Lagergeld, money issued by the Germans for use in POW camps. *Lagergeld* had little value to the prisoners as cigarettes became the recognized currency. Canadian POWs were relatively wealthy because they could, and did, obtain large quantities of cigarettes from their families and friends in Canada.

Kriegsgefangenenlager

Datum: 14 / 12 / 42

Above: Prisoner-of-war mail. This sample of German censorship is a postcard sent by Sergeant Sam Ebsary from Stalag VIII B, Lamsdorf, to his family in St. John's, Newfoundland.

Left: POWs with a *Kübel*, or barrel, of soup. This would be carried into their barrack block and the soup distributed among the prisoners. Note the laundry hanging on the barbed-wire fence at the right.

Left below: A typical Canadian Red Cross food parcel contained milk powder, butter, cheese, corned beef, luncheon meat, salmon, sardines, dried apples, dried prunes, sugar, jam, biscuits, chocolate, salt and pepper, tea, and soap.

Above right: A German news photographer snapped this picture of Donald Campbell of Halifax, a fighter pilot with 403 Squadron, just moments after Campbell was shot down and rescued from the English Channel, June 2, 1942.

Right: Dieppe, August 19, 1942. Captured Canadians were marched through the streets of Dieppe.

Below: Canadian POWs, Stalag VIII B, Lamsdorf. Most of these men were captured at Dieppe.

Left: The Germans ordered the hands of Canadian POWs tied, October 8, 1942. Although this order applied mainly to the soldiers who took part in the Dieppe raid, RAF and RCAF prisoners at Stalag VIII B, Lamsdorf, were also tied. Above are air force POWs attempting to cut their bread ration. (Note the homemade cups on the table.)

Below: Christmas, 1942, the first Christmas in captivity for the Dieppe Canadians. This is Barrack 19B at Stalag VIII B, Lamsdorf. The POWs made the decorations themselves with whatever they could scrounge.

One of the illegal radios at Stalag VIII B. Comparison with the matchbox at right shows how small the radio is.

K. Hyde

K. Hyde

Above: Believe it or not, there was an escape tunnel under construction here, at Stalag VIII B. It was being dug under the blanket-covered table which was ostensibly serving as a trading centre.

K. Hyde

Right: This is an interior shot of the same tunnel, showing one of the POWs at work. At this time, the tunnel had been under construction for three weeks.

Another reason why work parties were popular among POWs: three Yugoslav sisters befriended by a Canadian POW work party in northeastern Germany, 1944. The girls were brought to Germany as slave labourers.

Above: The orchestra in the north compound, Stalag Luft III, winter of 1944. The orchestra had a Canadian conductor, Flight Lieutenant Art Crighton.

Above left: A scene from one of the Death Marches, February 1945. POWs from Stalag VIII B in a barnyard at Prausnitz, Germany.

Below left: Canadian prisoners of war playing hockey at Stalag Luft III.

K. Hyde

Left: Flight Sergeant Ken Hyde snapped this illicit photo of *Unteroffizier* "Ukraine Joe" Kissel, the senior NCO in charge of the air force compound at Stalag VIII B.

Below: Ken Hyde's candid camera at work again. Inside the forty-holer at Stalag VIII B, Lamsdorf.

Bottom: Canadian prisoners opening Red Cross parcels, Stalag VIII B.

K. Hyde

Courtesy F. Morton

A Red Cross inspection team arriving at Stalag II D, Stargard, late 1944.

The Red Cross officials are the civilians being escorted into the camp by German officers...

...and greeted by Canadian NCOS representing the POWS.

A work party of Canadian POWS on a farm in northeastern Germany, 1944. Private Bill Larin of the Royal Hamilton Light Infantry stands fourth from left. The others are members of the Essex Scottish.

A blower, the small stove made by POWS. Its operation is described by Flight Sergeant Doug Hawkes on page 83. The blower here is demonstrated by Private R. J. McMahon, a Canadian POW at Stalag IX B.

Above: A working party, *Arbeitskommando* 1426, at a farm near Schönrady, Germany, 1944. Corporal Leo Lecky of the Queen's Own Cameron Highlanders stands at right. The others are all Canadian Dieppe veterans. The photo was taken by a friendly German guard in exchange for cigarettes.

Left: A little dog adopted as a mascot by a work party of Canadian POWs near Schönrady, Germany, in 1944.

Left: This RCAF Halifax bomber has just had part of its tail section knocked off by bombs released from an aircraft above. One of the three of its seven-man crew to escape was the pilot, Flight Lieutenant George Gardiner.

Below: Liberated POWs at Dulag Luft, Frankfurt, April 1945. Sergeant John Nicolaiff of Ottawa stands eighth from the right. The German camp doctor is kneeling fourth from the left.

Right: Sham Shui Po camp, Hong Kong. In 1943, the majority of Canadian POWs moved from Sham Shui Po to prison camps in Japan.

Courtesy D. Syvret

Below right: North Point camp, Hong Kong. This was where most of the Canadians were taken following the surrender of the colony on Christmas Day, 1941.

Courtesy D. Syvret

Below: Canadian and British POWs at Hong Kong awaiting their liberation by a landing party from HMCS *Prince Robert,* August 30, 1945.

PA 114811/Public Archives of Canada

Above: Canadians released at Hong Kong. The man in white, an officer from HMCS *Prince Robert*, is distributing cigarettes to the happy POWs. *Below:* Liberated Canadian POWs in Yokohama, 1945. These men still recall with gratitude the kindness shown by the Americans.

Above: Canadian officers following their liberation at Hong Kong, 1945.

Below: Lieutenant R. W. A. Dunn (with white towel around neck) of HMCS *Prince Robert*, about to sample the food eaten by Canadian POWs at Hong Kong.

XI/Nightmare At Buchenwald

The city of Weimar is located about two hundred and forty kilometres southwest of Berlin. Weimar is a cultural centre, the home of some of the giants of German culture: Goethe, Schiller, and Liszt. It is ironic that while Weimar represents some of the most creative aspects of German cultural achievement, the Nazis chose to locate nearby a monument to the darkest and most reprehensible side of the human mind.

North of Weimar is a forested plain. Eight kilometres from the city is Ettersberg, a mountain of about five hundred metres. In 1937, Ettersberg was chosen as the site for a concentration camp. Using forced labour, the Nazis cleared the mountaintop of its trees except for one oak tree where, according to legend, the poet Goethe would go for inspiration. Barrack blocks were built, and an electrified fence surrounded the forty-hectare site. Over the front gate was the motto: "Give the devil his due."

This was Buchenwald, and it would soon acquire a reputation as a chamber of horrors. Buchenwald started out as a work camp for the "undesirables" of Nazi society, mostly Jews and assorted political prisoners. Tens of thousands of these people would pass through Buchenwald's gates. They were put to work slaving in factories and in a nearby stone quarry, and they built "the highway of blood," the road linking Weimar and Buchenwald. The work was performed under the watchful eyes of sadistic SS guards. The camp commandant, an SS colonel named Karl Koch, amassed a fabulous, and illicit, fortune by farming out prison labour to private enterprise and pocketing the proceeds. So blatant was his criminal activity that Koch was finally arrested, tried, and executed by the SS. As if that were not bad enough, his charming wife Ilse was nicknamed "the Red Witch of Buchenwald." Besides indulging in endless sexual perversion, Ilse had the quaint habit of making lampshades out of the tatooed skin of some of Buchenwald's unfortunate inmates.

In 1942, Buchenwald assumed an additional role as a medical experimentation centre. A special building was set aside for this purpose. From the prison population, the Germans selected human guinea pigs for the study of diseases induced by injection, primarily typhus. German doctors were able to observe under controlled conditions the effects of typhus, test various strains of the virulent disease, and experiment with vaccines. Incredibly, this work was so ineptly carried out that, from a medical standpoint, the results were almost worthless. Later, the experiments were diversified as the doctors sought new surgical techniques, treatments for phosphorous burns, and even a cure for homosexuality.

The crematorium at Buchenwald had a capacity of four hundred bodies per day. It was a busy place. By the end of the war, Buchenwald had accounted for the deaths of as many as sixty thousand people, although the exact toll is unknown.

Buchenwald was just one of many concentration camps run by the Germans during the Nazi regime. It was a relatively minor operation. Much more sophisticated medical experimentation was conducted at Dachau; Auschwitz, with more than two million victims, was far more efficient. As already mentioned, these places processed certain people: Jews, mostly, and political prisoners, saboteurs, and anyone else considered to be an enemy of the state. It was very unusual for prisoners of war to be sent to concentration camps.[1] As a rule, the Germans kept prison camps separate and distinct, and POWs were allowed certain rights once they were recognized by the German authorities.

However, an exception occurred in August 1944 when 167 Allied POWs, including twenty-seven Canadians, were shipped from Paris to Buchenwald. This is their story, as told by two of the Canadian prisoners.

Flying Officer Cal Willis, 640 Squadron, RAF

We took off on my birthday, June 2, '44, and we dropped our bombs. Our target was a marshalling yard just southwest of Paris. I was the bomb aimer. I was feeling pretty good because I saw the bombs fall right into the heart of the target indicator. We were two minutes on our way home, and we were hit from below by night fighters. One wing was on fire, and one engine was on fire, and the pilot gave the order to abandon the aircraft.

I landed in a tree, two feet from the ground. I buried my parachute and started walking towards Spain, by the stars. After a day and a half, I contacted a French farmer in a field and he hid me in the bush and said, "Wait here." He went off and got some people with the French Underground.

The Resistance people took me to a "safe" house, a hideout. Before this, they had given me a change of clothes. Civilian clothes and a beret. They found the navigator, Ernie Shephard, and they brought him to this house too. This was about forty kilometres from Paris.

We were in this house on the night of the fifth. It was just like the movies — spies all over the place. There was a British agent there, there was a couple of French agents. That night, we were listening to the BBC, and they all got excited because the codeword came over the radio that the invasion was going to be within forty-eight hours. They had planned to get me back to England, but the fact that the invasion was starting — they all had different jobs, so they couldn't look after me. I was just excess baggage then, me and the navigator both. They had to blow up bridges and do this and that. So they put us in another car and moved us to a little town, Dourdan, and they hid us in a house. Then they went about their business.

In the meantime, the invasion had started. A couple of days later — it was a rainy day — the place was surrounded by twelve cars. I'd say there were about fifty Gestapo. I dashed upstairs — my navigator was caught on the stairs — and you wouldn't believe it. First, I was going to get under the bed, but I thought, "No, that's too obvious." There was a bunch of clothes piled on a chair, so I ducked behind it. The first guy in the room kicked the door open and came in with his gun. There were some cupboards up above me, and he came over and felt up there, looking for guns hidden on the shelf. He actually had pressure on me. Then his sergeant came up and said, "Lift up those clothes." And that was the end of me.

They took us to Paris, in this convoy of twelve cars. I had to sit between two of these guys, with their guns drawn. You wouldn't believe it. They looked just like gangsters out of a Hollywood movie — leather coats, big black boots.

They took us to Gestapo headquarters. I sort of had a half-smile on my face, and I don't think this went over very big. Because two of the Gestapo fellows took me down for more questioning, and I guess they wiped the smile off my face. The first thing I knew — wham! — one hit me hard enough to knock me down. I got up and he hit me on the other side, and knocked me down again. So after that, every time he hit me, I fell down. It makes me mad to think about it, because this guy was smaller than me. But I didn't swing back. I figured that wouldn't be too smart.

After they got tired of that, they put us up in a cell. Then the next day, they took us off to Fresnes prison. It's just outside Paris. It's a huge jail, huge. A lot of air force people that were caught in and around Paris usually passed through there. That was about June 19, and we were there until just before Paris fell, about August 19.

Pilot Officer Bill Gibson, 419 Squadron, RCAF

It was American Independence Day, July 4, 1944. We were bombing the marshalling yards south of Paris. We had seven fighter attacks before we got to the target, and one over the target. And shortly after we dropped our bombs, we were to go down as low as we could and get out as fast as we could. Somewheres around twelve to fourteen hundred feet, we were hit by a head-on attack by a Junkers 88.

All the crew got out, and my pilot and I came down in 'chutes together. I landed on top of a house and he landed in the backyard. And the next day we contacted the Underground, and they kept us for about two weeks and took us to Paris. We lived in a hotel for a while. And then, unfortunately, a collaborator had infiltrated the underground cell and we were captured by the Gestapo.

We were in civilian clothes when we were captured, so under the Geneva Convention they could have shot us. But we were taken to Gestapo headquarters and we were interrogated. We were locked in our cell, handcuffed back to back, in a little cell about the size of a telephone booth. I was punched once, but we weren't mistreated that much. I don't think I was expecting to be shot. When you're eighteen, you don't ever expect anything. It's an adventure.

We were taken to Fresnes prison in Paris. I think it was around the seventeenth of July. Spent thirty-two days in solitary there.

Willis: We were hoping we'd be liberated in Paris. But just before Paris fell, they put us all in these cattlecars. I think there was about ninety in our cattlecar, and we spent almost a week in that. Everyone couldn't sit at the same time. And there was one pail in the middle of the car for everyone to go to the toilet, and that was it. We didn't have a clue where we were going.

Gibson: We left Paris August 19. We had no idea where we were going, and the train ride was horrible. The engine was shot out the second day, and we were kept locked inside. They did give us some food. They gave us some loaves of bread that were so hard you couldn't break them. And very little water. Toilet facilities were practically negligible: a tin can, that was it. I remember up around Nancy or Metz, in that area, it was bombed out and we had to get out and walk around. A woman with the French Red Cross gave me a glass of something to drink, and I drank it down. I found out later it was the first and only time in my life I had buttermilk. I never tasted it before or since. Then we got on another train.

The trip to Buchenwald was very scary, because my pilot escaped off the train we were on. He and five Frenchmen got away. A sixth one was shot. And they stopped the train, and they were gonna execute seven for each one that got away. And since the rest of the crew were the only English people on this train, we figured we were it. They didn't execute

181

anybody, but they took all our clothes away from us. We were naked in the boxcar for the rest of the journey. They did kill a seventeen-year-old French kid the next day.

Willis: After we got over the French border into Germany, it just felt like a hundred pounds was taken off your shoulders. Everybody was relieved. You see, the Germans were afraid of being attacked by the Resistance while they were in French territory. And once they crossed the German border, it was just like a cloud lifted up. I guess we were relieved too, eh?

Eventually, they got us to Buchenwald. I believe it was late at night, and they just marched us through the gates. We had all kinds of civilians with us at this time because there was a trainload of them evacuated from Paris.

Gibson: I didn't know what Buchenwald was. I don't think any of us knew what a concentration camp was at that time.

When we arrived at Buchenwald, I don't think we were off the train five seconds when the fellow next to me got hit in the face with a rifle butt. The SS guard hit him because he didn't move fast enough.

First of all, they shaved us, our heads and our whole body. And then they gave us a pair of pants and a shirt and a little tiny hat. And we slept on the bare ground. This is the latter part of August, and Buchenwald is on a mountain, so it gets pretty cold. And we were there for I don't know how many nights. Quite a few, I know, and it was awful cold and uncomfortable.

Willis: The day after we arrived, the Americans came over and bombed a small-arms factory that was on the camp. But their aim was very good; they were pinpoint bombing. A couple in our group were slightly injured by bomb fragments, but nothing serious.

Gibson: That was a terrifying situation. We weren't allowed to move. We had to lay flat on the ground, and the SS had machine guns trained on us and told us not to move. And the bombs were falling. I think the nearest ones hit probably three hundred yards away from us.

And after the raid was over, we were all called up to the main square, to find out what we had all done in peacetime. The senior officer was a New Zealander and he told us to tell them nothing. So we told them we didn't do anything. And I remember a German saying, "We've got 167 hobos here." Then they said we had done the damage and we had to clean it up, but we didn't do too much.

Willis: There were some secret agents in there at that time. This here Pickersgill was one of them. They were not classed as prisoners of war, they were classed as terrorists. So they were automatically going to be hung, or shot, or whatever. A couple of them were allowed to come up and talk to us, mix in the camp. While we were there, I don't know how many of them were executed. It struck me as strange. They were all big specimens of men, healthy. And they were upset because they were going to be hung instead of shot[2].

Gibson: We had some contact with the people that were there. Buchenwald was one of the oldest concentration camps in Germany. It was built back in [1937]. And some of the prisoners there were Germans who had been there since then. They had some Jews there too.

I think the thing that frightened me most about it was the deaths every day. Because people would die, and they'd keep them in the huts to get the extra rations. And then the bodies were just thrown out on the street and a wagon came along each morning and they piled the bodies on and took them to a crematorium.

Willis: There were Germans in there, Poles, Russians, everything. They were dying every day. You could see them being carried out. They had three crematoriums in the camp.

Gibson: Buchenwald had a floating population of around thirty to thirty-three thousand prisoners. And they were every type of prisoner. Russians, just about every nationality in Europe was there, including a lot of religious groups like Seventh Day Adventists. And sex maniacs and criminals. And while we were there also, the whole Danish police force was brought in there because they were all purged and put in the concentration camp. And it was shortly after the attempt on Hitler's life, and there was quite a few Germans brought in there. And a lot of them were executed.

It was hard to believe, really. And it's doubly hard to forgive. Because it's absolutely unbelievable that there could be such inhumanity between human beings. The guards were maniacs. They would think nothing of setting the dogs on a prisoner, and that would be it.

I don't think people will ever believe what happened to us there.

Willis: As I say, you drifted through. I guess your mind must adjust to it after a while, and you drift through. I find it difficult to believe. It doesn't seem possible that that could have happened to me, or anybody else for that matter.

There were an awful lot of fleas and lice there. I've never had so many bites in all my life. My midriff, all the way around, was just covered in bites. Luckily, I had determination enough not to scratch. But a lot of fellows scratched, maybe unconsciously in their sleep, and they came up with great big sores all over their bodies.

They didn't make us work at Buchenwald. There was very little to eat, of course. You stood around for roll call for five, six hours. That would start about four in the morning. I think that was twice a day. The Germans are notorious counters, and they had to start re-counting every once in a while.

I guess we spent most of our time lying down, talking. By the time you got your two roll calls and the little bit you did get to eat, you'd be back to sleep and then up again at four in the morning.

Gibson: We were suffering from malnutrition, because all we got to eat was a little bowl of soup made from grass or cabbage leaves and an inch of bread and three little potatoes a day.

Afterwards, we were put into a barrack building that was originally designed for two hundred and fifty people, and I think they had somewhere near six hundred in it. Your beds were like shelves coming out of the wall, and there were four tiers of these shelves, divided into sections of five feet. And five men slept in each of those sections. So you couldn't really turn over at night, unless everybody else turned at the same time.

Willis: I've never found out how we got out of there, how they went about getting us out. Somebody must have protested, someplace.

Gibson: There are two questions that remain in my mind, and till the day I die, I don't know why we were put there, and I don't know how we got out of there. I haven't any idea at all.

We were there for well over two months. I think the thing that kept most of us alive was our youth. We were pretty healthy when we went in there, and we were young. I spent my nineteenth birthday in Buchenwald.

It was the latter part of October before we got out of there. And then we were called up on this square again, and the German sergeant-major from the air force said in perfect English, "According to the Geneva Convention, if you attempt to escape, you will be shot." But we couldn't figure that out, because under the Geneva Convention, we shouldn't have been put in there. However, we were then put in another cattlecar and taken to a prisoner of war camp, Stalag Luft III.

I remember when I got off the train at Luft III, the Germans came down to get us — the German air force — and a German colonel asked us where we came from. And we told him we came from Buchenwald concentration camp. He said, "Places like that don't exist in Germany." And at that time, our heads were still shaved, and we were a pretty sad-looking bunch of people. The prisoners of war in the camp, I think, believed us to a degree, but I don't think even they believed where we'd come from.

I get annoyed about it. As I mentioned before, people wouldn't believe where we were or what we'd seen. Even today they don't believe it. They like to shut their eyes on the fact that these things happened. I can remember right

185

after I got back to England in '45, I was in a movie theatre, and they were showing a newsreel of Eisenhower. And when the Americans captured Buchenwald, Eisenhower was taken there, and he made all the people of Weimar, which was a town near Buchenwald, come up and look at corpses and the graves and the state of the camp. And an English lady was sitting beside me — I guess she would be in her sixties — she said, "You know, things like that never happened. They'll do anything for propaganda." So, what are you gonna do?

When we came back to Canada, in fact, we were told by the air force not to say anything about our experiences at Buchenwald.

Footnotes

1. Many Russian POWs were sent to concentration camps because the Germans did not recognize them as prisoners of war. The Soviet Union was not a party to the Geneva Convention and, in any event, the Germans considered Russians to be subhuman. It made little difference whether Russian prisoners were kept in POW camps or concentration camps; they were treated miserably in both. Late in the war, a large number of Russians were sent to Buchenwald where they perished in poison warfare experiments. It should be pointed out that German prisoners in Soviet hands fared little better; hundreds of thousands of Germans died following their capture by the Soviets.

2. These were agents belonging to the Special Operations Executive. SOE was a secret British organization specializing in sabotage behind enemy lines. The Germans rounded up and shipped thirty-seven SOE agents to Buchenwald in mid-August, just before the POWs got there. Three of these agents were Canadians: Frank Pickersgill, Romeo Sabourin, and John Macalister. In early September, most of these agents were executed, including the trio of Canadians. They were garrotted, hung from meat hooks with piano wire. At this time, there was already another Canadian agent at Buchenwald. Georges Rodrigues spent more than a year there; he died shortly after Buchenwald was liberated.

186

XII/The Death Marches & Liberation

By January 1945, the war in Europe was clearly into its final stages. The western Allies were preparing for their final drive into Germany while the Soviets were doing likewise in the east. In December 1944, the Germans made their last desperate gamble for victory by launching an armoured attack in the Ardennes, the famous Battle of the Bulge, in a bid to break through the American lines and cut off the Canadian and British armies to the north. The attack failed and by mid-January it was apparent even to the Germans that they had suffered a crushing defeat. About this time, the Soviets began their offensive on the Eastern Front, capturing Warsaw on January 17, 1945. Germany was doomed.

For the prisoners of war in German hands this was a most miserable time. With the Third Reich reduced almost to its pre-war borders, the Germans began evacuating their prison camps, particularly those in the east. The POWs were put on forced marches and moved back and forth across Germany, into and out of various overcrowded prison camps. They joined literally millions of refugees moving westward to escape the ravages of the Russians. Just like the rest of the German war machine, Germany's POW system was breaking down, succumbing to the chaos of a nation in its death throes.

Pilot Officer Alden Magnus
Warrant Officer Arnold Dawkins
Flight Sergeant John Edelson, Stalag VIII B, Lamsdorf[1]

Edelson: We left the camp on January 17, 1945, exactly two years after I was shot down. And we marched two-thirds of

187

the way across Germany and a third of the way back, with no food, really. You were lucky to live through that.

The Germans, who were great organizers, really got screwed up on The March, because the bombing became so intensive. As the Russians closed in from the east, and the Americans came in from the south, and the Canadians were pushing in from Holland on the west, it just became a chaotic situation. The result was that all their food dumps went for a Burton. It got to the point where you lived by stealing. They didn't have any food, and you didn't get any to speak of.

Magnus: We were seven days at one point that all we had was the snow that we ate along the side of the road and bits of turnips that we picked up out of the fields. Occasionally we found a potato that somebody dropped on the road; we'd eat that.

Edelson: We slept in open fields. At times, we'd just fall down at the side of the road and go to sleep. We all had dysentery, which is really de-energizing. I had it real bad, so I couldn't keep up with the group. But my buddies would always get a place to sleep, and they put me in the middle. Remember, this is wintertime.

Magnus: There were lots of times I wondered if I'd ever make it home. It's forty below zero, and you could hardly walk and they forced you. You didn't care whether you got back or not. It was so darn cold, and you didn't have the proper clothing. Your feet hurt. Morale was very low. Guys would drop out, and they didn't care if the Germans shot them or not.

Dawkins: Leeks, we discovered, grew all year round. And when the snow left the ground, we dug them up and we ate them. We also found that in parts of Germany, they would harvest their crops and pile them and then cover them with straw and dirt, and then there'd be these huge mounds near the roads. So when we would stop for a rest, somebody would investigate, and then everybody would be helping them-selves to this food. We'd get spuds and onions that way. Several occasions, we were shot at.

Private Alfred Moody
Private Bill Douglas
Sapper Harold McConnell, Stalag II D, Stargard

McConnell: We were about fifty kilometres from the Oder River. And we knew nothing about how the war was going. All of a sudden, the Russians burst through, and this is where our release came.

Moody: We could hear them coming. Before the tanks got there, there was a guy come up the road, and he was armed to the teeth. Of course, the guards were gone. This Russian came in just like he owned the whole country!

Douglas: We were on this work party, and we knew there was something happening. All the guards took off. And we saw this fella coming down the road. He was an ex-prisoner of war from another part of the country. He'd been released by the Russians. And then the Russians came in. It was sort of a spearhead.

Of course, we went out and started raising a ruckus. We got into the wine cellar in the big house and we had a ball.

Then the following day, they were moving out, and a few of the Russian prisoners went with them. And a few others moved out with the Polish people. So there was fifteen, I guess, twenty of us, and we started off to go to the next town. And on the road there, we run into this tank corps. They were parked along the road.

The Russians, you know, were very forceful. They were issued alcohol. And they'd hand you a big enamel mug full of it and you'd have to drink it down. And if you didn't, they'd pull a gun on you. Straight alcohol. It really burnt you down! You were down on the ground shovelling snow in your mouth, you know, to cool it off.

McConnell: We were put on a train, and we started to get behind the Russian front lines. We went through Warsaw and from there we went through the Ukraine down to Odessa.

There was no explanation at all. We rode filthy, crappy trains to get through the country. And you don't tell Rus-

189

sians, at this time, that you're a Canadian. Because they don't know anything about a damn Canadian at all. We were Americansky to them, and that was it. We thought Canadians were pretty popular, but not in Russia — they weren't known.

Douglas: I guess it was about two weeks to get to Odessa. And we were put into a great big holding area where there was Americans, Italians, all kinds. We were there, oh, a couple of months, I guess.

Through that course of time, we didn't go anywhere. Every once in a while, we'd go get a shower or hot bath. You'd be paraded, with Russian guards.

Then the boat came in, the Canadian *Duchess of Bedford*, a CPR boat.

Moody: I'd say there were possibly forty or fifty of us. We had the whole ship to ourselves. It was a beautiful little trip through the Mediterranean. Just lie on deck there and soak up the sun. Until we got to Italy. Then we took on a whole mess of Canadian soldiers going back to England.

There was just one thing I resented. I had a pair of dice. I kept them through everything. Always had my dice and a pack of cards. And I threw them overboard when I got on the ship. Then all these guys get on there with dough and all kinds of stuff. They couldn't get rid of their money fast enough. And only one or two pair of dice on the whole boat. If I'd kept my dice, I could have made a fortune, just runnin' the game!

Douglas: I got back to Britain before the war ended. I went to a holding unit and got interrogated. Then finally they asked me, "Do you want to go fight the Japanese?" But I was in no shape to fight my way out of a paper bag. So they issued us with new clothing, and they started to give us all our decorations or whatever, you know, for service — ribbons and stripes. We looked like Christmas trees!

190

Flight Lieutenant Al Aldridge
Flight Lieutenant Art Crighton
Flight Lieutenant Al Hannah
Flight Lieutenant Anthony Pengelly
Flying Officer Joseph St. Arnaud
Flying Officer Keith Ogilvie
Flying Officer Ray Epstein
Pilot Officer Don MacDonald, Stalag Luft III, Sagan

Ogilvie: We'd been warned to be ready to move out on extremely short notice. We had in there with us a chap who was an ex-Mountie, and he showed us how to make backpacks. When the time came to move, we just crammed as much food in there as we could, and cigarettes, and whatever was most valuable to you.

St. Arnaud: Everybody rushed over to the library and went through the books and found the thinnest paper they could find, tore the covers off, and stuffed it into their kitbags — toilet paper, eh? Very, very practical.

And when we were sure we were going, I went back over to the library. And there was a great big wall map of Germany there, and I took a knife and I cut the whole thing up and I put it in my pocket. That became the most valuable thing on the marches. Everybody would look at my map, and I'd colour it in every day to show where we were.

Epstein: When they decided to evacuate that camp, they opened up the warehouse, and we discovered that they had fifty thousand [Red Cross] parcels. They didn't want the Russians to get it. And in weak, emaciated condition — like, I weighed ninety pounds when I got back to England — we'd pick out the condensed chocolate, or tea, or cans of butter. And it was bitterly, bitterly cold, eighteen, fifteen below zero Fahrenheit. And it was snowing.

MacDonald: We started on this Death March on January 27 or 28, 1945. Colder'n a polar bear's butt. And we marched for about four days with minimum stopovers. Every time you stopped, you practically passed out.

191

You know, I'd heard stories of the First War, guys walked in their sleep. I thought that was just a story. Don't kid yourself. You do walk in your sleep, and you're putting one foot in front of the other, and you don't know why.

Hannah: Lots of people got sick along the way. One chap, a friend of mine, he fell sick. We think he had appendicitis. And the last I saw of him, he was sitting beside the road. They wouldn't let us stop, of course. And what happened to him after that, I don't know.

Crighton: There was a fellow by the name of "Scruffy" Weir. Gee, I have a lot of admiration for that guy. If I ever saw him again, I'd like to thank him. I felt he kept us alive. It wasn't so bad when we were moving, we could keep warm. But we were standing there for hours on that freezing cold road, the wind blowing, and snow. It was just hell. And Scruffy was running up and down the column, yelling at everybody to keep moving: "Wave your arms! Wave your legs!" He was using foul language and everything else, just to make us do things. That, to me, was leadership. Scruffy was just one of us, but he had the guts to get up there and keep us alive, really.

Aldridge: All of a sudden, one night, the thaw hit. In just a matter of hours, the snow disappeared from the roads, so we had to throw all our homemade sleds away. That's when the Russians got held up, in the big thaw that year. We could hear the guns of the Russians when we left there. They were only about forty miles away, I think.

Epstein: I remember they put us on a night march one time, trying to make up time. Every hour they'd call a five-minute rest, and I remember sitting down on the curb in this small little village. I was sick, and I had diarrhea, and I was miserable. I said to my pilot, Al Aldridge, "Al, I give up. I can't go anymore." And I knew they were picking up those who were too sick to go on, picking them up in a wagon at the end of the line, and it was rumoured that they were being shot. And if it wasn't for Al saying "C'mon, Eppy, get up off your ass, we're going!" — I was quite prepared to die there. You know, I gave up, I didn't care anymore.

Aldridge: The Canadians were innovative, you know. Just myself, for example. I traded cigarettes or chocolate or something for a baby carriage. And I put my stuff in the baby carriage and wheeled it along the highway. Eventually two wheels on it broke. So then I got a pole and I tied the pole to it, and I pulled it on the remaining two wheels with this pole, for miles and miles and miles.

Pengelly: And we were just like a scourge across the land because we needed water, we needed turnips, anything that was edible: eggs, potatoes. And we just went down like a plague of grasshoppers, stealing everything. But in the little villages that we went through, there was no animosity.

Aldridge: It was just a miserable bloody trip, walking to Spremberg. We saw some very sad refugees on the road, on carts, horsedrawn, oxdrawn, on foot. We tried to give them what little food we had, but even the children were afraid of us. Eventually they would take a piece of chocolate if we had some.

We got to Spremberg on February 2. We went to a German panzer barracks and we were issued with some soup. And at 4:00 P.M. we boarded a train to take us, we found out later, to a camp near Bremen.

Epstein: I will never, never forgive the Germans for that. Never. That was the lowest depths to which I have ever gone. They put us in boxcars that were meant for — what do the French usually say? — *"quarante hommes ou huit chevaux."* And they took us across Germany, towards the Hamburg area. And put us on sidings wherever possible, so that trains going to the front and whatnot could get by. Bitter, bitter cold. We ran out of water, we had no food. Eighty to ninety people per boxcar, sitting on the floor with your legs apart and the guy ahead of you sitting in your crotch, you know, just jammed in. And in one corner of the place was the shit pile. And we were freezing, sick. It was degrading. Everybody was sort of in a semi-comatose state.

193

Aldridge: On February 4, we went nearly to Bremen, and then on a single line, northwest, to a place called Tarmstedt. Tarmstedt was a naval prisoner of war camp. I have a note in my diary that about nineteen hundred and fifty officers and NCOs made it to that camp from Sagan.

We got to the camp at 6:30 P.M. and we finally got into the camp at two o'clock in the morning. They conducted a thorough search of everybody and their luggage. It was bitterly cold, it was raining all the time. And many of the prisoners were fainting. You could hear them as they hit the mud and the water. Splat!

Now, this camp wasn't prepared to receive prisoners. The prisoners that had been there before had been moved out, and the bunks had been moved out, so we were sleeping on the floor. The place was filthy, full of bedbugs, cockroaches.

Epstein: The next day, they said, "Send somebody over to the cookhouse for a meal." We were absolutely ravenous. We'd had nothing, we hadn't eaten much for days. And they sent one guy over for, I think, fifteen people. And he came back with a tin can — like, a tobacco can size — filled up with pieces of turnip that had been cooked in horsefat. And that was the meal for fifteen people. And I don't particularly like turnip, but I ate the two or three little pieces that were my share, and that was it.

St. Arnaud: And I had dysentery for about three weeks there, very bad. In fact, it took me years to get over it. I think the greatest fear I had was falling in the toilet! I was so weak, and the toilets they had were great big metal tanks with a two-by-four running across the top. You sat on the two-by-four, and you had to hang onto the two-by-four because if you went over backwards, you'd fall into this goddam tank. So I used to have a great fear of falling in, because I was getting pretty weak by that time. I'd lost about thirty pounds.

I found that camp very dirty and very discouraging. It wasn't like Stalag Luft III, where everything was organized. There was nothing organized here, and the food was poor. And there wasn't many Red Cross parcels, either.

Pilot Officer Daniel Almon
Warrant Officer Ross Elford
Warrant Officer Keith Pettigrew
Warrant Officer Harold White
Flight Sergeant Soggy Norton, Stalag Luft IV, Grosstychow

White: January 29, 1945, we had our first inclination that big moves were on the way, because there was a column of prisoners of war marched by our camp who were further east of us. And as they were going by they were yelling, "Get ready for a move, you'll be on the road!" So we knew something was up, that the Russians were gradually forcing their way into Germany.

Elford: We started marching February 6, 1945. Roughly two thousand of us had to evacuate the camp. We marched until May 2, the day we were liberated. We marched 778 kilometres in forty-four actual days of walking. We were down to about eight hundred of us when we were liberated.

Almon: We found out after a few miles that we weren't in very good shape. So, before the day was over, everybody was throwing all their excess baggage away, including food, except what we could carry in our pockets of our greatcoats.

After, I guess, the second week, we started to get into a little better shape, as far as our feet were concerned. But the first two weeks were terrible because everybody's feet were blistered. Food was extremely scarce, only what we could gather when we stopped overnight on farms.

Pettigrew: The Germans would put us in a barn at night, most nights. We only slept in the open twice. We'd go into a barn, and the only thing they could get us for food from the farmer — things were tough then — they'd just take potatoes from the pigs. They used to have big boilers and they'd boil up last year's potatoes and feed them to their pigs. So we'd get some of those. And of course from that we got dysentery, and everybody had the shits, in different degrees of intensity. We walked twenty-eight miles one day, and I went sixteen times that day. Dysentery's an awful bloody thing, and it's tough on the morale.

195

Norton: We had nothing to eat. We were stealing out of farms. In Europe, they store their root vegetables in great big pits, then cover them with straw and earth — carrots, beets, potatoes, whatever. And when we saw these mounds, we'd wait till the guards weren't looking, then we'd dig in.

Pettigrew: We were warned against drinking the water because at that time in Europe, most of the water table was contaminated, from too much sewage and human waste not being properly looked after. But when you're thirsty, to hell with it, you drink it.

Norton: When we were marching, some Allied aircraft strafed a German convoy on the road — they used a lot of horses to pull their equipment — and killed some of the horses. And they let us have two carcasses. So the Germans said, "Anybody here a butcher?" And I put my hand up, just to make sure I got close to that meat, you know. Of course, I didn't know what to do, but there was a couple of guys that had volunteered that were butchers. So we made sure we got some of the best cuts off the goddam horse to eat. I never ate horsemeat before I went to Europe, but it's good, you know.

White: We finally ended up at Fallingbostel, Stalag XI B.

Sergeant Tommy Cunningham
Corporal Earl Summerfield
Corporal Leo Lecky
Lance-Corporal Don Craigie
Private Geoffrey Ellwood
Private Bill Olver
Trooper Jack Whitley
Sapper Wally Hair, Stalag II D, Stargard

Ellwood: The war started getting a little bit close. You could hear some small arms fire off on the horizon. Apparently the Russians were sending in flash patrols — they'd come whipping in and shoot up a place, then go back. So the Germans decided to evacuate the camp.

Lecky: Either the end of February or the beginning of March of 1945, our German guard commander came in and said, "Pack up! Pack up!" That wasn't hard, because we had few possessions. And away we went.

We marched and we marched and we marched. To make a long story short, it was terrible. Of course, by the fourth or fifth day, we were all lousy. And later on we began to have dysentery. And boys were falling off. Sometimes we used to hear a shot in the distance. I can't say for sure, but we presumed he was shot and left to die.

Ellwood: In those thirty days we were marching, they fed us three times. They didn't have anything, and they couldn't get it.

One of the first things we'd do when we got to a farm was check out the pig pen. Because right adjacent to the pig pen was always this thing where they threw their old vegetables, you know, rotten old turnips, corn, and things like that. This is what they fed their pigs. And we'd get in there and take something that's half-rotten, scrape some of the slime off, and chomp on it. And I never saw anybody that wouldn't fight to get at it.

Olver: The Germans, I guess, wanted to keep us and keep ahead of the Russians. And they pushed us and pushed us. Six o'clock in the morning; six-thirty at night before they'd stop. And one day, they pushed us forty-two miles and all I had was a slice of bread.

I got an awful blister on my foot. Of course, you couldn't stop. They'd keep at you, poke with the old rifle butt to push you on. I marched for I don't know how long on the toes of my one foot, with my heel off the ground, trying to save this blister. I would say four weeks I did this.

Ellwood: When we started out on our forced march, we came to a village. And the whole village had turned out. They lined the road, and as we marched in, they cheered us. We didn't have a clue what was going on, you know. And when we got in there, we found they had a great big iron *Kübel* of soup on the fire. And they'd already built latrines with screens

197

around them. Oh, golly, they treated us just like we were their own people.

We found out that just one week before we came, three German prisoners had been repatriated from Canada, in that village. They had told the people how well they'd been treated in Canada.

That was the only real sign of friendliness I ever saw in Germany.

Craigie: We just seemed to march back and forth, east and west, north and south, depending on the way the Russian Front was advancing. We were never far from the sound of the guns.

A buddy of mine from Toronto, a fellow by the name of Ted Musgrove, we thought we'd take off and escape to the Russian lines. They couldn't have been very far away because we could hear the guns.

So when night came, we knocked some boards off the pig pen where we were, looked around and waited till the guard went round the other side of the building, and away we went. This would be just before dawn. We got about a mile away when we came to a hill. We could still hear the guns. We just nicely got to the brow of the hill, popped our heads up to have a look and, Jimminy Crickets, there were bullets flyin' around our ears!

So we just turned around and crawled back to the pig pen and called it a day. We thought we'd wait till the end of the war if they were that close!

Ellwood: Our physical condition was worsening. And I started breaking out in boils. These were all down both legs, hips. They used to sort of erupt at night. You could see your underwear where it was all stuck to your leg, you know, where the matter was down your leg. Of course, by this time, you hadn't washed for so long, you were smelling pretty high. And then there was this putrid smell from the boils.

Whitley: At the same time that we were marching down the road, all the German civilians were being evacuated too. And they were a sorry looking lot, too. It's hell to see a nation like that on the move because of war. They were the enemy, but I still felt sorry for some of those women and children.

Summerfield: And the women we saw that were raped, you know. The Russians, the soldiers, when they rape, they just cut their clothes right down the front. And when you saw women with their clothes wired together or tied together, you knew they'd been raped. Dozens and dozens and dozens you'd see every day.

Cunningham: It was April 13, 1945. There'd be about a thousand of us. Six Spitfires came over and saw our column. They assumed it was a German column. Well, sir, they came in on us and they strafed us. And I guess they killed about eighteen guys. I think the RAF greatcoats were lined with white, and this one guy whipped off his greatcoat, and he stood up in the road and turned it inside out and waved it. And he was just cut down.

It's a funny feeling, you know. It's your own guys shooting at you. Are you mad, or are you forgiving?

Summerfield: We got through Swinemünde. We bypassed Lübeck, and then they rounded us up and put us on boxcars. I don't know the names of all the places we went through. Then we got out, and they made us march to this camp. Sandbostel. It was a concentration camp. They kicked all the Polish guys out, put them on the road. Sandbostel was all wooden huts — no beds, no bunks, no nothing there. But bedbugs! You never saw so many bedbugs in all your life. Billions of them. I guess they were glad we came, for something to eat!

We were there, I'd say, about nine or ten days. Then they kicked all the Canadians out. They gave us a Red Cross parcel each and started us down the road. And just as we started down the road, up comes the SS with political prisoners. And they were just walking skeletons. Let me tell you, you wouldn't think a guy could get so thin and still be a little bit mobile. That's why the Germans kicked us out of Sandbostel, so they'd have some place to put them.

Hair: And I actually saw these people. They were just skin and bone. They were so far gone, I saw German guards bringing in blankets with food rations and laying them on the ground, and those fellas just stood around and drooled. They didn't have the coordination to go pick up the food to feed themselves. They were that far gone.

Summerfield: So we went from there to Marlag [und Milag] Nord. It was a navy camp. They put us in the officers' compound, because they'd evacuated the officers.

Private Cecil Cook, Stalag VII A, Moosburg

We had to get up at four o'clock in the morning, and we marched down to a station — there'd be thousands of us — and we'd board the boxcars for Munich, to work all day. We'd be cleaning up the damage done by our planes the night before. And in the afternoon, about three o'clock, we'd line up and get some horsemeat soup. We'd start the day at four o'clock in the morning, and we didn't get back to camp until eleven o'clock at night.

So then one day, I went in to work and I come back that night, and there's a line-up at our sergeant-major's office. I said to Bob Cole, "What's the lineup?" He said, "They want volunteer truck drivers." So we both put our names in and two or three days later, my name was called to go to Constance on the border of Switzerland and Germany. I think there was fourteen of us, with a sergeant-major.

We were supposed to go there and pick up loaded trucks. Red Cross parcels. This was an agreement that the Germans and the Red Cross made. This was near the end of the war, and they tried to get these parcels down from Switzerland to the stalags. We landed there, and people from Geneva brought the trucks through to Moosburg. So we had to jump in the train and go back. I think it was a two-day ride. And then when we got there, we took the trucks and took off to different stalags, in a convoy. We went all over, dumping our parcels.[2]

Sergeant Bert Gnam, Stalag IV B, Mühlberg

The war ended in May, and I escaped in March. We were

having trouble. No electricity, no food. All of us got diarrhea. So this American and two of us decided we would take off and see if we could reach the American lines. We were not alone. Every night, there'd be twenty, thirty, maybe forty guys would take off. The stench in that camp was awful. You have no idea, when you have that many men with diarrhea.

We got underneath the fence after midnight, got to Mühlberg, stole bicycles, and started heading west.

I saw some terrible things. Once we were looking for food, and we stopped at a little farmhouse. The house was empty. There was a trapdoor leading to the basement, so we went down there. There were three women down there, and these women were hung by their ankles. And they were cut from their thighs down to their neck and there they hung, just like a side of beef. And I believe they were alive when this happened to them. This was done by Russian prisoners of war.

We got to a little place, maybe five, six thousand people. And what we used to do when we came to a town was to ask for the mayor. And we would ask for food. They were terribly afraid of the Russians and they would give you food hoping you'd stay there. We used to tell them we were the advance party of the Allies. They couldn't have really believed it. One look at us and they must have thought they were winning the war, not losing it!

Our bicycles by this time were pretty well worn out, so we asked for a car instead of food. The mayor gave us his car and filled it full of petrol, and away we went. We kept that car a good three weeks. Had no problem getting gasoline. Go to the Americans, get all the gas you want.

We stopped at Wurzen and went into the beer parlour. When we come out, someone had stolen our car!

Flying Officer Wilf Blewett
Flying Officer Dave Mackey
Flying Officer Allister McDiarmid, Oflag XIII A, Nürnberg

Mackey: The Germans decided to move us. They were actually taking us as hostages, and they were intending to take us up into the Alps. We started out marching about April 8.

201

McDiarmid: We were moved to Moosburg[3], which is just east of Munich. And it took us about fourteen days to get there. And in that fourteen days, the Germans were able to give us one meal. We were able to get some food as we walked down the road. There'd be the odd farm, and we'd eat dandelions and roots and anything else we could lay our hands on.

Mackey: On our march, we used to break away from the column and trade soap and such for food. That was the only way we got some food to eat along the way.

I got a bottle of pop at one farm. We used to go in and offer soap and get the bread, and then not give the soap — walk out and have screaming Germans coming after you! But they were always afraid to go too far, because if they were ever caught trading with you, they were in trouble.

Blewett: There were some tense moments on the march because the Gestapo were retreating behind, making sure their own people didn't retreat too quickly. And they weren't averse to shooting anybody. We had a few people dropped off. They said they weren't going to march any farther, they would hole up in a barn or a field and wait till the Americans came by. Well, they were discovered by the Gestapo and just shot, you know, as escaped prisoners.

We crossed the Danube there, and they had their field guns there, and they were manned by kids that looked about sixteen, fifteen. And scared to death, by the appearance on their faces, you know.

McDiarmid: About three or four days out of Moosburg, many aircraft appeared above us. We could hear them. Then all of a sudden, about five of them came down through a hole in the clouds and opened up on us, thinking, of course, that we were German troops. There were a few killed and quite a few wounded.

But it was either the second or third aircraft realized who we were and got the firing stopped. And from then on, we had an escort of our own fighters watching over us, all day and all night, until we got into Moosburg.

Warrant Officer Harold White
Flight Sergeant Clem Hawkins
Sergeant Gilles Lamontagne
Sergeant Jim Sampson, Stalag XI B, Fallingbostel

Hawkins: On April 7, they moved us out of the camp. We had to pack everything, any food we had, clothing, bedding, we had to pack the whole thing. By that time we were getting so undernourished and suffering from malnutrition that when I went to bed at night, I felt like I didn't know if I would wake up in the morning. Then to go packing a load was a real strain on you.

Lamontagne: And so we walked the last month like this. That was terrible, because everybody was sick and weakened, most of them by less food and less food. Because the Red Cross could not get to us as easily as previously.

Sampson: They'd put us up in farms along the way. Well, we stole everything that was on the farm to eat. We killed the chickens and the pigs, ducks, anything that was edible, we'd steal it. And so, before long they realized they couldn't keep doing this. So they started just leaving us out in the fields.

Hawkins: On April 19, we got to a Red Cross depot, and they issued us with one Red Cross parcel to four guys. Of course, there was chocolate and raisins and sometimes they had cheese, butter, biscuits. It was a pretty good type of food parcel. It was designed for one person, but we hadn't seen any of that for several weeks, so even to get a quarter of one was a real treat.

After we got our ration, we moved out onto a long, straight road, and they told us we could take a rest and munch on our goodies. We had just finished when we heard planes. I heard somebody say, "They're coming in on us!"

Sampson: Before we could do anything about it, we looked up, and just over the treetops come these airplanes. And they were Typhoons — our own — and they came in on top of us and started strafing us.

Hawkins: I dived behind a tree just as these planes came in and strafed the roadway. Right where I had left the roadway they dropped an anti-personnel bomb, and they were firing fifty-millimetre cannons. And one of these bombs lands in the roadway right where I had been. Lobbed a guy right in half.

Sampson: Well, this Andy Rodgers and I reacted quickly, and we went into the ditch and we started running to get over to this field. This Englishman stood by the wagon and he had a white towel and he was waving it, you see, at our own airplanes. Well, they shot him — the bullet went right through his head and out the other side — dropped him right there.

Hawkins: I never got hit or anything, but I remember getting up and there were dead people all around. I was pretty shaken up. I guess that was about the most traumatic experience that I had during the war. That was worse than getting shot down.

Sampson: There was dead and wounded laying everywhere. And we had one medical officer. This fellow gave Andy and I some needles and we went around shoving them into guys. There were fifty-six or fifty-seven of our guys killed, and about nine of the guards.

They were our own airplanes that shot the shit out of us. They were just over the treetops, and they made eight attacks on us.

White: We were on the road until we were released by a column of motorized American soldiers. We were in this little village on this particular morning — I believe it was May 2 — and we heard a lot of cheering and yowling and whatnot, and we went out to the road to see what was going on. And here's this column of motorized American troops going through. Nobody stopped or anything, they just kept going. Of course, we all went crazy. But nobody waved to us, nobody looked at us, or anything. And the whole column just disappeared, away they went. And we wondered what was going on, 'cause they were supposed to be on our side!

Then we started to look at each other. And you know, we'd been on the road for months, and we were the dirtiest, lousiest bunch of men you ever laid eyes on. Well, about twenty minutes later, the second column comes through. And the same thing happened, for about halfway down the column. Then somebody must have realized that we were ex-POWs. Anyway, they kicked out two of those wooden crates of K rations. And of course, the crates hit the roadway and broke open, and tins flew in all directions, and we were just in there like a bunch of dogs.

So, actually, we were liberated at that time. Of course, we took over the village. I don't mean to say there was any rough stuff; there wasn't. The German people knew the end was there as far as the war was concerned; they treated us halfway decent and we treated them halfway decent. Of course, they lost a lot of chickens and whatnot, and we took over the houses.

Flight Lieutenant Al Aldridge
Flight Lieutenant Art Deacon
Flight Lieutenant Anthony Pengelly
Flying Officer Joseph St. Arnaud
Pilot Officer Don MacDonald, Marlag und Milag Nord,
Westertimke-Tarmstedt

Aldridge: We left this camp Tuesday, April 10. Now, this march was a picnic compared to the five-day one in the winter, because it was now spring-like weather. We were camping in the fields. We did have some food and we were able to do some bartering with the German civilians to get a little more food.

St. Arnaud: This is where we really lived outside for about a month. We slept in fields most nights. And this is where I taught all sorts of Englishmen how to light fires and build lean-tos. My Canadian know-how, eh? The things I'd learned in Scouts.

We had a poor old guard with us, about sixty-five years of age. He treated us very well. And he got so tired and worn-out that one guy took his pack and another guy took his rifle, so he just had to walk, and the prisoners carried everything for him.

We stayed off the main roads. And we averaged five or six kilometres a day, you know, four or five miles at the most. We didn't want to walk by then, 'cause the weather was nice. The first march, we walked to get out of the rain and the snow and the cold.

Aldridge: We knew it was just a matter of time. It was just a question of when. Eventually, we reached this farm just south of Lübeck. Our Senior British Officer was a Canadian, Group Captain Wray, Larry Wray. He insisted that the Germans leave us there or face dire consequences. So we were billeted on this farm, and that's where we were liberated.

St. Arnaud: Then one morning, all of a sudden a jeep appeared with a British lieutenant and a sergeant. Just drove right into the camp. The lieutenant said, "Who the hell are you?" And I said, "We're POWs, British airmen." And he says, "Okay, fine. We'll have some trucks up here to get you within twenty-four to forty-eight hours."

MacDonald: When that day came, it was a funny reaction. Some guys just broke down and cried like babies, and I must admit there was a bit of excess perspiration came down the side of my cheeks, too. There was an artificial lake there, and some of the boys just ran like hell and dove into the lake, clothes and all, screaming and hollering, "We're going home, we're going home!" I remember looking at Hardy deForest and all I remember saying is, "Home." If I'd said one more word, I'd've probably bawled like a baby. And I buggered off, went for a walk out in the country.

St. Arnaud: As soon as we were liberated, I said, "Well, I haven't had a bath for six months. I'm gonna go into town and I'm gonna find a bathtub!"

So three or four of us went into this little village about a mile away, and we came up to this little house with a white picket fence, beautifully well-kept, and I said, "That's the place for a bath." And we walked in. Of course, the Germans came and took one look at this bedraggled, dirty, bearded, filthy bunch. One of our fellas spoke pretty good German, and he said, "We want a bath."

Well, the Germans were so relieved that's all we wanted, that we weren't going to rape and pillage! And we took turns having a bath. The woman boiled hot water for us and filled the bathtub, and she had nice clean towels for us. When we finished the bath, she had nice tea and cookies and bread and butter for us. Then we said, "Thank you, and goodbye." And away we went. But, oh, that bath was just something! Funny, the little things you miss, eh?

Pengelly: The ammunition trucks that were coming up and the army store trucks had to go back empty. So, as they went back, they took us. And the first stop was the nearest British army base that had total bathing facilities because they were all convinced that we had, probably, typhus and everything else. And the first thing they wanted to do was take all our clothes, burn them, and give us new army battledress. Hot showers. You were supposed to use special lice soap for your hair. I mean, they all assumed we were totally contaminated. Actually, we weren't, but they assumed that.

Then the next day, they'd put you in trucks and move you again. Wherever we went, they'd assume the same thing. So they'd take all our brand new army battledress, burn 'em, put us through the delousing, and issue us with new uniforms, and so on.

Till finally we got to Lüneburg, which was a big Luftwaffe training college. A big one, enormous. Not unlike a university grounds, really. That would be May 6, I guess. We didn't have any idea how we'd get back to England at that point.

We had much better rations. They were obsessed with our health. Doctors were coming in and examining you every hour, on the hour, to make sure you were still alive. I was down to ninety-two pounds. But I was in good health. You know, we'd been outdoors since January.

About six o'clock that morning, we heard the rumble of Russian tanks. It was a welcome sight to see, the Russians coming in with their tanks, horse artillery, women with

207

machine guns. We thought, "Well, we're free at last!" But later on we found that we were not.

One morning we woke up and were surprised to see about forty American trucks all parked on the road outside. The Americans came into the camp and said, "Okay, let's go." But they were turned away at riflepoint by the Russians. All the forty trucks had to turn around and go back to American-occupied Germany.

We didn't know what our fate would be. We were all finger-printed by the Russians, interrogated by the Russians.

Rogers: The Russians were a little reluctant to let us go. They said they had to wait for word from Moscow.

Davies: Just about that time, the "organization people" came through. These were the Russian organization people. They were big, they were well-dressed. Just the look about these people, the terrible feeling they gave you, you just sort of shuddered for the people they were going to get hold of and what they were going to do to them. If there was anybody I was ever glad to get away from, it was them. Just a terrible, omnipresent feeling about these Russians.

Some of us managed to get away. We managed to get across the Elbe River at Torgau, at one of the bridges that the Americans put across. I think it was the 82nd Airborne, one of the American crack divisions, they were on the other side of this bridge. They had a small post there, and they were very surprised to see us. I think we must have been ten or a dozen.

So, the first thing they did was to sit us down and give us something to eat. And they had this mess tent and a couple of tables, and they put out bowls of canned peaches and stacks of white bread. And I still remember that poor old corporal no sooner put this bread down than all of us just gorged ourselves on it. We were just like animals, going after this white bread, and the poor guy kept bringing loaves and loaves of it.

Deacon: I remember the first piece of white bread that I saw. And, you know, it just looked like angel food cake. Gosh, I didn't realize that bread could be so white.

208

Pengelly: We were sitting in Lüneburg. Bomber Command in England at that point hadn't anything to do. I mean, there was nothing left to bomb. So Bomber Command volunteered to fly the air force out.

They were all flying Lancasters. Based upon the date on which you were shot down, that was the order in which you went back. So, obviously, I was kind of far up the list.

That was May 7. They took us by truck to this airfield and flew us back to England. And we landed in a big reception field. And they assumed we were all lousy and did the same routine. Took our army battledress, burned it, and gave us air force battledress. We were in these big hangars, and the hangars were filled with cardtables and chairs. And they had an afternoon tea for us. And the local ladies of the community and Red Cross people and nurses just swamped us. You know, from seeing no women at all to being swamped — hundreds of them. And here we were with teacups and scones. It was the most absurd scene!

Deacon: Having got back to Britain, the RAF, I said, "Well, how much leave do we get?" The fella said, "Two weeks."

"Two weeks, after five years?" "Yes, you'll be going out to the Far East, probably." So we went down to London, and we found out we could transfer to the RCAF. So that's what we did.

Flight Lieutenant Ivan Anderson
Pilot Officer Jim Davies
Pilot Officer Russ Rogers, Stalag III A, Luckenwalde

Anderson: Stalag III A. This was a large camp near Potsdam, just outside Berlin. There were Russian prisoners, Polish prisoners, all types of prisoners in that camp. We were in that camp from February '45 until May.

You could hear the artillery getting closer and closer all the time. One evening, we saw a lot of activity around the German guards' camp outside the camp proper. And at midnight — that was April 21 — the Germans sabotaged all the electricity, water, everything they could, and left the camp. Left us to fend for ourselves. We were, of course, prepared for

209

this, and we were all set up with our electricians and plumbers and all sorts of tradesmen. In three hours we had everything working again. This would be about three o'clock in the morning.

Anderson: About ten days later, we woke up one morning, and there was about sixty Russian trucks all lined up. We all jumped into the trucks. About six hours later we were at the banks of the Elbe River. The Americans had a pontoon bridge across, and we all walked across into the hands of the Americans. That's when we felt free.

Flight Sergeant John Cox
Flight Sergeant Doug Hawkes
Flight Sergeant Bill Rowbotham
Sergeant Bob Charman, Stalag IV B, Mühlberg

Cox: We got released by the Russians. It was about April 22, 1945. There wasn't a guard in the camp. They'd all taken off. You see, we were on the east side of the Elbe River, and they'd all taken off to the west side of the Elbe River to escape the Russians.

Charman: It was Cossack horsemen that liberated the camp, riding down through the camp just like it was the eighteenth century. We were more afraid of them than the Germans! The Russians mounted guards in the sentry boxes to keep us in there.

Rowbotham: They were on scrawny little ponies. They didn't look like a first-line attack force to me, whatsoever. Talk about a rough bunch of desperadoes. But they weren't quite as strict as the Germans. Whereas the Germans were unprepared to feed us towards the end, the Russians did let us get out and scavenge around and find what we could.

Hawkes: We went into Mühlberg and found the army stores that the Germans had left, perfectly intact. My God, the food in there! Some of the nicest cheese I'd ever seen. You'd see guys going back to camp with bushel baskets full of strawberry jam. I brought back a case of condensed milk. Then we'd divvy it all up and trade amongst ourselves.

Charman: We stayed around for two, three days, but we got fed up with that after a while. So about ten of us, early one morning, cut a hole in the fence and escaped.

We made our way into the little town of Torgau. This was where the Americans and the Russians first linked up, General Bradley and General Zhukov. They put a pontoon bridge across, because the main bridge across the river had been blown. And we saw Bradley come across to meet Zhukov. They had a big powwow on the eastern bank of the Elbe River.

The Russians wouldn't let us use the pontoon bridge at Torgau. So we walked down the river about four miles. We saw a boat anchored out in the Elbe River. One of the American fellows that was with us was a very powerful swimmer, so he swam out and got hold of this boat. We all got in it, and it capsized in the middle of the river. We all scrambled ashore on the west bank. Then we "liberated" a farmhouse, dried off, and had a big meal.

We walked from there to Halle, which is north of Leipzig. From there, we were flown back to Brussels in an American transport plane.

Cox: [The Russians] kept us there for about a week, and then they moved us down to the town of Riesa. But they wouldn't let us go. Well, one night in Riesa, a New Zealand officer came in, and a Yank, and they told us if we could get away from the Elbe River to the Mulde — this was about fifty kilometres west of the Elbe, it was like a no man's land for the Americans and the Russians, a buffer zone — if we could get to the Mulde, they'd be waiting for us.

So we took off, and the Russians were shooting over our heads, trying to scare us back. But after that, they didn't bother us too much. In fact, we hitchhiked the last five miles on one of their trucks to this neutral zone. And we got across a pontoon bridge on the Mulde and, sure enough, the Americans were waiting for us.

The Americans took us by truck to Halle. We were there a day or two, and then we were flown back to England.

211

Flying Officer Wilf Blewett
Flying Officer Dave Mackey
Flight Sergeant Bob Collins
Trooper George Hailes, Stalag VII A, Moosburg

Collins: Guess who liberated us? General Patton. We heard the gunfire the night before, and we went to bed as usual. And the next morning, we got up, and in the distance we could see these hills. And the first thing we saw was American tanks coming over these hills. Oh, what a sight to behold! And, of course, the guards just took off, they were throwing their guns away.

Blewett: General Patton came through and stood up on his tank with his pearl-handled revolvers and said, "Well, you're brave men, you've made it. My troops will help you as much as they can, but we've got work to do." Just like John Wayne, you know, and away he went.

Mackey: But we were worse off now, under the Americans, than we were before. Because we were getting a little bit of rations from the Germans before we were liberated. But once we were liberated, we lost that, and the Americans didn't have anything to feed us. So we had to go out and scrounge in the small town there, Moosburg. We did get some potatoes and got some margarine.

Hailes: Eventually, after a week or so, some British planes came to the camp, about seven or eight of them. We went from there to Reims. And we got white bread. That's the thing I remember about that place. First bread that wasn't black that we'd seen in about three years.

Then we got back to England. Threw us all in a hospital compound, where they were checking us all over.

Mackey: Then we had to go through a very embarrassing process of being dusted with powder, to kill the lice. And we were going around like snowmen for a couple of days, because they kept coming up to us every once in a while, saying "We've got to give you another shot." And this went all through your clothing and inside your drawers, and really, it was very embarrassing.

Then we were sent back to Bournemouth to be rehabilitated, put on special diets to build us up. And after about three weeks of that, I had to get out because they made me so fat I could hardly walk!

When I did get home, eventually, I found out that I had been reported "missing in action, presumed dead" because there hadn't been any communications out of Germany the last six months of the war.

Trooper Cliff Hooey, Marlag und Milag Nord, Westertimke-Tarmstedt

The Russians were only about two hundred kilometres away, and the Germans tried to move us on foot from the camp we were in. You've got a column of, for a guess, two thousand men, and maybe twenty-five or thirty guards. They tried to stick to what prevails in the military — on the march, you walk for fifty minutes and rest for ten minutes. So somebody at the back of the column would be shouting all the way up to the front: "Sit down and rest! The officer back here says, 'Sit down and rest!'" Even though the officer had never said it. So we were continually sitting down and having a rest. On the third day, we were surrounded by the British army, so the guards told us to go back to the camp. So we went back to the camp in about four hours' march — the same distance it took us three days to get there!

Then the British liberated us. The 17th Hussars, I think it was. They rode in about ten o'clock in the morning. They kept on going down the road. We took off with them, myself and three others. We went up to as close to the front as we could. The camp where we were was approximately twenty kilometres from the Bergen-Belsen concentration camp, and we were there when it was liberated. You couldn't believe it. There was stacks of dead bodies, emaciated bodies, four feet high, sixty or seventy feet long, where they'd crawled up on the stack and starved to death. The stench was unbelievable. They'd throw male and female into the same camp, and there were sacks full of newborn babies — they'd killed them

213

because they couldn't feed them. You can't believe that one human could treat another in such a manner.

Flight Lieutenant George Gardiner
Flying Officer Arthur Low
Flight Sergeant Ed Rae, Stalag Luft I, Barth

Low: Things started to get pretty tight and off in the distance we could hear cannon. And we really started watching them, because we thought there was a chance the Germans might just come over and start shooting us.

We had some New Zealand paratroopers in there with us. And these were death on two feet, these guys. And they trained us to defend ourselves. So you take your table knife, break it off till the blade is three inches long, no more. Find yourself a stone or a brick, and you start rubbing that thing till you get it to a point, and sharp on both sides. Get some string and wind it around the handle for a grip. That was your only weapon. And the paratroopers said, "All we're teaching you is how to kill, and how to stay alive."

Gardiner: We thought we might be in the midst of action. So we were busy digging slit trenches. The next morning, the guards had vacated. We sent a patrol out to make contact to the east, and we sent another group to the west to make contact with anybody.

Low: I was on the crew that took over the aerodrome. On the edge of the airport was a hospital. And there was two German doctors and five nurses who stayed. It's a good thing they did, because on the airport itself was a concentration camp. All Polish and political prisoners, Polish Jews. They got out, and they got food, and they died. There were five or six hundred people in there, and we were ferrying them over to the hospital, and the German doctors and nurses were doing what they could to save them. And we were out scrounging up food to make up into a broth to feed them.

We got a bulldozer and got it going and made a pit, and we started laying the bodies down in the pit. It's a cruel thing to say, but we didn't even try to drag them down the stairs, we

214

just tossed 'em out the windows. We had a lot of bodies in that pit.

Rae: The Germans went out the back gate and the Russians came in the front gate. They went through the town — anything that walks, they shoot it, you know. Even shot their own guys. And they were all drunk.

Low: There were regular Russians. There were Siberians, who were big, good-natured guys who chewed tobacco and stunk to high heaven, just like billy goats. And then there were Mongolians. A Mongolian was death waiting for a place to happen. I watched them go up to a house. They didn't even try the door, just took their tommy guns, went br-r-r-r, and kicked the door open. The only person in the house was an old lady about seventy years old. And the five soldiers and the officer all raped her.

Rae: They came in on horseback, horsedrawn wagons full of straw and vodka bottles. They were relatively short runts with no hair, and a burp gun over their back — and no hesitation to use it. These were actually Mongolians, shock troops, or cannon fodder. Their officers were Russians, but the men were Mongolians. They were a mean lookin' bunch of buggers.

Most were on horsedrawn wagons, and bicycles, motorcycles, cars of all descriptions. There'd be about eight or ten of them in a car, all whoopin' and hollerin'.

Low: There were a few Junkers 88s at the aerodrome. And they were booby trapped. I got into one of them and got the compass out of it — very carefully — and I just got that, and the Russians came along and kicked me out. And in go the sappers to defuse the booby traps. Bang! And two more guys went into the next one to get the booby trap — bang! All these aircraft, one by one, they managed to blow them up and two people with them each time. And there were half a dozen Focke-Wulf 190s in a line. And the Russians blew up every one of them, trying to defuse the booby traps.

215

Gardiner: The Russians wanted to take our camp back through Russia. But the Americans and British wanted no part of it. For four days this arguing went on. It was tight.

Low: Come V-E Day, May 8, and I managed to trade cigarettes for two bottles of firewater. We were marching up and down through the town, all stoned to the eyeballs. And the Russkies put on a dance. They commandeered any women they could find for this dance. I danced with a Russian army nurse who was armed to the teeth — good Lord — hand grenades, pistols, knives. I woke up the next morning. For a pillow, I had an opera hat. And I had a Russian tommy gun. Probably some Russky got drunk and gave it to me. I brought it all the way home with me.

Finally, five of us piled into a car; our goal was Lüneburg, British army headquarters. We knew that the First Canadian Paratroops were at Wismar. Rostock was all bombed to hell, the streets were full of shell holes and bomb holes, and a Cossack on a horse took us through the sidestreets and put us on a road out of town.

And there were barriers manned by Russian soldiers about every two miles. We had a lot of cigarettes, and we bribed our way through them, till we got to the one just before Wismar. There were two officers on there. And they thought we were Luftwaffe, and they had their guns pointed at us, and they're not about to let us through.

Well, only about twenty yards away are the Canadians, with their own barrier. So I hollered across, "We're Canadian POWs. They're not gonna let us through!"

Up came every rifle, every tommy gun, pointed right at the Russians. And somebody said, "If we yell 'hit the dirt,' do it, 'cause we're gonna kill those bastards!"

I guess the Russians understood English. Because all of a sudden, they stepped back and waved us on.

Gardiner: But finally the U.S. Air Force came in with their B-17s. So we evacuated the camp in two days. This was May 11 and 12.

Corporal Earl Summerfield

They flew us back to England. After that, they put us in barracks in Farnborough. And they tried to take our combat jackets off us. They said there was lice in them, and disease. And we'd had more shots of white disinfectant up our tunics and down our pants — every time we met anybody, that's what they did to us! And they wanted to take our clothes off us. No way would we give them up.

Second day, they'd set up field kitchens in the big transport garages. And there was steak and chops and mashed potatoes and peas, custard and bread and everything else. They'd give us plates, and we'd go through the line. We'd go over and sit down and eat as much as we could. Then we'd go outside, and they had all the garbage cans lined up, and we were all sick in them! The food was too rich. And then we'd go line up for more food.

Flight Sergeant George Thom

I was liberated on April 12, and we got into England in May. But we had been eating, really, off the fat of the land. Anytime we wanted, we could eat. We could have American rations or anything, you know. When I got to England, I weighed a hundred pounds. I couldn't sit down, not comfortably, because the bones of your ass just cut through your skin.

Pilot Officer Daniel Almon

I spent V-E Day in London. That was quite a day. It was quite a couple of days, as a matter of fact. We had quite a party. We had gotten paid, we had lots of money. We got a couple of bottles of Scotch on the black market. I think we paid quite a bit for it, but that didn't worry us at that time.

The party lasted two or three days. It was a very unwise thing to do because we weren't in any condition to celebrate to that extent, after three and a half years in prison camp.

Pilot Officer Gord King

About ten of us landed in England on the night before V-E

Day. They took us from this aerodrome through London, by rail, on the way to Bournemouth. And we were just in our old rags, you know, coming out of the camp, we'd been walking for a month. And we jumped the train, we said, "There's no way we're going to miss this party!"

So we got off, went to a hotel. We got cleaned up a bit and went out to Trafalgar Square, and there were wall-to-wall people. And we celebrated.

And then we really got into trouble! A couple of drinks would put us under the table, 'cause we weren't used to it. So we were in pretty bad shape when we got to Bournemouth.

Flying Officer Joseph St. Arnaud

The prisoners were going to be the first ones home. They just told everybody, "You're a Canadian, you're going home." What they failed to realize is that a lot of these people had married English girls. They didn't want to go home.

About two thousand of us went by train down to this ship. It was a very dirty ship, an older ship. And by the time we got there, everybody else had got there ahead of us. So we were right down in the bottom of the hold. And some of the prisoners, you know, got together and about four hundred of them walked off the ship.

The British army was called out and they were threatening the prisoners. And, of course, having been a prisoner, they'd had machine guns shooting at them and guards prodding them in the ass with bayonets for four or five years. They were sure their own people wouldn't do it to them. They just sat down and wouldn't move.

And finally, they sent for Larry Wray. And he came down from London — he was an Air Commodore, I think, by this time — and he talked to them. And, of course, he'd been with them as a prisoner. So he asked them what was wrong, and they told him. And he said, "That's wrong." And he got on the phone, the Air Ministry in London. And within half an hour, he says, "Anybody that wants to stay in England, get over here. Everybody who wants to go back to Canada, get on the ship." Settled it, just like that.

Of course, I didn't get off the ship. I wanted to go home!

218

Flight Sergeant John Cox

When I got to Bournemouth, they found out I had tuberculosis. So I was sent to Number Eleven Canadian General Hospital, Lady Astor's estate. I know I was supposed to go to a garden party which I never got to because I was in hospital. The King and Queen were having a garden party and they invited a bunch of Canadian prisoners of war, and my name was on the list. But I never did get to it. Woulda been nice.

Trooper George Hailes

Eventually, we got on the boat and went home. I had to make a dollar going home, so I had my groundsheet and Crown and Anchor dice. And on the inside of my groundsheet was all the Crown and Anchor figures. I made a few bucks there.

Lance-Corporal Don Craigie

We came back on the *Queen Mary*. They had the CPR passenger train waiting at the dockyards in New York. They took us to see the New York Yankees and the Detroit Tigers play baseball that afternoon. It came over the PA system that we were there and the fans gave us a standing ovation. They wanted to give us all the hot dogs we could eat and all the beer we could drink. So I enjoyed the ball game!

We got on the train and four days later we were in Calgary. That was on the Sunday morning after the Calgary Stampede had just finished. You never saw a deader city in all your life. But I was mighty happy to be there!

Footnotes

1. In the late stages of the war, Stalag VIII B was re-designated Stalag 344. Similarly, Stalag XI B at Fallingbostel in northern Germany was renamed Stalag 357. For the sake of simplicity, the original designations of these camps will be retained.
2. In early March 1945, fifty POWs volunteered for this duty. Thirty-two were accepted.
3. Stalag VII A.

Part Two: The Far East

XIII/The Horrors of Hong Kong

It is ironic that although Canada directed its primary war effort against Nazi Germany, the first major battle fought by the Canadian army was not in Europe, but in the Far East. And it was a disaster.

In the fall of 1941, the Canadian government made a decision that sparked a controversy that survives to this day. On the recommendation of its top military men, the Mackenzie King government agreed to a British request to send Canadian troops to reinforce the garrison of the Crown Colony of Hong Kong. Why the British even made the request is a mystery, because their experts had long since decided that Hong Kong was indefensible; that, while the loss of the Colony would be a blow to British prestige, Hong Kong would not be vital in any war with Japan. As a result, the British War Office decided as early as 1937 there was no purpose either in building up Hong Kong's defences or in reinforcing the four Regular Army infantry battalions posted there (two British, the Middlesex Regiment and the Royal Scots, and two Indian, the 2/14 Punjabis and the 5/7 Rajputs). Even as late as 1941, British Prime Minister Churchill was advocating reduction of the garrison to merely symbolic status.

Nevertheless, the British government reversed itself in September 1941, and with war in the Far East growing imminent, Canada was asked to make available two battalions of infantry to bolster the garrison at Hong Kong. For reasons that are not altogether clear, Ottawa agreed. The popularly-accepted reason is that, at the time, the Canadian army was still languishing in Britain with no prospect of immediate action against the Germans; if that was indeed the reason for sending Canadians to Hong Kong, it was an awfully poor one. And it does not explain the choice of the two units given the Hong Kong assignment, the Royal Rifles of Canada and the Winnipeg Grenadiers. Neither was combat-ready; in fact, they were chosen from a list of units considered unfit for operational duties. To this point in the war, the Royal Rifles had been on garrison duty in Newfoundland, while the Grenadiers were fulfilling a similar role in Jamaica, where ironically, one of their tasks involved guarding German prisoners of war. Both battalions had to be heavily reinforced with raw recruits to bring them up to fighting strength.

On October 27, 1941, the Canadian contingent sailed from Vancouver. Commanded by Brigadier J.K. Lawson, the bulk of the 1975 Canadians sailed on board the Australian liner *Awatea*, with one company of the Royal Rifles on board the armed merchant cruiser HMCS *Prince Robert*, which was escorting the *Awatea*. Five hundred and fifty of these men would never see Canada again. Two hundred and ninety would die in the ensuing battle for Hong Kong. Almost as many would lose their lives in cruel captivity afterwards.

Private Don Nelson, Winnipeg Grenadiers

I proceeded overseas in '41 with the Winnipeg Grenadiers. We arrived in Hong Kong in the latter part of November 1941. My understanding is that we were supposed to be garrison troops. Our government never thought there would be a war that soon.

Private Arnold Graves, Royal Rifles of Canada

I feel we were sent to Hong Kong because it was considered a safe place. Ours was a "million dollar" regiment. There were a lot of very prominent people in the Royal Rifles. We had two Price brothers — the Price Brothers Lumber Company. Clark Steamship Lines, his son was with us. "Chubby" Power, Minister of Air, his son was with us. A regiment with five or six millionaires' sons, I can't see them throwing it away. Money talks.

221

Company Sergeant-Major Cecil "Red" Windsor, Winnipeg Grenadiers

On our arrival in Hong Kong, we were greeted enthusiastically and paraded from the docks to our camp in Kowloon. With us being Canadian, we were paid more money than the English, and we dominated Hong Kong. Where the English would take a rickshaw to go downtown, they'd give him a penny or two pennies; we'd be giving him a dollar or two dollars. So this created a little bit of discontent between the English and Canadians. And a riot ensued in a place called the Sun-Sun Hotel. It was good fun while it lasted.

Private Don Nelson, Winnipeg Grenadiers

On December 8, we got word that the Japanese had hit Pearl Harbor[1]. At that time, a lot of our boys were sent up into the New Territories. The rest of us were sent from Kowloon to the island of Hong Kong. The fighting was fierce, hand-to-hand. And most of our boys were driven back and onto the island after about three days. We had a lot of casualties, Canadians especially. There were other units with us: the Royal Scots, the Middlesex, Punjabs, and of course, your Hong Kong Volunteers, which was mostly Portugese and Chinese troops. We had no air force and no gunboats to help us, so it was just a matter of time before they overran us[2].

Lance-Corporal Harold Englehart, Royal Rifles of Canada

We lacked in weapons, especially three-inch mortars. We had only two-inch mortars and not a great supply of ammunition. The Japanese were using three-inch mortars, so they could lob mortar shells in on us a great deal farther off than we could. We had to more or less storm the hills at night, but as soon as daylight came they could see where we were and lob in those mortars.

The equipment that we had was very good: the Bren gun, which proved itself in Europe, and we had a supply of Vickers guns. The lack of training was noticeable. I had one day's training on the Vickers gun. I could use a Vickers gun, but if it broke down, I wouldn't have known how to repair it.

Private Stephen Kashton, Winnipeg Grenadiers

The whole thing was disorganized confusion. Nobody was prepared for it. There was no communication. We didn't have transportation. You carried everything on your back.

I managed to shoot a plane down with a Bren gun. He was dive-bombing, and when he came over our position, he was no more [than] a hundred, hundred-fifty feet above me. I opened up — two magazines. And he finally burst into flame and went down into the water. I thought that was quite a big thing. But I got shit for it, because I didn't get permission to fire off the Bren gun. They were going to court-martial me, but that never materialized.

Private Fred Reich, Winnipeg Grenadiers

I think it was [December 18] when we were told that some paratroopers had landed and everybody was ordered in full marching gear to look after these few paratroopers. It proved to be one of the main invasion points of the island. There were untold thousands of Japanese there. It was just a question of us retreating to the point where we couldn't go back any further. And we were forced to surrender. This was the morning of December 19.

The wounded, not being able to walk, were automatically cut out of the ranks and just bayonetted to death. Even some that weren't wounded. I recall one incident where one of our guys threw a hand grenade into one of their machine gun nests and destroyed three or four of their soldiers. They in turn bayonetted fifteen, possibly twenty, of our people in retaliation.

They took us back to a ferry and over to the mainland to a place called Argyle Camp. Argyle Camp was an officers' camp prior to this. We were there until the island capitulated on Christmas Day.

Sergeant Ed Schayler, Winnipeg Grenadiers

You talk about fear. This is when it first struck me. I heard this crackling sound, and for a little while I couldn't understand what it was. Then it dawned on me. It was bullets going past my ear. If they come close to you, you won't hear the ping like they make in the movies. You'll just hear a little crackle.

They couldn't move us off this mountain, so they started to strafe us with airplanes. I remember seeing the machine guns from the airplanes going and I could see the dirt kicking up right in front of me. So I knew what fear was. I often wondered how I would react, and I shocked myself because I became quiet. I didn't shake, my mind worked well. I didn't shake until I got out of that place.

We kept getting smaller numbers, smaller numbers, regrouping. And I don't say there's such a thing as a coward in that kind of situation. I have seen men do stupid things, and they're called brave.

Private Walt Jenkins, Royal Canadian Corps of Signals

I was a telephone lineman. We laid lines at night, mostly. A friend of mine and I, we laid a telephone line through the Japanese lines at night. The only time I ever heard a machine gun being fired before this was in the movies. I didn't know nothing about being a soldier. Never had any training. Never fired my rifle. All of a sudden, some bastard is firing at me. I didn't like it! It was awful, just terrible.

CSM Red Windsor, Winnipeg Grenadiers

We shouldn't allow our youngsters to go overseas. It makes you feel awful sorry, and you get emotionally upset and disturbed when you see them trying their damnedest and crying like little babies because they haven't got no equipment to fight with.

Private Bob Lytle, Winnipeg Grenadiers

Well, it became obvious pretty quick that we weren't very well trained. Secondly, all we had was our small arms: rifles, and Thompson machine guns and Bren guns, and some grenades. I honest-to-God think, with what little we had, we did put up a pretty good show. But the surrender was a terribly desolate feeling.

224

Lance-Corporal Ralph MacLean, Royal Rifles of Canada

I ended up being taken prisoner just across the bay from Stanley Peninsula on Christmas Day. We were defending a hill, and we were overrun. Within the next hour, through a loudspeaker across the valley, a Japanese officer speaking perfect English told us if we came across with a white flag, we'd be given safe conduct. We decided to surrender.

Most of the fellas had their hands tied behind their backs, and we were marched back behind the lines. We went by different groups of our fellas that had been bayonetted. They were tied up in groups of six to ten and butchered. We figured we'd end up the same way.

Corporal Ken Gaudin, Royal Rifles of Canada

Just about dusk, the shells stopped coming, the aircraft disappeared from the air. The last shell hit the remaining truck and the gas tank exploded. It was so quiet. The only noise at that time was the crackling of the burning truck.

Up on the hill there were the Stanley Barracks. A lot of the wounded and the dying were up in these buildings. The word "Christmas" was mentioned. Although they were wounded and dying, from up in those barracks up on the hill, the strains of those men singing "Silent Night, Holy Night" is something I shall always remember.

We had with us kids who hadn't yet turned sixteen. They were thinking of home, their fathers, their mothers. And I could see by the light of the burning truck the big tears trickling down their cheeks.

Private Bill Savage, Winnipeg Grenadiers

Late on Christmas Day, there was a runner sent around to tell us it was all over, and that we were to march to Wong Nei Chong Gap and give ourselves up. When we got up there, there was a Japanese officer, and he was the wildest looking character you ever did see. Straight out of a comic book. He had this big Fu Manchu mustache, swinging this long blooming sword around. Kind of scared the hell out of all of us.

They lined us up, and they took *tenko*, numbered us off.

225

There was one fellow they found with an army issue knife in his pocket. They opened it up and stabbed him with it. All of a sudden it dawned on me that I had a grenade in each blooming hip pocket of my coveralls! I broke out into a sweat. But I managed to flip them into the blooming ditch behind me.

Rifleman Donald Geraghty, Royal Rifles of Canada

I guess I fought in two skirmishes. I fired at them, where I thought they were. But I never did see a Jap until Christmas Day up in Fort Stanley. I looked out and here's this carload of little wee fellas. And I'm six foot one. It was a blow to my pride to be captured by these little yellow creatures.

Christmas night, we were up on a ridge in front of Fort Stanley waiting for the attack. There was no attack because there was a truce at the time, pending negotiations between the governor of the island and the invading forces. The most frightening thing was looking out and seeing the glow of thousands of cigarettes. The Japanese down below had been told [we'd] surrendered, so they all sat down and started smoking cigarettes. Then we realized how close they were, and how many they were, and how impotent we were.

I was only seventeen at the time. And that first night, I had only a feeling of outrage. The next day, I think, was when it really hit. To see these little fellas strutting around there with their rifles which were almost taller than they were. Slapping people. That was the most alarming part.

Bandsman Art Munn, Winnipeg Grenadiers

I was a non-combatant. Being in the band, our duties involved stretcher-bearing and first aid.

As it turned out, I spent the duration at Peak Mansions Hospital, until the surrender. The surrender came the afternoon of December 25. There was an advance guard of Japanese came in, and they committed atrocities upon our nursing sisters in that hospital, such as rape. They bayonetted a few patients in bed.

Just a matter of hours later, the main body came in with an officer in charge, a lieutenant. Major Crawford was our

226

senior officer and he reported these atrocities and slayings to this lieutenant, who could speak perfect English. And he in turn asked our doctor to identify the men who created these atrocities. These Japs were identified. That officer executed them on the spot. After the execution, he says, "Make it be understood that we deal out punishment to anyone who disobeys the Nippon army. I do it to my men. I do it to you more willingly. Just give me an excuse."

That sort of shook us up. We were even afraid to talk back to them.

Private Sid Vale, Winnipeg Grenadiers

The day of the surrender, I was in the Peninsula Hotel in Hong Kong. They turned that into a military hospital. My right foot was broken, and I was on crutches for three months after we were captured. I remember the Japs coming into the Peninsula Hotel and turning the beds over. Didn't matter who was in them or how badly wounded they were. They were looking for arms. And I remember a nurse — I don't know if I should even tell this or not — but I remember listening to the screams of a nurse getting raped in the room next to us. That is something that has always stuck in my memory. I couldn't walk or do anything at that time. I don't know whether I would have had the guts to do anything had I been able to walk. But that's something I'll never forget.

Private Stephen Kashton, Winnipeg Grenadiers

Something hit me. This was the morning of the twenty-fifth, and I don't remember nothing till two weeks after. Bowen Road Hospital. There's a sort of loading platform where they put the stretchers. A medical team goes around. When you get hit in the head, with your brains showing, they say, "Well, there's not much hope for this guy, we'll leave him till last." Apparently I was there for a couple of days before I was taken in.

I don't remember nothing till January 7. When I opened my eyes I had double vision. First thing I remember, I asked a nurse, "How's the boys up in the hills?" "Oh," she says, "it's all over."

227

And I was in that hospital for three years. My doctor, his name was Bowie. British. With what the doctors had to work, they were damn good.

I was paralyzed on one side for about six months. The right side of my face is still paralyzed.

Sergeant Ed Schayler, Winnipeg Grenadiers

Finally the day come, Christmas Day, when we surrendered. I didn't give a damn, personally. I was tired. We hadn't had any sleep. We had nothing to shoot with. I was a little ashamed of our senior officer; he was pissed. Anyway, we were put in this big building, and the Japanese set up sentries.

Next morning, they had their victory parade, and we had a front row seat. We saw not only the army we were fighting against, but we saw their dead. They carried these little white boxes, and there were hundreds of them. They woke us up in the morning with their boots on the stone streets. And when it got dark, they were still marching. How the hell we were able to hold them back as long as we did, I don't know.

Private Gordon Durrant, Winnipeg Grenadiers

In the morning, I remember I was put out on guard duty. And I seen this guy sitting with the rifle, and he was rocking back and forth. All of a sudden he says, "We're not gonna make it." He says, "The Japanese don't take any prisoners. They're gonna line us up and shoot us." Then he says, "They're not gonna get me." Then he put his rifle under his chin and he reached down and pulled the trigger. Blew his whole face off, right in front of me. All over the wall.

There were quite a few others that were the same way. One guy hung himself.

Private Don Nelson, Winnipeg Grenadiers

They were pretty rough on us. They tied our hands together with barbed wire. A lot of the boys that fell and couldn't walk because they were wounded so badly, they were cut loose and bayonetted right there. They don't believe in taking too many prisoners.

But you've got to give the Japanese credit. They're a fighting little race. Their camouflage was marvellous. And there's no fear among them, because it's drilled into them from such an early age they don't know what fear is.

Private Al Martin, Royal Canadian Army Dental Corps

Some of the troops were taken to North Point, which was a refugee centre built by the British for Chinese refugees before the war. Those people were moved out, and they moved in captured troops. Then some of us were ferried across the harbour to Sham Shui Po, which was our original camp when we first arrived in Hong Kong. It had, of course, been looted of everything of any value. In fact, they'd even stripped the wooden frames around the windows and doors. So it was a pretty desolate place. And we were there for some time before most of us were transferred over to North Point. It became pretty well an exclusively Canadian camp.

Sergeant Howard Donnelly, Winnipeg Grenadiers

I think it was either the fourth or it could possibly have been the fifth day that the Japanese backed a truck up to the fence and dumped off a load of gasoline barrels and twenty or thirty bags of rice. We were then informed these were our rations for ten days. And the gasoline barrels were our cooking equipment.

We'd fill a barrel about half full of water, get it boiling, dump a bag of rice into it. We used five of those barrels, and we were cooking for around seven to eight hundred guys. The only rice I had ever cooked prior to that was rice pudding. And this is exactly what we got, a gooey paste, because we weren't aware how to cook it. And the smell of gasoline! Eventually, we got a Chinese person to show us how to cook the rice. But it didn't take the stones out of it, and it didn't take the maggots out of it.

Private Walt Jenkins, Royal Canadian Corps of Signals

All the different diseases, tropical diseases, in Hong Kong are fantastic. It never ceases to amaze me that so many guys got out of prison camp.

Major Gordon Gray, Royal Canadian Army Medical Corps

North Point camp was a bad spot. It was overcrowded. That's where we began to have a lot of dysentery. We had very little to treat them with. That's one of the terrible things about being a doctor in that situation. We knew there were just tons of sulpha drugs in Central Medical Stores in Hong Kong, but it appeared later the Japanese moved this stuff out of there for their own use.

Our dysentery hospital at North Point was an old "go down," a warehouse. In that part of the world they call warehouses "go downs." So we had these poor fellas on stretchers on the floor. We had to use latrines and buckets, and for people with dysentery, this was pretty bad. There wasn't much we could do for them. It got to the point where we were amazed that a little bit of something would seem to go a long way. Now, whether this was because they were becoming rapidly undernourished and a small dose of a drug had a greater effect, I'm not sure.

Rifleman Donald Geraghty, Royal Rifles of Canada

That's also when we started getting the "hot feet." First of all, it was just a burning sensation in the feet. Shove your feet under a tap, the feeling would go away. Well, the next day you'd do it again, but gradually it got to the point where you had to do it ten minutes, twenty minutes. It was addictive. No one could explain what the heck it was, other than it was the "hot feet." I would have to say this was the most demoralizing part of the whole thing, because we had that pain twenty-four hours a day and for a minimum of two years before we started to get better food.

The nerves in my feet are completely shot. I've had tests on them three times, and there just are no proper or normal nerve functions in my feet.

Lance-Corporal Harold Englehart, Royal Rifles of Canada

Our primary concern was the food situation. We were always

hungry. That's all people used to talk about: food, or the lack of it. We didn't work at first. All you could do was walk around and talk to your friends. The boredom was pretty bad.

Rifleman Donald Geraghty, Royal Rifles of Canada

Our officers were with us, and they ran the camp almost as if it was a Canadian army base. We had defaulters, an orderly room, all this kind of nonsense. And NCOs were putting fellas on report. That didn't sit well but, in retrospect, it kept the morale up a little bit inasmuch as the discipline was maintained. At the time, though, I thought the rules should have been relaxed.

It didn't sit well that officers were paid the equivalent amount of money that the Japanese officers were getting, and they were able to buy food. And they had batmen, servants, looking after them. There was resentment in the ranks but it was the resentment of, at that time, people with nothing to do but complain about loss of freedom, loss of food, loss of booze, loss of women. Plus, the unknown. You did not know what was going to happen next, because at that stage of the game, the Allies were being swept away.

Private Bill Ashton, Winnipeg Grenadiers

I was walking around North Point camp one day, and ran into Corporal Brezinski, George Brezinski. He says, "I'm gonna need four guys. Guys that would not be connected in any way with an escape." So we walked around, and he said, "You see that ladder in the sergeants' building, right opposite the washroom with no walls? There's a garage on the other side. That's where we'll be taking off."

So I got the most unlikely characters. Billy Moore, who was a real hot shot wheeler-dealer-trader. Then there was George William Fobister Stevenson, the battalion runner. And our postal corporal, "Tiny" Martin, who weighed nearly three hundred pounds.

The four of us walked around, and I told them what was going to happen. Four guys were going to come out of the hospital, an old tin garage in one corner of the compound, and I says, "When the first guy arrives, two of us are going to have the ladder off the sergeants' wall, through the washroom, and up against the building. And as the last man steps on the roof, the ladder comes down and goes back on the hooks. And this all has to be timed between the time the guards make their circle."

Tiny Martin was always dealing, and Billy Moore was always dealing. These two guys were going to be dealing with the Japs, to get the Japs used to seeing them around in the middle of the night. It worked perfectly. The Japs got so used to seeing them, they were calling them by name. We were in preparation for weeks. So it got to the point where the two Jap guards would meet when they passed the washroom, and when they got to the furthest point, I had Moore and Martin talk to the guards. They'd wait till the guards were right at the furthest extremity, then they'd signal. Stevenson and I grabbed the ladder, walked through the washroom, put it up on the wall. The guys came through. By that time, Tiny and Billy Moore had arrived at the washroom. They took the ladder and hung it back up. We all washed our faces and away we went. Four men gone without a sound: Sergeant John Payne, Corporal George Brezinski, Corporal P.J. Ellis, Private J.H. Adams.[3]

We don't know for sure how far they got. There were some coal barges just a few hundred yards down the coast from where our camp was. They were going to steal a painter from there, you know, a little rowboat? Row across to the mainland and make their way to Chiang Kai-Shek's forces. They never made it. They were caught and shot.

The first night, the Japanese didn't know they were four men short. But the second night, we were on parade at four o'clock that afternoon, and we stood at attention till eight o'clock the following morning.

Major Gordon Gray, Royal Canadian Army Medical Corps

There was grave concern about people trying to escape and the reprisal tactics that the Japanese were taking. One of the codes of being in the army is that you do all in your power to escape. Every time someone did try, rations would be cut.

Our senior people, and I think rightly so, said nobody should do this, because it meant tipping the scales in the balance of living or not living for some sick people, if their rations were cut.

I think also the officers tried to maintain a feeling of pride, and this is one of the ways of doing it, by having people look smart. I think that's all right under the circumstances. Because it was so easy just to let go, even early on.

Rifleman Donald Geraghty, Royal Rifles of Canada

The Japs also had this system, what they called the "buddy system." The idea was that you were in groups of five. And if one person in the group did anything, the other four got it. So they used a little bit of psychology in making you responsible for your fellow prisoners.

Private Bob Lytle, Winnipeg Grenadiers

I have a note in my diary. September 26, '42. "We got moved from North Point to Sham Shui Po." We went back to Sham Shui Po and we were mixed up with the British. But I have a note here: "Three English guys died of malnutrition. Their weights were forty-nine, fifty, and fifty-two pounds."

Rifleman Donald Geraghty, Royal Rifles of Canada

According to my diary, it says, "We've just come into Sham Shui Po. The barracks are the filthiest thing I've ever seen in my life. No wonder the English are dying."

The Canadian attitude was, "Well, here we are. We're in China. We don't look Chinese. We don't know the language, so there's not a hell of a lot we can do except make the best of it." According to the information that we got in Sham Shui Po where the British were, the general there, Maltby, just said, "We want proper European rations. We don't want this Asiatic food that you're giving us." So the Japanese said, "Well, you're not going to get European rations, and if you don't want this, that's fine with us." And they lived on plain rice and water. And they had disease and malnutrition all over the place. They did not get the rations we were getting because they were uncooperative.

Now the Japanese came around and asked us to sign a declaration that we would not escape. I signed mine, "Don Geraghty, u.d." Under duress. And everybody did the same. It was a joke.

Sergeant Howard Donnelly, Winnipeg Grenadiers

The Japanese had it figured out that we were to get eight ounces of rice per day per man. We would line up every morning and cook a rice porridge. That was breakfast. Then at noon hour, we either had a tea — which we figured was made out of dried cherry leaves — or if we had real good luck, there would be enough vegetable greens brought in. There would be chrysanthemums, sweet potato tops, Irish potato tops, buttercups. And the Japanese would dump a truckload of this stuff. We'd chop that up and make what we called "green horror," a soup. Then at suppertime that night, we would try to cook the other four ounces of rice. We'd use a measuring tin, and a guy would dish it out. He was watched just like a hawk, and if somebody got a half a tablespoon more than another guy, there was hell to pay!

To see these great big guys standing there waiting for that four ounces of rice — they would eat it in three mouthfuls. Every day, you could see them wasting away. I think that was the most traumatic part of it.

Major Gordon Gray,
Royal Canadian Army Medical Corps

The sudden change in diet from meat, potatoes, and vegetables to one of ninety per cent rice, and some unrecognizable green things in it, and little unrecognizable pieces of fish — it's quite a shock. I was lucky in that I could eat a lot of rice. A lot of people just couldn't tolerate it. We ate in groups of maybe eight, and just about everybody left rice, and I ate theirs too, whatever they left. Damned if I was gonna have this thrown out. I'm sure this stood me in good stead later on. I didn't get as much swelling of my feet and so on as other people did that didn't eat enough.

Corporal Lucien Brunet, Canadian Postal Corps

I ate with chop sticks. I had a spoon and fork, but do you

234

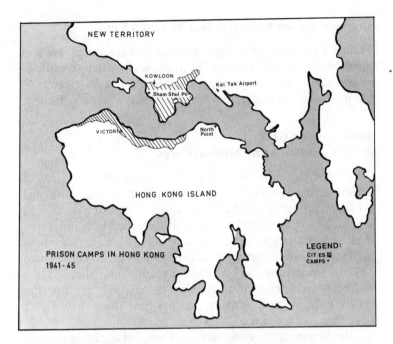

PRISON CAMPS IN HONG KONG
1941-45

NEW TERRITORY

KOWLOON
Sham Shui Po

Kai Tak Airport

VICTORIA

North
Point

HONG KONG ISLAND

LEGEND:
CITIES ▨
CAMPS ✛

know the reason why I ate with chop sticks? It took me longer to eat my meal that way. Seemed to me I had more enjoyment!

Corporal Jack Willis, Winnipeg Grenadiers

They'd bring in sprats, three little fish not much bigger than a sardine, once a week. Cook them in soy sauce without gutting them, you know. With rice. Or you got whale meat, and sometimes they brought in porpoise carcasses that they had already taken the good meat off of. Just enough to make soup. And there was always this white fat floating on top of the soup. But, you know, when you get real hungry you can eat an awful lot of different things.

Private Al Martin,
Royal Canadian Army Dental Corps

We had very little salt, and without salt that type of fare is not very appetizing. So salt was a very valuable commodity. Almost as valuable as cigarettes.

235

Corporal Lucien Brunet, Canadian Postal Corps

I know a sergeant who sold everything for cigarettes. He was dead within three months. If there was a little chunk of vegetable or meat in the soup, he would sell it for cigarettes. He would sell his ration of rice. There was a few like him.

Major Gordon Gray,
Royal Canadian Army Medical Corps

We got to Sham Shui Po, and people started showing signs of undernutrition, vitamin deficiency. Then we had this outbreak of diphtheria. The Hong Kong expedition had been organized so hastily that many of the boys had not completed their inoculation program before leaving Canada. I went to medical school in Toronto, and they hadn't had a case since 1912 or something. So I had never seen a case, then all of a sudden we had seven hundred or so. If somebody got diphtheria in addition to dysentery and malnutrition, they didn't have much of a chance.

We knew there were tons and tons of diphtheria antitoxin in Central Medical Stores. But the senior Japanese medical officer involved with our people, a lieutenant by the name of Saito, was very interested in the skin complications in some of the diphtheria lesions, and he was more interested in taking photographs of some of these things than treating them. A lot of people started dying, and the Japanese wouldn't allow us to put down on the death certificate sent to the International Red Cross: "Cause of Death: diphtheria." We put down: "Cause of Death: laryngeal croup." Any medical person would know that was diphtheria, because that's what it used to be called.

Private Bill Savage, Winnipeg Grenadiers

There was no medication. And the Japanese blamed our doctors! Doctor Crawford was one of them. He was a pretty tall guy, about six-foot-five. And the Japanese blamed these doctors for letting the men die. One day, they lined them up out there and whacked the heck out of them. The guy doing the whacking wasn't too tall, and he couldn't reach Crawford. So he ordered one of his men to bring a box. He stood up on that and whacked him across the face.

Lance-Corporal Harold Englehart, Royal Rifles of Canada

I contracted dysentery about two weeks before the Japanese decided to move us over to the mainland. I was so sick, I guess I fell unconscious, because I don't remember too much. I woke up one morning about three o'clock, and I had a terrible pain in my throat, a burning sensation. I knew immediately where I was. We had a little shack out in the corner near the guardhouse, and the guys who were going to die, they used to put them out there, in this little death house. There was another soldier there, but he was dead. So about ten o'clock in the morning, I heard somebody coming. I was so mad I started cursing the hell out of them. They ran off and came back with a doctor.

They brought me into another hospital, and a Doctor Banfill examined me. He said I had diphtheria. So I asked if I could have some serum, but he said, "The amount of serum it would take to cure you now, because you've had diphtheria for several days, I could save ten guys' lives with that amount of serum. You'll have to take your chances without it."

I had trouble swallowing, my throat was paralyzed. Doctor Banfill knew that I wasn't eating. I just couldn't get the rice down. So he told me, "I'm going to try to get this drug for you, and it'll make you eat." And finally one night he came in and said, "Englehart, I have the drug." So he gave me a shot of this drug, and he said, "I don't think I'll have to give you any more, because it's pretty powerful." The following morning it seemed like I could get some food down. That went on for a couple of days, and each day I was able to get a little more food down. The officers, they got paid by the Japanese, and they had a little canteen fund. So Doctor Banfill said I was one of the ones selected for this. They were giving me a little bottle of milk. I don't know where they got milk from. And they were giving me some rice with milk and sugar in it. So this went on for a week, and this picked me up quite well.

The strange part about this was, the orderly that worked

with Doctor Banfill, I had asked him afterwards, "What kind of drug did Doctor Banfill get for me?" He said, "Plain boiled water."

Major Gordon Gray,
Royal Canadian Army Medical Corps

These kids from Quebec volunteered to help as hospital orderlies. Some of these kids couldn't even read or write. They were terrific. Of course, they were subjecting themselves to very close exposure to getting things themselves, but they volunteered for it.

I knew I wouldn't get diphtheria. I had immunity to it. I did get malaria, but not badly, and that was after we got some Red Cross supplies and were able to treat malaria. Dysentery, I got one kind, but I didn't get amoebic dysentery. Amoebic dysentery is a parasite, and it has other complications of liver problems and so on. The other one, which is called bacillary dysentery, responded very quickly to even small doses of sulpha drugs. And we were able to get small doses, sometimes.

The Japanese would always say, "Well, give us a list of what you need." So we'd give them a list and we'd ask for, say, a thousand tablets of one gram sulpha drugs. They'd send in a hundred tablets, maybe a tenth of a gram. So then you'd spread it out, trying to make it go as far as possible.[4]

Rifleman Donald Geraghty, Royal Rifles of Canada

They were burying fellas six a day. Originally, they were supplied with wooden boxes, but a lot of the fellas were bloated from beriberi, and they would have to fit them in as best they could. And they would blow "The Last Post." Well, they stopped that, because that was demoralizing the people.

Bandsman Art Munn, Winnipeg Grenadiers

Pellagra struck us. Pellagra is open sores on the mouth. That's from lack of vitamins, and a lack of food. And you get these blisters on your lips, and tongue and mouth. Running blisters. And also, sores on your legs and your feet.

238

Private Al Martin,
Royal Canadian Army Dental Corps

And we had an affliction they called "Hong Kong balls." Due to malnutrition, your testicles would enlarge to a great, red, swollen mess. Some guys could hardly walk.

Rifleman Donald Geraghty, Royal Rifles of Canada

Of course, when we got to that camp, the British wanted to put us under their jurisdiction. And of course, the Canadians said, "Hold it. We're Canadians. We're staying Canadians." And that did hold for quite some time. We did remain separate units, and we did maintain our identity.

The Japanese appreciated that difference in identities, inasmuch as there was a "hate list." And on a scale of one to ten, the Americans were ten, the British were eight, and the Canadians were one. They did not dislike us, or hate us. If you were American, you got the worst treatment. The British got the next worst.

CSM Red Windsor, Winnipeg Grenadiers

This is something the Japanese couldn't understand, why the Canadians were there. It was explained to them to the best of our ability that Hong Kong was an English colony, and we were a member of the Commonwealth of Nations, and we felt it was our duty to help England out. The Japanese couldn't understand that.

Sergeant Ed Schayler, Winnipeg Grenadiers

Another thing I experienced was the respect Canadians had from other people. I'm speaking of English, even the Indians, the Hindu. We were well received by men in the other armies, I think because of the men themselves, their attitude. To me, there's something about Canadians there's no fooling around about. An Englishman gets hurt, he moans. An American, he cries. A Canadian, he swears.

Corporal Dempsey Syvret, Royal Rifles of Canada

We weren't recognized as prisoners of war. Not officially

recognized by the Japanese, like, under the Geneva Convention. That's what the Japanese told us. They could do anything they wished with us, because we weren't recognized.

Private Don Nelson, Winnipeg Grenadiers

If the Japanese asked you to build a ladder to the moon, you started to do it, because they have a one-track mind. We would come off work parties, and maybe we'd have cigarettes in our possession, but this night they were looking for soap. If you were caught with soap, you'd get a beating. Next night, they'd come looking for cigarettes. But they would only look for one thing at a time.

Corporal Ken Gaudin, Royal Rifles of Canada

I think the one everybody will mention is our first interpreter, "Kamloops Kid." He was a Canadian citizen, he came from Kamloops, B.C. He said, "When I was back in Canada and going to schools, they called me 'slant eyes' and 'yellow' and all the names you could think of. I've got you SOBs now where I want you. You're going to pay for it." And believe me, we paid for it. He would do everything possible, that man, to make life miserable for us. Make us stand out at night in the rain at attention. He was a sadist, no question about it. He was so evil against the white man, against the Canadians, particularly. It's awful to say you hate, but there's no way you could keep from hating anybody who would do everything possible to make life so miserable for you.

Private Claude Corbett, Winnipeg Grenadiers

We had a guard, we called him the Kamloops Kid. He was the cause of three, I think, Canadians to be killed in the camp. By beatings. He was hung at the end of the war, in the war crimes trials.

I remember this one day we were playing poker. We made our own cards. We were allowed to play cards, but we weren't allowed to gamble. And the Kamloops Kid jumped in through the window and caught us. And he took "Red" Patterson, a fella with one arm, and he punished him by making him carry these bloody building blocks. They weighed about seventy pounds. And he'd have to lift one with his one arm, put it on his shoulder, and run the whole length of the camp. He had to move a whole pile of these blocks. All day long he did this. Yeah, the Kamloops Kid was a sadist. He liked to pick on somebody that was already crippled.

Private Bill Ashton, Winnipeg Grenadiers

We used to walk around that camp to the waterfront and see the bodies floating around in the water there. Chinese. With their legs and hands tied up behind their back and a noose around their neck. They'd garrotte themselves. Just dozens of bodies like that. You could smell them half a mile away.

Major Gordon Gray, Royal Canadian Army Medical Corps

One of the biggest problems of my whole career as a medical officer was trying to play God. Trying to decide who was going to get what. The Japanese finally consented to bringing in small amounts [of diphtheria serum], and instead of thousands and thousands of units per case, we may have had just a few thousand. Then we would have to decide who would get what we got. Or we'd have to decide who was going to go on a work party, who was fit enough to go on a work party, who was fit enough to be carried to go on a work party, to make the numbers. Because that's all the Japanese wanted, was numbers. They would call for 500 men to work on Kai Tak airport. Maybe there'd be 475 that could walk. Now of the 475 that could walk, 150 shouldn't be walking, for starters. Then you'd have to come up with another twenty-five that couldn't walk, that had to be carried. But you had to have 500 bodies out there, whether they were walking or not. This, to me, was the worst — trying to decide who to label. And I must give these boys credit. I have the greatest respect for them, all of them. Because never once did they complain about your judgement.

I thought the morale was surprisingly good for what they were going through. These lads really had it much, much worse than the officers, because they had to provide these work parties and do hard, physical labour.

Bandsman Art Munn, Winnipeg Grenadiers

Now some of my comrades in arms felt when we were taken prisoner, "About a year and we'll be out of here." I didn't want to be a wet blanket, but I figured two, three years, at the least. As it was, it was four.

A lot of them lived on morale that way. "We'll be home for Christmas." And when Christmas came and went, "Well, we didn't make it this year, but next year for sure."

Private Walt Jenkins,
Royal Canadian Corps of Signals

All the time they had Hong Kong, the Japanese published a newspaper in English. I was working on Kai Tak Airport one day, and this guy showed me the paper. He showed me where the Japanese claimed to have shelled the west coast of Vancouver Island. Of course, the guys from down East don't know about Vancouver Island, and they asked, "What's there?" And I said, "Trees, as far as I know." Then another part of the article was, they'd blown up the bridge between Vancouver Island and the mainland. And the guys from down East were asking, "Is there a bridge there?" And I said, "Hell, no!" They didn't know, so who the hell in Japan's gonna know there's no bridge to blow up?

Private Bill Ashton, Winnipeg Grenadiers

We had a lot of good concerts there. We were very fortunate in our unit. We had the best swing band in the nation. Our marching band were all professional musicians that played in dance bands around Manitoba. We had George Sweeney, rated the top clarinetist and saxophonist in all Canada in 1938. We had Johnny Matheson, who could make a trumpet drip honey. We had just sixteen of the best. God, they were good!

I had the privilege of singing with the band. The Japanese let the band have their instruments. Well, we started having little concerts in North Point. And after the second concert, the camp commandant ordered lumber brought in to build a stage. We put on a real variety show. There were comedians.

There were some guys that danced, even. We'd put on skits, play all their favourite numbers. We'd go like that for two, three hours. The camp commandant would sit there in his chair, front and centre, his two interpreters interpreting for him.

Then we moved over to Sham Shui Po. The church had been bombed out, the roof had been blown off. But the stage was still there, and the walls were still there. And we decided that would be the place to have our Christmas concert. It was a beautiful concert. As a matter of fact, the concert broke off for roll call, and we all went back to the church and continued on after roll call.

**Major Gordon Gray,
Royal Canadian Army Medical Corps**

We saw a big improvement when we finally got some Red Cross supplies. There was a lot of good stuff in the way of medication and vitamins. We also got a few Red Cross parcels. A little bit of something out of those food parcels made a lot of rice go a long way!

Private Stan Baty, Winnipeg Grenadiers

I guess the big thing was when the Red Cross came. It was the SS *Gripsholm*, a Swedish ship. They came just prior to Christmas of '42. There were lots of rumours that we were going to be repatriated. But they were pipedreams! Although the two nurses that were overseas with us, they were repatriated at that time.

We actually never saw any of the Red Cross officials. Bulk Red Cross food was trucked in. The British got so much, the Hong Kong Defence Corps got theirs, the Hindus and whatnot, and we got ours, except there was so much for Christmas dinner held back. It was bulk Red Cross: condensed milk; ghee oil, which I believe is water buffalo butter; and there was dried peaches and pears, powdered milk — KLIM — and tea.

There was a great flurry in the manufacturing of electrical heaters. You get a big can and a small can. You hook one wire to the small can, one to the big one, scrape both lines bare, then put each one over one of the bared wires with the power on. The big can's filled with water. And it's amazing how fast it heated up. But there was a lot of power outages due to that.

Then we had Christmas dinner. Even to this day, I don't think I've enjoyed Christmas dinner as much as that one. It was a lot of this dried fruit and whatnot, mixed in a big patty. It was sort of like a little loaf, three by three by twelve inches. I have to admit, that was the crowning point of the whole thing.

(Most Canadians captured by the Japanese were taken in the fall of Hong Kong. This is the story of one of the few Canadians captured elsewhere in the Pacific theatre.)

Leading Aircraftsman Elmer Graham, RAF

I was attached to an RAF radar station in Singapore. I got there August 6, 1941.

We left Singapore on the Friday the thirteenth because the RAF were evacuating all the technical personnel. February '42[5], I was evacuated on a riverboat. We had a very nice anti-aircraft gun on board, except for one thing. We didn't have any ammunition!

Our orders were to sail during the night and tie up in the daytime. We were tied up against an island, and I was on shore cutting camouflage. And the Japs came over and sank the bloody boat. We lost an awful lot of people. The sea turned red.

We stayed on this island for about ten days. Eventually, we got some Chinese junks to pick us up, and they took us to Sumatra. The Dutch co-operated, and they took us over to the west coast of Sumatra. A place called Padang. Then on March 17, the Japs came in. Of course, we had no arms or ammunition, we couldn't fight. There were about five hundred in my group, mostly British and Australian. There were also two Canadian civilians. They'd gone out to Singapore as rubber planters. One of them died. The other one got back to Canada.

We might have got away. Before the Japs got there, a ship

came into Padang. But the British Consulate [had] burned all his codebooks, and we couldn't answer the ship's challenge. So it just turned around and went back!

Actually, I made two trips across Sumatra. One when we were free, and one after the Japs had taken us prisoner. And the second trip, I ate a hell of a lot better than I did the first trip! Because I knew what I could eat. We could eat tapioca root. I remember coming back across Sumatra, they parked us beside a bunch of tapioca trees. And there wasn't a goddam root left after!

First, we were captured in Padang. Then they moved us to Medan. And then they moved us up in the mountains to build a military road.

We were there about three or four months. Then they moved us back to Medan, and they gave us about a month's holidays. They gave us quite a bit of food, and no work. Then they sent us to build a railroad. That was near Teluk, in Sumatra. We worked there until the war was over.

We got very little news. I got quite a few postcards from home, but there was no real news about the war in them. When we were in Medan, we used to get the Malay paper. And we had a school inspector from Malaya — of course, he was in the British forces — and he could translate the thing. If we believed everything they said in it, they'd sunk the whole British navy and the American navy about fourteen times!

There was no point in trying to escape. I mean, you could get out of camp, that was no problem. I was out of camp several times. In fact, we mounted our own guards. The Japs went to sleep, and we had to mount guards because the natives would come in and steal what little stuff we had left. But where in hell could you go? You had eighty miles of water to get across, and you had two thousand miles of jungle to get through to get back to our own lines. So, we never escaped.

Footnotes

1. Because of the International Date Line, Pearl Harbor occurred December 7 in Canada but December 8 in Hong Kong.
2. The battle for Hong Kong was a two-stage affair. It took the Japanese until December 12 to drive the Allied forces off the mainland and onto Hong Kong Island. The Japanese then spent the next six days softening up the island's defences with a massive artillery and aerial bombardment. They followed with an invasion of the island on the evening of December 18.
3. August 20, 1942
4. By the time the diphtheria epidemic had run its course, it had claimed the lives of fifty Canadians. They were among 128 Canadian prisoners who succumbed to the terrible conditions in Sham Shui Po and North Point camps at Hong Kong. In 1946, the Japanese commandant, Colonel Tokunaga — who was dubbed "the White Pig" by the POWs — was found guilty of war crimes and sentenced to be hanged. That was later commuted to life imprisonment and later still to twenty years in jail.
5. Graham was among the last to be evacuated from Singapore. The colony surrendered February 15, with the loss of one hundred and thirty thousand British, Australian, Indian, and local troops.

XIV/The Land of the Rising Sun

By the beginning of 1943, the Japanese juggernaut sweeping across the South Pacific had reached its high-water mark. On January 4, 1943, following a prolonged and bloody battle with US Marines, the Japanese began evacuating Guadalcanal. In the face of determined American and Australian opposition and with Japanese advances being checked in New Guinea, the threat of invasion hanging over Australia subsided. The only uncertainty was in the China-Burma-India theatre, where it would be the autumn of 1943 before the Allies finally forced the Japanese onto the defensive.

To assist with the insatiable demands of its war effort, Japan was becoming increasingly reliant on prisoner-of-war labour. In 1907, Japan joined forty other nations in signing a pact at The Hague agreeing, among other things, not to use prisoners of war for work that was either excessive or war-related. As the Canadians at Hong Kong found when they were put to work levelling a small mountain to expand Kai Tak Airport, the Japanese chose to ignore their 1907 agreement. British and Australians captured at Singapore also discovered this the hard way. In the summer of 1942, the Japanese moved thousands of POWs to the jungles along the border between Thailand and Burma, and forced them to build a railway linking Bangkok and Rangoon. Eventually, forty-six thousand prisoners were employed on this project, and one-third of them died in the horrendous working conditions.

In 1942, the Japanese began shipping POWs to the home islands. The prisoners were put to work in mines and factories and shipyards, and they were accommodated in about a

247

hundred and twenty prison camps — there would be a hundred and seventy-five by war's end — established in Japan. Some Americans captured in the Philippines were taken to Japan in the summer of 1942, and in September, the Japanese selected two drafts of British prisoners at Hong Kong.

With the arrival of 1943, the Japanese were seeking new sources of potential labour, and the Canadians imprisoned at Sham Shui Po in Hong Kong were considered prime prospects. By now, the diphtheria epidemic that had raged through the ranks of the Canadians had subsided. So, in mid-January 1943, the first draft of Canadian prisoners of war embarked for Japan, where their lives were to take an unbelievable turn for the worse. Before the year was out, 1184 Canadian POWs would be shipped to Japan as slave labour. One hundred and thirty-six would not survive the ordeal awaiting them.

Sergeant Alec Henderson

They gave us a physical test. They lined us all up on one side of the road, and if you were able to make it across to the other side of the road, you were able to go on the draft.

And I made it. I didn't want to stay in Hong Kong. I thought it couldn't be any worse in Japan.

Private Bill Ashton

Just shortly before we left, there were about eight hundred British guys blasted out of the water. They were on their way to Japan. I guess the American ships caught up with them. And these boats weren't marked as Red Cross boats or as carrying prisoners of war.[1]

They got us going down this long ladder into the bowels of the ship, an old freighter. I think the first day they let us up on deck for fifteen minutes. After that, we were in the hold. They used to send our food, a real watery rice concoction with a vegetable in it, once a day. The only toilet facilities was a bucket. We were jammed in there hip to hip and knee to knee and back to back. Little wonder that none of us like to be in a crowded room anymore. If there were twenty people in this room right now, I'd get up and walk out. Four days and four nights of that. Just a hell hole.

248

Sergeant Alec Henderson

On January 19, I left Hong Kong on the *Tatuta Maru*. Arrived in Nagasaki, Japan, on January 22. Nagasaki is on the south end. We went by train up to Yokohama. We arrived in Yokohama on the twenty-fourth. We had lovely seats, and they gave us a *bento*, a little box of food. The only thing was, we had to pull the blinds down on the windows so the Japanese couldn't see us in there.

Private Bob Lytle, Kawasaki Camp 3D

We went to a place called the Kawasaki district, outside Yokohama. This was a brand new camp.

There were 500 Canadians, and Captain Reid was our commanding officer. This man was a really fine Canadian. And, my God, I don't know what we'd have ever done without him! He looked after us when we were sick, but he also stood up to the Japanese. He was the only Canadian officer taken from Hong Kong to Japan.

We went to work in the Nippon Kokan shipyards. Some guys were riveters. Some fellas were putting nuts and bolts in the plates of ships. I was on what they called "the hot steel gang." We worked with Japanese in shaping the ribs for the ship.

The food fluctuated. Sometimes we would get a cupful of barley. We didn't get rice there. And sometimes you got some greens. I remember they used to give us this seaweed. The first time I ate it, it just slithered down and it slithered right back up again.

Sergeant Alec Henderson, Kawasaki Camp 3D

There were two huts, 250 men in each hut. And it was just a long, flat deck covered with a woven rice mat. And you had three feet on that deck. Then there was a shelf up above where you could put your gear. Down underneath, there was a little shelf where you could put your shoes.

Corporal Dempsey Syvret, Kawasaki Camp 3D

The Japanese that we worked with weren't too bad, they were all pretty good. The civilian guards — a few of them were dirty. We called them "seven ups" because they wore a Japanese figure that looked like a seven on their arm. You didn't have much to do with the military on the job. It was in the camps that you had the army types. The majority of them were old soldiers that had fought in China. Some of them could be pretty mean.

CSM Red Windsor, Omine

I wound up in a place called Omine, roughly sixty miles from Nagasaki. The camp itself wasn't too bad a situation, compared to what we'd been living in in Sham Shui Po. We were put into huts, and different what they call *shotais*. My *shotai* was Number Three Shotai. I had approximately thirty-eight men.

If you had anybody that was sick and couldn't go down in the mine, you were forced to take him down in the mine on a homemade stretcher.

Sergeant Ed Schayler, Taira

We arrived in this coalmining town called Taira in May 1943. I remember the day because it was my wedding anniversary. Looking down a Canadian coalmine, even in the days when I was young, they had these automatic machines. Not in their coal mines. They had jackhammers, and airdrills, and shovels. You were two miles underground, and I've been in shafts where the temperature reading was 130 Fahrenheit. And it's all volcanic ash. And you get sharp coal, it cuts you; then you get heat rash in there and you got stinging all the time. We had another thing called "night blindness," where artificial light is no good. Now, you try and tell the Japanese this guy's got night blindness. They think he's trying to get away from going down the mine. I experienced night blindness. My eyesight came back pretty good, but some guys went totally blind.

Private Fred Reich, Sendai

Sendai is a major seaport in Japan, but it's also a huge coal mining area. They had, I think, over a million Korean forced labour[ers] in the coal mines.

We worked in the coal mine, down at the 750-metre

level. You worked in the mine fourteen days in a row. The fifteenth day was *yasume*, day of rest. But on your day of rest, they worked you a hell of a lot harder up on the surface than you ever had to work down in the coal mine. Incidentally, you had the day shift and evening shift. The day shift, you went down in the mine at six o'clock in the morning. Everybody was given a quota of coal to do, depending on how far you were in the mine. Everybody had to produce their quota of coal, everybody was kept down there until the slowest group was finished.

In the mine, the clothing — don't forget, you get down 750 metres underneath the earth, it's hot — all we wore was a running shoe, the same as the Japanese issued their army. We weren't even given socks. We used to wear what we called a "g-string," like a diaper with two strings. And we had something like a baseball cap.

We lost numerous people there by cave-in. There wasn't a nail. All the timbering we put up as we dynamited and went further in, the thickest diameter of the trees we used was something three, three and a half inches. They were short of lights, so they'd take two out of three out. Still, we produced an awful lot of coal.

Private Bill Maltman, Niigata

The lowest I ever weighed was ninety pounds. Normally I weighed 170. A lot of people were the same way.

We were pushing a ton to a ton and a half of coal on these little coal cars. We were unloading ships. They were V-shaped hoppers, and you pulled a pin, and the hopper turned sideways. Some of the guys fouled up their arm when the hopper turned over. Crushed their arm, and then they would get off this job. And there were several that jumped off trestles just to get hurt, so they wouldn't have to work.

Private Gordon Durrant, Oyama

When we got off the train at [Oyama, there] were some guys that had left Hong Kong before. And they looked horrible! They were black from coal dust, and they were skinny. I said, "God, what happened to you guys?" They said, "You work from six o'clock in the morning till six o'clock at night. You get nothing to eat. We'd just love to be back in Hong Kong!"

Anyway, they said, "Your brothers will be glad to see you." So, sure enough, when we got to camp, my two brothers were there. They left Hong Kong before me, and I figured I'd never see them again, until after the war.

This friend of mine, he got off the train, he come into the camp, and he said, "Gordon, I won't last a month in this camp." He says, "Look at these guys. I couldn't go through this." I said, "You'll pull through. You just get that out of your mind." Three weeks later, I carried him out to cremate him.

Private Claude Corbett, Sham Shui Po

I stayed in Hong Kong. I was on the draft to go to Japan [but] I was on the boat when my appendix ruptured. So they rushed me over to Bowen Road Hospital. It was bombed out, but they let us use it. And so I had my appendix operated on with no anaesthetic, just guys holding me down.

And I was just getting over it, walking around the hospital grounds, when this damn Japanese officers' car drove past. And I didn't salute it. So they stopped, and this sergeant got out. He threw me on the ground and kicked me. He broke open my stitches. And he broke my nose, broke my arm. So back into bed I went!

My eyesight was failing, and I went totally blind. This was caused by vitamin deficiency. Right now, I still have under ten per cent vision.

Lance-Corporal Ralph MacLean, Niigata

I believe it was the first New Year's that we were in Japan, they built a new camp for us. We'd just occupied one of the buildings, a two-storey building. During the night, a heavy snowfall had started, and the building that I was in collapsed. There were about two hundred men in there, and I think eight were killed.

Corporal Jack Willis, Oyama

In the morning we got approximately eight ounces of boiled

rice. Green tea. And they gave us sourdough buns, which would be maybe six to eight ounces, made out of barley flour. And we were supposed to take the bun with us, and that was going to be the mainstay of our lunch. Then at noon, they would bring us into a "go down," they called it, with benches in it, and a couple of pots in the corner where they made soup. And I would say four or five times out of ten, why they would just have soya sauce and water. Plus this bun. And they always had lots of green tea. After we finished the tea, we'd eat the tea leaves, because it was food.

One day they brought us in some fish heads and guts. And they put that in the soup. There were maggots floating on top. It was about the thickest soup I'd had so far. The guy next to me said, "Those are maggots, aren't they?" I said, "Yeah, but they're cooked." And so I ate them. And the poor guy, he hit for outdoors. He couldn't take that!

Private Don Nelson, Kawasaki Camp 3D

All in all, you were slowly starving to death. I weighed approximately 183 pounds when I joined up, and when I came home, I was ninety-eight pounds. But in one sense, they weren't doing much better themselves, because they didn't have much to eat either.

Private Fred Reich, Sendai

Sex! God, a dirty old crust of bread, or the most glamourous young movie star in Hollywood, there'd be no choice! You'd go for the bread, even if it was fourteen weeks old. The most luscious broad, you wouldn't even give that a thought.

CSM Red Windsor, Omine

The Red Cross, to my knowledge, came three times to our camp. Each time they came in, the Japanese would prepare a nice meal, potatoes and everything else. And they'd have a man sit in the mess hall. They would let the Red Cross come in and interview this fella, and they'd let him take a little piece of potato. And then usher the Red Cross officials out quickly. With the result, the Red Cross was printing that we were being well looked after.

We had Red Cross parcels. We had three. The last one was eight men to one Red Cross parcel. And we drew. I managed to get the coffee. I had never been fond of coffee. But for that coffee, I was able to trade for eight quantities of tea. So for approximately a year, I didn't do without any tea. When the tea leaves became useless, you just let them dry out and mix them with your rice.

Private Sid Vale, Sendai

We never did get a full Red Cross parcel. We got about, in the two years we were in Japan, either three or four parcels divided amongst four men, I think. That was after the Japs had taken out the sugar, the chocolate, anything that they wanted for themselves. We got the balance and, really, there wasn't a hell of a lot to it. It was nice at the time, and you would look forward to getting it, and the pleasure would last maybe an hour or two after you got it.

Corporal Lucien Brunet, Kawasaki Camp 3D

We were there about four years, and we got about three or four Red Cross parcels. We had, sometimes, a parcel between seventeen men. You know what that meant? You had a can of bully beef, or a can of milk, you had to divide between seventeen men. It was good, though. I wish we'd had even one a month. So many people would have come back alive.

And the Japs had warehouses full of Red Cross parcels that they never gave to us. Some prisoners of war saw a Japanese open a parcel with a bit of cheese in it. He was trying to wash his hands with it. He thought it was a piece of soap!

Private Fred Reich, Sendai

If you could steal something, you did. We used to go out on work parties. All the stuff from latrines is put on the fields. Say, if it's an onion field, and you found an onion, it's covered with muck and shit, but you'd wipe it off and eat it right there.

You'd automatically steal. Of course, grain — you'd make a hole in the bag and tie up the bottom of your pant leg

254

and put some grain there. But you'd steal anything that was edible. Even a half rotten apple on the street, you ate it.

Private Bill Savage, Oyama

You do all kinds of darn things when you're hungry. Like, on the way to work, there was sort of a swamp near the camp. Whenever you got a chance, you'd stuff your pockets with frogs. At break time, you'd hold them over the bloomin' fire, and roast the bloomin' things, and down the hatch!

CSM Red Windsor, Omine

One of my boys caught a rat and cooked it, and he saved me a small portion. I sat it on top of my rice while it was still hot, so I could taste that flavour through the rice. When you're starving, anything tastes good.

Bandsman Art Munn, Kawasaki Camp 3D

At times, just prior to eating, it was not uncommon for prisoners of war to faint. Just from the anticipation of getting ready to eat something. Get so excited that you'd pass right out.

During our years in Japan, I was always conscious of everything I ate: what is the vitamin content of that? It got to the point where, if I could find grass, I would cut it and chew on the grass. Over the period of time, I got down to about eighty-five, ninety pounds. Now, I'm of small stature, and my normal weight was about a hundred and thirty pounds. So I held my weight between eighty-five and ninety, which is not too bad, considering men of over two hundred pounds were holding the same weight.

In season, they'd give us the Japanese orange, say, one orange a month. Now, a Japanese orange would last the average prisoner of war two weeks. What we'd do, we'd peel it, and we'd take the peel and string it up and let it dry out. When it dried out, you'd grate it a little bit and put that on your rice. There's citric acid in that. I think there are seven segments to an orange, so you're looking at fourteen days' rations there. Because you'd have half a segment a day. This is the way to get the most benefit out of it.

255

The body does not store vitamins. So if you take an apple or an orange and eat the whole thing, the body would take what it requires and pass the rest away. But the way we dished it out, it didn't pass anything away. I'll tell you, we learned survival the hard way.

Corporal Lucien Brunet, Kawasaki Camp 3D

I, personally, was starving to death. And I was eating garbage. I would go into the garbage in the shipyard, and look to see what the Japs would throw away. Sometimes there were tangerines — I would eat the peels. Fish heads are good. We had forges, and you'd put it over the forge. I was chewing it, trying to get all the oil out of it, to get some kind of protein. Chew it all, and spit out the scales.

Private Walt Jenkins, Niigata

Funny thing about Japan. People always think of cherry blossoms and oranges and beautiful countryside, kind of tropical. The Japanese are a northern, vigourous people. The only reason they get oranges is the Japanese Current comes along in the south. You get about a hundred miles away from that current, they get plenty of snow. In Niigata, where we were, we were up to our ass in snow for two winters.

The thing is, when you're on a low-calorie diet like that, if you get a cold, you die.

Corporal Ken Gaudin, Kawasaki Camp 3D

One of the saddest things that I remember, again in the same camp, 3D, we had a father and son team with us. Sergeant Elmer Cole and his son, Rifleman Bliss Cole. They came from the Lac Saint Jean area, Kenogami. Bliss and his Dad slept side by side, and his Dad took a very bad cold. And I guess it was more advanced than he had let on. And Bliss — he'd be only eighteen or nineteen at that time — woke up to find his Dad dead beside him. This hurt all of us, because we thought the world of the two of them. You see a young boy with tears rolling down his cheeks and his Dad lying dead beside him.

Private Bill Savage, Oyama

We were there in the bloomin' winter. Several guys were getting frozen feet, you know, and toes amputated. So they got the idea then they'd give us knee boots. This was better, but they were all from size twelve up. You could almost turn around in them. But they came in handy. In our hut, they had a coal heater. But they would only allow you to have a fire in there every rest day, which was once every ten days. Unloading coal was part of our job, so then guys would stuff coal in their bloomin' boots! And they'd have enough for a bloomin' fire all evening!

Private Don Nelson, Kawasaki Camp 3D

A lot of us were sick with beriberi and things like that. The Japs let us off work, but they believed if you bled that you were cured. They used to have long sticks for lighting fire-crackers. They'd break off little pieces and place them all over your body and set a match to them. If you bled while your skin was burning, they figured you were cured. I've still got holes all over my body from being burned.

Corporal Jack Willis, Oyama

Another thing we had lots of. I had four kinds of worms. You see, these worms were microscopic. You get them from walking in the gardens where they're using human faeces to fertilize their gardens. Then you walk in that in running shoes, and it's wet, and you get into water, and it goes into your shoes. And apparently these worms get into you through your pores. The poor old worms were starving to death, too, you know. You'd go to sleep at night, and you'd get a worm just like a two-inch earthworm, and he'd come up your esophagus. Once I scratched my nose and pulled a two-inch worm out of my nose. He was hungry, because he had nothing in me to eat.

Corporal Lucien Brunet, Kawasaki Camp 3D

In Japan, if there were five hundred men in the camp, and if you had three hundred men working, the ration was for three hundred men. The Japanese don't believe in a person not working having to eat. You don't work, you don't eat. And we had a lot of sick people. But the more you had sick, the less rice you would have.

Sergeant Howard Donnelly, Oyama

It just was too dangerous to say, "I'm sick and can't go to work." You just could not afford to go without that bowl of soup at noon. It wasn't so bad during the summer months, you could maybe get by all right. But during the winter, where you shivered yourself to sleep in that cold weather at night, you had to have every cotton pickin' ounce of rice or anything, to keep you alive.

Private Fred Reich, Shinagawa

Shinagawa Hospital was the base hospital for all the prison camps in the Tokyo area. The death rate in this camp was, I'd say, four, five, six every day. I was in the dysentery ward there. Every dead body was given a post-mortem and you could see them on the table there. They had a slab, but no sanitation whatsoever. They'd cut the bloody head, and brains would come out. They had pickled hearts and they had pickled livers. They were always comparing.

They had an incinerator, and I remember they used to come in and take these bodies away on a bicycle with a sidecar. Then the Americans blew the incinerator all to hell. Then *we* had to go out and burn these bodies! You had to bring back the ashes from the bodies. When a body burns, it snaps and crackles like a pancake. And, hell, you'd eat your lunch right there, and it wouldn't even bother you.

Private Bert Delbridge, Kawasaki Camp 3D

I should tell you about the bathhouse at 3D. It was a big bath, about half the size of a regular swimming pool, eh? The camp commandant would go in, and his officers, and they would have their bath. Then the Japanese troops. Say there are fifteen sections. Well, by the time you got down to the last section, the water would be ice cold, and it would be so darn dirty. Then the next week, Section One would be the last in, and Number Fifteen would be first.

Of course, soap was scarce. The guys used to swipe the soap on the skids of a ship laid down to go into the water. It used to burn.

Sergeant Howard Donnelly, Oyama

When we were working in Japan, we got paid. Every rest day we got a cigarette for each day we worked, and one yen. A package of cigarettes at that time was running about two or three yen a pack, for ten cigarettes. That's when we first arrived in Japan. But when we left Japan, we were paying as much as ten yen for one cigarette. And there was absolutely nothing at any time that I can ever remember that we could have bought, other than cigarettes.

Private Fred Reich, Sendai

The funny part about it, they even used to pay us. You'd work fourteen days straight and you got a day off. So they paid us five cents a day for the day shift and ten cents a day for the night shift. At the end of the month, they might bring in a few little items. They'd bake something like a cookie. You eat that bloody cookie and you weren't sure if you had a piece of lead or something.

Corporal Lucien Brunet, Kawasaki Camp 3D

Christmas, we were lucky. We were off at Christmas. We tried to make the best we could, because that was about the saddest day of the year. Sometimes you tried to sing songs or talk about what you would have been doing if you were home.

Private Bert Delbridge, Kawasaki Camp 3D

You found a lot of fellas, if they didn't keep their hopes up, they just got depressed and passed away. I know a good friend of mine — he was on a work party with me — and he says, "I won't be on this work party tomorrow morning." I says, "Come off it, Cec, what's the matter?" He says, "I've had it." Next morning, he was dead. No will to live.

259

Private Al Martin, Kawasaki Camp 3D

One day, somebody sabotaged the shipyard. The tool shop. They set an incendiary device of some kind, possibly a candle in some shavings. And when we left, the candle evidently burned down and started a fire and burned out the tool room. That stopped work, I think, for about three days.

The Japanese had their ideas about fighting, and to be taken prisoner was a terrible thing. You're supposed to fight until you die. So, in many cases, they looked down on us as being subhuman. They thought we should never have surrendered, that we should have fought to the last man. Their theories were a little bit different than ours, unfortunately.

Bandsman Art Munn, Kawasaki Camp 3D

The water treatment. They'd force you to drink water until you blew up, then jump on your stomach to force the water back out again.

Corporal Ken Gaudin, Kawasaki Camp 3D

You would question whether the Japanese did know very much about Canada. We laughed at it at the time, but I remember one day the camp commandant had us all lined up. The commandant was speaking in Japanese, and we had another interpreter, Koneche Kondo, "Mushmouth." He spoke English very poorly and it was very hard to understand. Koneche Kondo would translate: "You may wonder how long you're going to be prisoners of war. Well, I will tell you. Japan will burn up and destroy your country with balloons we are sending over. And when that goal has been achieved, then you will be freed." You know it's impossible. Yet, when the chips are down, you're down and the morale is down, and something of this nature doesn't exactly pep you up.[2]

Private George Price, Oyama

We had a couple of people that were accused of being collaborators, Harvey and Tugby. They were tried in Winnipeg after the war for collaborating, but they got off with a slap on the wrist. Like, they did it under duress, sort of thing.

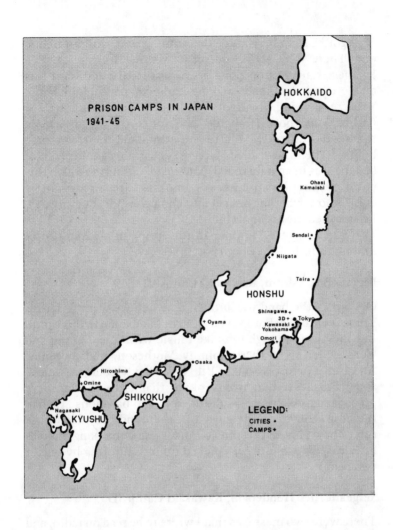

PRISON CAMPS IN JAPAN
1941-45

HOKKAIDO

Ohasi
Kamaishi
+

HONSHU

Sendai •

• Niigata

Taira •

Shinagawa +
3D + • Tokyo
+ Oyama   Kawasaki •
Yokohama •
Omori +

• Osaka

Hiroshima
• Omine

SHIKOKU

Nagasaki
KYUSHU

LEGEND:
CITIES •
CAMPS +

I got beat up by Harvey one time. It was close to lights-out. There were about four of us sharing a cigarette. The Japanese sentry came along. I was last in line and I had this cigarette in my hand, and he came in and collared me. "You're smoking after lights-out." So, he gave me a couple of bashes, you know. He hauled me out to the bloody parade square and he says, "You're going to stand there for three hours." Then they called Harvey. I guess they got him out of bed, he was in an ugly mood. They said, "You got to give this guy a licking, because he was smoking after lights-out." I don't know whether he had any choice or not, but anyway, he smashed me around a bit.

I had to go to Winnipeg in the spring of '46 and testify against him. But they both got off.[3]

Private Bill Ashton, Kawasaki Camp 3D

Of course, the band was broken up when we went to Japan. There were only about seven or eight bandsmen in our camp. But there was enough to make music with! I had Elmer and Gerald McKnight there, Johnny Matheson, and Sweeney. And Elmer wrote a song, "I'll Never Say Goodbye Again," and I broadcast that from Tokyo, thanks to the Japanese propaganda machine. We did it from the bathhouse; it had the best acoustics. The guys all sat around the edge of the tub. They played the music, and I sang the song. It was broadcast live, and it was picked up in California by one or two people.

Sergeant Alec Henderson, Kawasaki Camp 3D

There were two messages that I wrote to be read on radio, and one that I recorded in the prison camp. Now, these messages got home to my parents via ham radio listeners in America that recorded the messages and then were good enough to mail these messages to my parents. Anybody who wanted to try to send a radio message put their name in a hat, and the names were drawn. And I was fortunate enough that I was one of the five, three times.

The first one was in June of '43. I remember saying how things were here, and when I get home, I would certainly

262

enjoy spending a holiday in Stoney Mountain! Stoney Mountain, here, of course, is a penitentiary [in southern Manitoba].

I don't recall the date of the second message. But the first two were read by Japanese interpreters.

April 25, 1944, now that's when I made a radio broadcast. It was recorded, then broadcast, my own voice. I had so much time, a minute and a half or whatever. The Japanese brought all the equipment into the camp, and they had a room set up for a recording room.

I don't know what the intent or purpose of it was. I got a thrill out of getting this message sent out. It was very nice for me. Of course, the governments over here weren't so sure how they could accept it, if we were doing it under duress or what.

Lance-Corporal Ralph MacLean, Niigata

I believe I had about three letters during the time I was there. It was just a very basic letter, with lots of big black censor marks on it.

Private Don Nelson, Kawasaki Camp 3D

You had no news, no letters. A fellow by the name of Ambrose was allowed to write home, and in one letter he wrote that "Don Nelson says to say 'hi' to his folks." Then his parents got in contact with my folks in Prince Albert. But that's the only news they ever got about me.

Private Fred Reich, Sendai

I'm sure a cat in an ordinary household in Canada exists one hundred per cent better than we existed over there.

This was a completely different world. I couldn't even begin to picture what it was like to live in Canada.

Private Gordon Durrant, Oyama

After you were in there for a while, you got the idea that Canada never existed. After the years went on, you thought it was a dream, Canada was just a dream. It didn't exist. It couldn't exist. Canada and your life before was just a dream.

Footnotes

1. This was the second draft of British POWs, 1186 on board the freighter *Lisbon Maru*, sailing from Hong Kong to Japan. The *Lisbon Maru* was torpedoed by the submarine USS *Grouper* on October 1, 1942. Eight hundred and forty-three POWs lost their lives.

2. The Japanese mounted their balloon assault in the fall of 1944. Nine thousand balloons were launched from Japan, each with high explosive or incendiary bombloads of about fifty pounds. Only 296 of the balloons reached North America, eighty of them getting to Canada. For the most part, they caused only minor damage. In April 1945, the Japanese abandoned the balloon attack, considering it to be an operational failure.

3. The case of Tugby and Harvey is one of the most bizarre involving Canadian POWs in the Far East. Marcus Charles Tugby was a senior NCO with the Winnipeg Grenadiers, while Corporal (Acting Sergeant) John Harvey was a member of the Royal Army Medical Corps. Upon their arrival at home after the war, both were charged with collaborating with the Japanese. In all, Tugby faced nineteen charges, ranging from collaboration to assaulting fellow prisoners. Harvey faced twenty-nine charges of a similar nature, but he was also charged with manslaughter in the death of Private John Friesen of the Grenadiers in Oyama camp in February 1944. Being British, Harvey received an all-British court-martial in Winnipeg in the spring of 1946; Tugby, a Canadian, faced an all-Canadian court-martial. Three of the charges against Tugby were thrown out of court, and he was acquitted of eight others. However, he was convicted of the eight remaining charges, all of them assault. For this, Tugby was sentenced to be "severely reprimanded." Harvey was acquitted on nineteen of the charges against him, including the manslaughter charge. Found guilty on the remaining charges, he was moved to England for sentencing. On his arrival, Harvey was told the guilty verdict had been quashed and instead, he was mentioned in despatches for his conduct as a POW.

XV/The Final Year

For Canadian POWs in the Far East, the beginning of 1945 marked the start of their fourth year in captivity. The majority of the Canadians captured at Hong Kong had been transferred to Japan in 1943, although three to four hundred remained in Hong Kong.

They were vaguely aware that the war was being won, but since radios in Japanese prison camps were a rarity, the information the POWs received was sketchy and often inaccurate, particularly if it came from Japanese sources. Along with British, American, Australian, and Dutch prisoners, the Canadians were virtually slave labourers in Japan, working in coal mines and factories and shipyards. Now, as they entered their fourth year in enemy hands, Canada remained a distant dream. Time lost much of its meaning; the POWs were totally preoccupied with survival.

And survival in Japanese prison camps was no mean feat. The POWs never received more than subsistence-level rations, and they saw few of the Red Cross food parcels that meant so much to the prisoners in Germany. To make matters worse, by 1945 the American naval blockade was strangling Japan; the Japanese themselves had little to eat, let alone food to spare for prisoners of war. In any event, the health of their prisoners was never a real concern of the Japanese.

Early in 1945, the Americans began their fire raids on major Japanese cities, as a prelude to the expected invasion of the home islands. The POWs had no way of knowing that the Americans proposed an invasion of Kyushu, the southernmost Japanese island, for November 1, 1945, with the inva-

265

sion of the main island of Honshu to take place in March 1946. It is doubtful whether many prisoners would have survived if they had been forced to wait that long to be liberated. Fortunately, their misery was cut short by the atomic bombs dropped on Hiroshima and Nagasaki, August 6 and 9, 1945.

Private Bill Maltman, Niigata

It's very easy to die, you know. It really is, when you get a little bit low. And there were times when everybody got a little bit more depressed than they should. I think you had to be very strong, mentally as well as physically, and have friends to help you.

Rifleman Donald Geraghty, Sham Shui Po

The real, true heroes of all prison camps were the comedians. They kept you going, kept your spirits up. You had to laugh, even if it was a stupid remark. Like a guy could fall and break a leg: "Well, I guess I won't have to do any work parties now!"

Lance-Corporal Malcolm Gillis, Omori

I was sent to a camp near Tokyo called Omori. It was all British and Americans there except for one guy, Wing Commander Birchall, the Canadian "Saviour of Ceylon."[1] By this time, the air raids were getting heavier and heavier. Our camp was on a piece of reclaimed land right in Tokyo Bay. There'd be an air raid one night and everything would be burnt for blocks around. The civilians were trying to salvage what they could. We used to get pelted with rocks.

Our chief worry was that the Americans would miss and hit us.

Lance-Corporal Harold Englehart, Kawasaki Camp 3D

It was March, the big raid on Tokyo, the fire bombing[2]. We went through a pretty rough night that night. We had just got home from work and were having our bit of rice when the bombers came over, which they did quite often. But that night seemed different. There seemed to be no end to the bombers, and they were dropping HEs and then incendiaries. Finally the fire was just about up to our camp. Our great fear was that the civilians would break in, because there were thousands of them just outside the camp. The big problem with a lot of incendiary bombs like that is that the fire burns up the oxygen in the air. You had to get right down on the ground before you could breathe. But they never bombed the plant where we were working, because it was an American-owned plant.

So after that big raid, we weren't able to work a great deal, partially due to bombing and the problem with the Japanese civilians against prisoners. You had to keep looking over your head — they would drop a load of steel on you, the civilians would. There was a number of our boys killed that way.

Private Stan Baty, Kawasaki Camp 3D

We dug an air raid shelter. Oh, it'd be about three, four feet deep. Had a bamboo ridge down it, and bamboo poles over, and then the sand piled over top. I think if you'd stepped on it, you'd have fallen through.

They kept us in for three days. The place is surrounded by at least a ten-foot wall, and you couldn't see a thing. But when you stepped out, you could see from horizon to horizon. The place was just burnt to the ground. We were between a railway and a canal, so we were safe.

Sergeant Alec Henderson, Kawasaki Camp 3D

After the Americans bombed Yokohama, we were broken up into groups of about two hundred. I was in a group that went north to Sendai, a coal mining area. We at first thought, "Oh, gee, this is great. We're going to a Red Cross camp. They're going to fatten us up before they send us home!" What a disappointment!

Major Gordon Gray, Sham Shui Po

We treated some of the Japanese, but it was in the form of a bribe. We would treat their venereal disease if they'd bring

267

the drugs, and we wouldn't tell anybody if they'd do this, this, and this. And our dentist did dental work for them on the same basis. Mind you, by this time a lot of the guards were Formosans, and they'd been taken over by the Japanese themselves earlier in their lives. Sometimes I felt the Japanese had more trouble looking after the Formosans than they did after us!

Rifleman Donald Geraghty, Sham Shui Po

I was in hospital about two and a half years. I was down to ninety pounds.

Here again, we used to put our feet in the water. It was the only way to relieve pain from the "hot feet." The doctor said, "I don't want to see this man again. I haven't got time to help those who will not help themselves." That night, I said, "Fellas, I'm going to quit the water." I know exactly what it's like when people go off drugs, the withdrawal symptoms, because this is what happened to me. These water treatments were addictive. And I did quit the water.

But a funny thing happened. A fella by the name of Jim Cook, a corporal, was doing orderly work. I was in agony. So he said, "Don, do you believe in prayer?" At that stage of the game, I didn't believe in the Lord, because no Lord would ever allow us to be in that position. Cook said, "I'm going to pray for you." And he knelt right down beside my bed. And I went into a coma. I never moved until the next morning. And I had, I guess, passed the crisis point, where I did not have to depend on the water to control the pain in my feet. So that was almost a religious experience. I'm not a Christian today, but that was an experience I'll never forget.

The day came when I asked to go on working parties, because I could get extra food [and] cigarettes with which to buy extra food. Also, it was something to do.

At one time, they had duties around the camp which consisted of collecting the "honey buckets." You pulled them out, put them on a truck, and threw them in the water. Well, there was a big tract of land next to the camp which they talked the Japs into using for a garden. They would dig trenches across it. So instead of putting the "honey buckets" into the ocean, we started putting the "honey buckets" into these trenches. And by God, we got the greatest fruit and vegetables! And that way, we started to supplement our diet.

By about the third year, anybody that hadn't died had adjusted to the situation. When the war started to go our way, things changed as far as the Japs were concerned. Our mental attitude and our physical attitude changed, and we started an upswing.

Private Stephen Kashton, Sham Shui Po

Morale was pretty good. The Japanese used to bring in a little paper in English. They lied about all kinds of things. When I first read it, the Japanese were in the Solomon Islands, New Guinea. And pretty soon they put a piece in the paper about fighting in Luzon, one of the Philippine Islands. Well, the Solomon Islands and the Philippines, that's a hell of a long way apart. So I knew the Americans had landed, that they must be coming back. And this helped morale.

Somebody in the camp had a radio. Once in a while you'd get news, and since then I have found out it was pretty accurate. That was good for morale too.

Sergeant Ed Schayler, Taira

We got our news via the "Bamboo Wireless," we called it. Where it came from, I don't know. We got to know, for instance, when Roosevelt died, when Doolittle flew over Tokyo. We knew when Germany quit. The trouble is, there were so many rumours you couldn't sort fact from fiction.

As time goes on, a kind of hopelessness and helplessness creeps in. In spite of things, you still have memories. And I had a wife — that was important to me. I also read the Bible from beginning to end, and I think that helped me a lot.

Major Gordon Gray, Sham Shui Po

Mail was another sore point. I think I got my first mail some time in 1943, and then it was a year old. We were allowed to pen these little twenty-five-word postcards. We tried to devise some between-the-line messages. The worst thing is that after it was all over, we found tons of mail still in camp. It had never been sent off.

Private Claude Corbett, Sham Shui Po

I got one letter all the time I was a prisoner. It was a picture of my daughter that was born after I left Winnipeg. And by the time I got it, she was three years old.

Company Quartermaster-Sergeant Bill Laidlaw, Ohasi

We had a radio for those last five months. The American boys did. A chap by the name of Bunch. He was a radio operator on the cruiser [USS] *Houston*. I don't think there was more than half a dozen in that camp knew that there was a radio there. And I only did by chance. They asked me to bring a battery in for the radio. I carried a wet cell battery into the camp under my hat.

Of course, we knew the war was over right away, because we heard in on the radio.

Corporal Lucien Brunet, Sendai

The morale there was finished. We had no news. Nothing. We didn't care. Death would have been a relief.

Private Stephen Kashton, Sham Shui Po

We were digging defense tunnels. The Japanese figured the Americans would land at Hong Kong, so they started digging tunnels all in through the hills. You had to do two metres in every day.

I think it was August 6, the bomb on Hiroshima dropped. Anyway, the Japanese were saying a lot of planes came over and dropped a lot of bombs. But they said the Japanese would never surrender. Then another bomb dropped, and they told us about the atomic bomb and how barbaric the Americans were. Two or three days after that, we got up in the morning, no sentries, no nobody.

CSM Red Windsor, Omine

We were roughly sixty miles from Nagasaki. When that bomb went off at Nagasaki, we all thought it must've been three hundred, four hundred, five hundred B-29s. Three or four days afterwards, one of the Japanese broke down and told us that one plane and one bomb had blown the whole of Nagasaki up. We kind of laughed, and he was very serious. He was going to beat us up because we were laughing.

Private Arnold Graves, Yokohama

No way we were going to get out of there if the war continued. Even with the bombing, I felt the war would have gone on another two, three years if they hadn't dropped the atomic bomb. The Japanese had their mountains tunnelled out, gun positions set in. I feel they saved thousands of lives by dropping the atomic bomb.

Private Sid Vale, Sendai

We had an idea the end was coming. We could tell, just by the way they were acting, something was coming up. All of a sudden work was called off. They called us out on the parade square. Then the Jap commandant came out and two of his guards — I can still see them doing it today — one on each side, and they lifted him up on this box. [He] told us the war was over. And with that, he turned around, jumped off the box, disappeared out the gate, and we never saw him again. I don't think there was a dry eye in that crowd that morning.

Private Stan Baty, Sendai

The last three days, we knew there was something going on. The guards kept telling us, "Just rest." Then Captain Reid told us the war was over. You know, for forty years, I've been trying to analyze my thoughts, but it's almost impossible to put into words. I think, disbelief after all those years.

Private Bill Ashton, Ohasi

Sergeant John Malloy was one of the POW bosses. One morning he comes in and says, "No outward signs of exuberance, old chaps, but at noon today, peace will be signed in Tokyo." Did we laugh! We thought it was a joke, but John was serious.

So we're waiting. Ten minutes past working time. Half an hour past working time. The Jap guards are standing off to one side, talking and smoking. Finally, one of Jap guards comes, big grin on his face: "Okay, let's go to work."

We marched down the road. We got down to where we were loading the gravel and muckin' about. The little guard says, "*Yasume*, rest." So we sat down, and we sat there for over an hour, until we just couldn't sit any longer. Some of us got up with our shovels and started working. After all those years of work, work, work, we just couldn't sit there.

And Johnny is still saying, "You know, guys, the war is over." After all these years, we had trouble making ourselves believe there was such a place as Canada, let alone that the war was ever going to end. I mean, this was our life.

So we're sitting there, and I heard the most glorious sound of my entire life. Way off in the distance, I could hear a bunch of young voices. Guys that were still working in the mine were coming down the road, singing "O Canada" at the top of their lungs. God, it was beautiful! We sat there and we listened to them coming down. Then they were in sight, shovels and picks over their shoulders, singing "O Canada." My God, I wish Trudeau could hear that! Maybe he'd realize what Canada is all about.

Our officers gave us the word, officially, it was indeed over. We were going home! Billy Moore and Price and I went back to our hut, climbed on our bunks, and sat there side by side. Moore says, "I'm not going to be a sissy. I'm not going to cry."

So we all did!

Private Bert Delbridge, Sendai

I made up my mind that the first Jap that I found when I was liberated, I was going to beat the shit out of him. This is one thing that made me keep living. But I didn't do it.

Private Arnold Graves, Yokohama

The Americans flew in big drums of fruit salad, boots, clothes. Dropped them by parachute. Two men were sitting in their bunk in the prison camp. They dropped a drum of boots — come through the roof and killed the two of them. The day the war was over.

Private Bill Savage, Oyama

The morning after this, the Americans came over, a two-man plane off a carrier. They'd made up some bundles of bread and butter and jam. The cookhouse door happened to be right at the end of the parade square, and they were divebombing. They'd bounce this stuff right into the cookhouse. I tell you, that stuff really tasted good after all that time.

Next day, they came over with bombers, and they had forty-five-gallon drums loaded with supplies. They tried to dump it outside the camp. The things hit a pile of bloody rocks. Talk about a mix! But anyway, our cooks got hold of it. There was just a mish mash. Canned peaches and canned tomatoes and pork and beans. They dumped it all into this bloomin' big vat, heated it up. What a mess, but it tasted good!

Corporal Derek Rix, Sendai

I pretty near ruined myself, because a Jap guard brought meat into the camp. I knew the cook, it was Ed Schayler. So I asked him, "How about cooking me some steak and onions?" I ate the steak and onions, and I walked it off and went back for some more! It's a wonder I didn't bust, you know. Then I had K rations and candy dropped by the Americans.

Corporal Jack Willis, Oyama

The Americans dropped all this food, and of course, a lot of guys ate too much. I remember one fella told me that he ate all the peaches out of twelve cans. And he had ten Hershey chocolate bars on top of that. You know what happened to him, eh? I mean, it was just like a laxative. The poor guy, he didn't know whether he was coming or going or being sent for, for two days.

Lance-Corporal Malcolm Gillis, Omori

These landing barges pulled right into the canal. It was the Americans, and they told us they were evacuating the camp. There were two or three thousand POWs. So anyway, by about four o'clock the next morning, we were all aboard a hospital ship. They took off the clothes we were wearing and threw them overboard, and issued us with American fatigues, gave us a meal. Then they transported us to different ships.

I went to an American destroyer first, the USS *Reynolds*. Then I was transferred to a British aircraft carrier, the HMS *Speaker*.

On September 2, we sailed out of Tokyo Bay. We sailed past the *Missouri* when MacArthur was signing the surrender. They were right up on deck. We could see the whole thing.

We come down to Manila, in the Philippines. There were five Canadians on this carrier: myself, Billy Day, Arnold Graves, and Eric Maloney. I can't remember the other. They took us into this big camp outside the city of Manila, a big American base. There was a kitchen wide open, any time we wanted to go and eat.

[Eventually] they put us on a boat. Three days out of Manila, I had an attack of appendicitis. They had to stop the ship for the operation. We were twenty-four days from Manila to San Francisco.

So I got home on October 28. Matapedia, Quebec, right on the border of New Brunswick.

Private Bill Savage, Oyama

They loaded us on a bloomin' train, and they took us down to Yokohama. They had all the darn windows nailed shut but we managed to open up a window, and we took a peek as we were coming through Tokyo. That place was flat. There was the odd girder sticking up here and there. The only houses you saw were made out of rice bags, hunks of tin, scrap whatever the people could scrounge together.

Corporal Jack Willis

When we got into Yokohama, we got into the place where they had congregated all these prisoners of war. They were delousing us and giving us new clothes. We saw this big, long Plymouth sedan drive up, an army staff car. And we saw these officers get out of it. And we were just elbowing our way through, and I bumped right into MacArthur! And he turned around and looked at me. And I said, "Oh, excuse me, sir." And I came to attention. He said, "That's okay. You know what you're getting for breakfast, do you?" And I said, "Yes, sir, I hear that you are giving us bacon and eggs and toast and coffee." He said, "That's correct." So I actually had close contact with MacArthur. He was quite a boy.

Private Stan Baty

We get to Tokyo. You get into this room, you undress. They give you a shot of this DDT. Then you have a shower. They give you new clothes. And then you were debriefed.

They took us out to the USS *Iowa*, which is the sister ship to the *Missouri*. All I heard there was, "I can't understand why the peace treaty wasn't signed on the *Iowa*. Because this ship is half an inch longer than the *Missouri*!" I think the greatest sight I ever saw was the massed naval power in Tokyo Bay. There was the *Missouri*, *Iowa*, the two American battleships; then the *King George V* was there. There was literally hundreds there.

Of course, we went through the full treatment, as far as needles were concerned. We were there for four days. Then they finally flew us to Guam. I guess we were there about two weeks. We got the same needles over again. We went home on the USS *Hedi Lamarr*. It was a Liberty ship. We went to San Diego. Roy Rogers' wife, Dale Evans, was there. That was before she was a born-again Christian. She had about as much stuff on her, enough material on her, to make about three small handkerchiefs.

Anyway, we left on October 25, 1941. I arrived home October 25, 1945. So it was four years to the day.

Bandsman Art Munn

I was put aboard a battleship for a day. Then we were turned over to the Fleet Air Arm, and flew from Tokyo to Guam. I stayed in Guam for a week, and then from Guam, I flew to Honolulu. I was in Honolulu for a couple of days, and then from Honolulu we flew to San Francisco. We stayed in 'Frisco for a few days. From there we went to Vancouver, and we were given Canadian uniforms. We were in American uniforms, some dressed like navy, others like army. The Americans really did treat us like you wouldn't believe.

From Vancouver we were sent home. My place was Winnipeg. Boarded a train, and we arrived back in Winnipeg about September 28. I was given extended leave and back pay, and we just had one big bash-up for about five months until we got discharged!

Major Gordon Gray, Sham Shui Po

We knew they had dropped the atom bombs. And then there was a rapid change in the attitude of the Japanese. Then some planes started flying over and dropping things into the camp. Then there was a great big delay. We heard the navies were sitting outside Hong Kong and they were arguing about who was going in first. But the first people into the camp were from the [HMCS] *Prince Robert*, which was the boat that came over with us! Of course, there was a lot to be done, because there were still a lot of very sick people. They had to be sorted out — who could travel and who couldn't. You couldn't just pack up the place and move out.

We were put on the old *Empress of Asia*, and went to Manila. The Red Cross and the Americans looked after us just beautifully. Got us cleaned up and fed and outfitted. Then they put us on an American troopship, the *Admiral Hughes*. It was supposed to go to San Francisco. They decided they were going to take us into Seattle. So then we're heading across the Pacific, and they decided they were going to drop us off at Esquimalt. Better still! So that was the first stop, and they let off all the Canadians in Esquimalt. Then my wife arrived. So it was great.

Leading Aircraftsman Elmer Graham, Sumatra

We were finally released August 21. The Japs all of a sudden said, "No working party today." Then the Japs told us that there would be rest, more food, and holidays for us. We still had no idea the war was over at this point.

Then one of the Jap guards told some of our boys that the war was over. At that time we had two captains with us, a Dutch captain and a British captain. And they finally went to

276

the Japanese lieutenant that was in charge of us, said, "Look, we're not going to tolerate this situation any more. We've got guys dying here, and we believe the war is over." The Jap said, "Yeah, the war is over. But tell your prisoners not to get rambunctious, because we're still in charge."

Then they put us on trains and sent us to Pekanbaru. We had working parties out and they got the airfield serviceable. On September 15, four Australian Dakotas came in and they took out, I think it was, twelve stretchers and thirteen walking, each. The MO read off the names, and I was number ninety-nine on the list! They flew us to Singapore.

I weighed 107 pounds. I had malaria, dysentery, and beri-beri. I wouldn't have lasted another six months.

CSM Red Windsor

This is my own personal feeling. If we'd been prisoners of war any longer, the way the men were desperate for food, starving, I don't think that we would've buried anybody. I have a funny feeling that they'd have been eating each other. I don't think they'd have killed to do it. But I think if a person died, they would have done it.

Footnotes

1. In fact an RCAF Squadron Leader, Leonard J. Birchall won the Distinguished Flying Cross while on patrol over the Indian Ocean in early April 1942. In command of a Catalina flying boat, Birchall detected a Japanese fleet approaching Ceylon. Birchall's aircraft managed to radio a warning before being shot down. Birchall was captured but his message alerted the defenders of Ceylon. A few days later, a Japanese attack on Colombo harbour was repulsed with heavy losses.
2. March 9-10, 1945, 345 B-29 Superfortresses attacked Tokyo. An estimated eighty-five thousand people died in the firebombing, with most of the city being burned to the ground.

Part Three: Epilogue

XVI/Coming Home

Nearly four decades have passed since the end of World War II.
The young men who found themselves in enemy prison
camps are now much older. The former POWs are, for the
most part, in their sixties now, with a few in their late fifties
and a sprinkling in their seventies. Many are retired, and
others are getting ready to retire. Their hair is usually greyer
and often thinner than it used to be, and their waistlines are a
little thicker, although you won't find many who are over-
weight. A lot of them have health problems resulting from
their POW experience; this is particularly true of the Hong
Kong veterans.

Every year their numbers dwindle steadily. This is only
natural, of course, but studies have shown that the POWs,
depending on their prison experience, have a shortened life
expectancy.

Many of them attend reunions held regularly by groups
formed after the war, such as the Hong Kong Veterans'
Association of Canada, the National Prisoners of War Association, and the RCAF Prisoner of War Association. They tend to
recall the good times they had, and they can sometimes
laugh at things that seemed so bad when they happened. The
really terrible things they witnessed or experienced, they
have managed to forget, or at least they simply prefer not to
talk about them. And, of course, the years have dimmed
many of the memories, good and bad.

How do they feel about their experiences as prisoners of
war? Was there any value or benefit in the experience? Why
did they survive when others didn't? Did it change them in

any way? Did they have any difficulty adjusting to life in Canada after spending time in prison camp? Are they still affected by what they endured? These are some of the questions posed to the ex-POWs during the research for this book. The answers are influenced not only by individual personalities, but by the experiences they encountered. Not surprisingly, there are some dramatic differences between the answers given by Hong Kong vets and those given by the Kriegies. The differences are sharpened by the terrible treatment the Hong Kong vets suffered at the hands of the Japanese, as opposed to the relatively more reasonable treatment given Canadian POWs in Germany. To keep the comments within the context of the experience that is responsible for them, this chapter has been divided into two parts, one for the Hong Kong vets and the other for the Kriegies.

THE HONG KONG VETERANS:

Ken Gaudin When we meet now, I've often said we're closer than blood brothers. We were together in very cramped quarters lots of times, where people were so hungry that they were going into the garbage bins. Eating fish heads. One man eating another man's vomit.

This was the hardest part. I came back with quite a number of people into Oakland, California. A train there went north to Seattle, and we went over on the *Princess Alice* over to Victoria. It all felt very good. Then we came over to Vancouver. They named the train *The Hong Kong Special*. All across Canada, there was a gnawing fear about what it was going to be like to get back home. Many of us, when we got home, there was just one big welcoming party after another. It just kept on going, and there was a fair amount of alcohol consumed. Some, unfortunately, weren't able to stop.

Sid Vale We had a lot of back pay coming to us at the time, and the dollar bill was worth a dollar. You could buy a hell of a lot of booze, and that's what most of us were doing. I think the drinking became a problem for some, but not for me. Once I got out of uniform and off to work, I was okay.

Emile Van Raes One bad thing it taught me: self-sufficiency, which was great trouble to my wife when I first came back home. I was very independent, and I was very selfish. I felt I had to look after myself, same way as I looked after myself over there. And it was kind of rough at first for my wife, until I got out of it and started realizing what I had to do. But I would say it took two or three years.

Aubrey Flegg There's been an awful lot of divorces in our gang, a hell of a lot. I know I've given my wife some very bad times that are most uncalled for, and it was not fair to her. But it wasn't my fault that I did it, any more than it was the fault of the other boys that did it to their wives.

Arnold Graves If you were to leave your home and go to another part of Canada, and you go back in four years, you see a lot of changes. That's how it was with us. Your girlfriend's married to someone else and got a couple of kids. Some of your relatives are dead. Somehow you feel that it's going to be the same when you go back, but it's never the same. And that's what throws you off more than anything else.

Donald Geraghty As far as Canada was concerned and the Canadian way of life, I left seventeen years old, and I came back four years later, seventeen years old. A seventeen-year-old mind stepping into a world that had gone from a depression era into a world that had gone through six years of war, and the poverty was gone, pretty well. And I could not cope with the people as they were then. We went thinking 1941 Canada, and when we came back to 1945 Canada, there was such a vast change. The women were liberated, they had more money. And when I came back and I tried to talk to people, they had changed so drastically and I had not. I didn't know the world I was stepping into, and for a few years, that was the big problem.

People would ask, "Oh, you were a prisoner of war. How was it? Was it really as bad as they said it was?" All people cared about was the atrocities. If you tried to tell them anything else, they lost interest and turned away. But if you could tell them of some brutality, they lapped it up. That was 1945 Canada, '46, '47.

I don't fear death. I've seen too many people die under too many bad circumstances. Diphtheria, it's a horrible death. I saw a man sit on a can for five days and just drop dead — shit himself to death. I've seen bullets, bayonets, decapitation. So what's there to fear? Sometimes I worry that maybe I'm a little bit too cold-hearted about it.

Claude Corbett I was blind until I came home. Right now, I can't read a newspaper or anything. I have under ten per cent vision. So I'm resigned to it.

Tommy Dewar When I lost the use of my hands, my arms, and was paralyzed from the waist down, I was put on a vitamin pill every day. Finally, my hands came back. But my legs never did.

Stan Baty I came home with pellagra sores around the ankles. And when you look through my file, it's always "the alleged pellagra." Well, I mean, they treated me here for it. Yet they still use the word "alleged." It's things like this that cheese you off about DVA.

Bill Laidlaw Now they tell us some of us are likely to have contracted strongyloid worms or something. After all these years, they're going to start testing us for them. What they do, I don't know. And if they haven't done anything in the last thirty-five years, what the hell are they gonna do now?[1]

Howard Donnelly I go to bed at night and only sleep for an hour and a half, two hours, and then one of my legs will kick, involuntarily, just like an electric shock went through it. I wake up, and it gets hot and it starts to ache. You lay there and start wondering, "Why in the hell did them bastards have to starve us to the point where we still suffer?" You know, I didn't mind being a prisoner. I felt I joined the army, goddam it, and it was my luck to get caught. If I live, that's fine; if I don't, I've agreed to this. But goddammit, I didn't agree to suffer till I was seventy-one years of age! I felt when we came back, the medical people would say, "We can fix you up." But nobody's ever done a cotton pickin' thing, except a prescription for some Valium to let me get some

281

sleep! I've talked to my friends — every damn one of us is the same.

Our big problem at first was getting the government to agree that we should have been pensioned for heart condition. You see, this is what really started the Hong Kong Veterans' Association. We came back and the doctors said, "You're gonna be fine. Here's a ten per cent pension." So we've got a pension that'll give us about eight dollars a month. And then our guys started dropping dead. The first one that I can recall was an officer, Jack Norris. Dropped dead of a heart attack.

When we first started [the HKVA] the idea was to get together for a few drinks. But when these fellows started dropping off, we asked, "Is there a reason for this?" One thing we found, that a hell of a high percentage had hypertension. So this is what really sparked us to fight for our pensions and benefits for the Hong Kong veterans.

We got our first real breakthrough in 1971, when we got our wives covered to the extent where, if a Hong Kong veteran dropped dead, his wife would receive the widows' pension. That was our first aim, to make sure that our wives and children would be protected in case of an early death.

Then in 1976 we finally got our POW Compensation Act through. I think the lowest pension right now would be a twenty-five per cent disability pension and a fifty per cent prisoner of war compensation, for a total of seventy-five per cent of the total pension.

Back in the sixties, there were a couple of major studies. One was the Richardson brother survey. That was when they compared a hundred Hong Kong veterans with a hundred army personnel from the European theatre. They were blood brothers: one went to Hong Kong, and the other fought in Europe. Richardson compared them as to their mental state, their physical state, their financial state. He came up with the recommendation that the Hong Kong people should be considered separate and unique, and in need.

That was followed by the Wood Committee. [It] merely recommended that the recommendations of the Richardson Report be adopted. It is just ironic that it took the government so long to act.

282

I would say, now, we are the best treated veterans in Canada, and that Canada's veterans are treated better than any other veterans in the world.

Gordon Gray If I had to be there, I'm glad it was as a doctor. I felt that I did do some good, or the best I could, under the circumstances. That's a sense of satisfaction. So, really, it wasn't a complete waste of time.

Being a prisoner of war was often as hard on the relatives, maybe more. I'm sure that's what killed my Dad, trying to find out what was going on. He was a busy doctor in Edmonton. He'd bust himself working, then spend the rest of his time worrying about me. He'd get a rumour or some lead somewhere, and he'd write or telegraph or whatever. As a result, I got home in October [1945] and stayed for about four weeks. Then I went back down East because I wanted to get going on my interning. Early in December Dad had a coronary. I came home, and he was getting on reasonably well, so I went back East the first of January. Dad got out of hospital, but had a massive heart attack again in February of '46 and died at the age of sixty-three. I had always wanted the opportunity of working with him. He was known as a great teacher and I was looking forward to the day when I could come back here and work with him. Never did.

Red Windsor I had a wife, and I think everybody else that was in my circumstances in a prison camp would dream consistently of home, what it was going to be like. And I think this kept us going. I know it kept me going. I thought there was nobody like her, and I was going to come back to my wife, come hell or high water.

I came back, all right. But my wife had cancer. It was eleven days from the day I got back till I buried her.

Bob Lytle I was greatly appreciative of a country like Canada when I got back. I don't know how anybody could be there and not appreciate this country a lot more.

Alec Henderson I came out of it alive, anyway. I served my time as I had volunteered to do. We wound up over there, we did our bit, we made the best of it. You can't have any feelings of resentment or regret about that.

THE KRIEGIES:

Don Morrison A very large percentage of the fellas that wound up in prison camp were lucky to be alive. They all survived being shot down or crashing or being fished out of the drink or whatever. So that most of the fellas came pretty close to being killed at that point. So I think we all realized we were lucky to be alive. At this point, I've had almost a forty-year bonus.

Allan Glenn It took me a long while to get used to traffic. Other people, too. I don't know why.

The worst part of the whole thing was the uncertainty. If you'd been told it was going to be three years, okay, you could settle down to it. But you don't know if you're going to be there three months, three years, or thirty years.

Roy Bourne It was a great experience at the time, but it's something that I would never ever want to do again. You're scared all the time. I don't know anybody that wouldn't be.

George Thom It was a hell of an experience. So many didn't live through it. Really, it just scares you when you think of them. I was lucky, that's all.

Ray Eaton I was in action in Italy. For a year and a half, I was in all sorts of battles, right up to the time I was taken prisoner. And I can tell you, I'd much rather be fighting than be in a prison camp. I value my freedom too much. I go crazy when I'm cooped up.

Lou Pantaleo It was like a dream. It still feels like a dream. I can't believe I was really there. I was never looking from the inside out, I was looking from the outside in.

I know I did a lot of foolish things when I came back home. I had several jobs. I couldn't settle down. I had a lot of drinking to catch up on, and a lot of partying. That went on for about a year, a year and a half. Then I met my wife and got married, then started living a normal life again.

Forbes Morton I spent my twenty-first, twenty-second, and twenty-third birthdays in a prison camp. I figured those were the best years of my life. And I swore to God that from then on, every year I was gonna get drunker'n a skunk on the day we were liberated. Which I proceeded to do. And not only that day, but many other days too. In fact, I eventually turned into an alcoholic. But I overcame that. I joined A.A. I haven't had a drink now for going on twenty-four years.

Sam Dunn I found it hard to adjust to the fact that I was free. You know, you'd been under that strain for so many years that you'd wake up at night and wonder if you were home or where you were. I don't think you ever really get over it. I still have the odd nightmare. But in those days, you had quite a few, because it was so damn fresh in your memory.

Fred Woodcock A lot of the adjustment that has to be made, not only us to our disabilities, but then, too, our wives. I left my wife. I'll take my hat off to my wife any day, I'll tell you that. We'd been married fourteen years before the war. You leave a wife behind like that, and she has to assume the responsibilities and make all the decisions that you took care of when you were present. So the wife has to make an adjustment when this four-years-away husband comes home.

Wally Floody I think probably the average POW was better off than the average guy who came back [from overseas]. Now, I'm talking mainly about air force people. They had to come back from being sort of war heroes and they had to live up to that. I came back from the absolute bottom of the barrel, everything was a plus. And of course, I had one big plus. I was married before I was shot down, and I came back to an already stable marriage.

Alex Masterton I was captured when I was nineteen. And one thing we didn't learn — prisoners who'd been in for a long time — was how to behave in the presence of women. And I don't mean that facetiously. We didn't even know how to approach a woman. I mean, we were fumbling, bumbling stumble-bums, really, when it came to the presence of women. And I think that took a long time to get over. Oh, we were really stupid. I think we lost a sense of civilization.

Marcel Lambert As a prisoner of war, you develop a psychosis that you must not let any food go to waste. In a restaurant, if the platters have got anything on and that food's going back to the kitchen, I all of a sudden feel hungry for it. Same at home. My wife says, "Here, you finish this." And I will not tolerate food going into the garbage. The net result is, as you grow older, you just pile it on. I know what you should do is just eat to appease your hunger, then cut it off. But that's easier said than done when it's deeply engrained that you must clean your plate.

Arnold Hanes I don't ever want to see another grape. I can't even look at a pizza. You can't get me in an Italian restaurant. I just got a hate for Italian food. Funny thing, though; I just love German food!

Gilles Lamontagne I remember 1948, the first time I went back to Germany. I could hardly stand hearing a German talk, because in my mind it reflected where I was, and they were not always nice, you know. But after that, it went away, and today I have no hate.

Bill Larin I'll tell you, I think there was a lot of character formed in those camps. They weren't the greatest hosts, the Germans. At times, they could be awfully mean and miserable. It taught us a lot. It taught us how to get along, for one thing. You had to have a lot of self-discipline. Because you're all in the same boat.

Art Deacon Five unforgettable years. Outside of being crazy ever since, I think it made me more tolerant with people, about people, about things. I am sure my understanding of so many things was broadened the way it never could have done in ordinary civilian life or if I hadn't been taken prisoner.

My experience as a POW was an education that you can't buy any place. You met some interesting people in camp, some well-educated people. I even learned some French in there.

Lots of friendships built up. You know, you don't realize it at the time, but it's a situation where little things become so big, and big things become so little.

Bill Douglas It's an experience I don't want to forget. It broadens your mind. All those people in there, I imagine a lot of them gained an awful lot of experience of being able to cope with, not only living, but getting along with people. In all walks of life. There was different types from all over the world, and whether you could talk their language or not, you still got along with them.

Brian Filliter You only remember the funny things anyway. You don't remember the daily grind, standing out there in the bloody rain while the Germans can't count properly and you're freezing to death. You don't remember those things, just the funny things.

Bill Haslam The odd letter that fellows got from people at home shows that they just had no understanding of what was actually happening. I can recall one mother writing and saying she was so glad that her son was shot down before flying became dangerous! Because we were going in on targets with maybe half a dozen aircraft and, of course, the papers by that time were full of the one thousand bomber raids. So she thought it was very good that her boy had been shot down before it became dangerous!

Al Hayward It certainly made me more tolerant of my fellow man. I really think a lot of us got a lot of good out of it. As long as you didn't suffer some longlasting medical effect, as far as I'm concerned, it was good.

Stew Saunders When I got back home, the only thing I had was stomach trouble. Eventually, I had an operation for ulcers. Now, whether that was caused by camp food or whatever, nerves, stress — I don't know.

Herb Krentz I'm still being compensated for chronic bronchitis. Just before the liberation, I was about a month in bed with pneumonia, unattended by any physicians. It left a large scar on my right lung, and the doctors diagnosed this as being chronic bronchitis which I still have difficulties with in cold weather.

John Cox They found I had tuberculosis. They had to take out two-thirds of my right lung. But it spread over to the left lung after the operation. But this was just at the point when streptomycin was introduced. I was dead lucky. It worked on me like a charm, and I haven't had any trouble since.

Ray Epstein The only mark that it's left, really, is claustrophobia. And if I'm on a street, if my wife and I go to Toronto or Montreal, and we're walking along, let's say, Yonge Street at lunch hour and the street's loaded with people and you're working your way through crowds, I just start to break out in a sweat occasionally, and I have to duck down a sidestreet to get away from this sense of everything closing in on me.

Roger Teillet

(After the war, Teillet entered politics. In 1963, he joined the cabinet of Prime Minister Lester B. Pearson and was Minister of Veterans' Affairs until 1968, when he retired.)

During my term as Minister, I set up the Wood Committee. It was a ministerial committee to examine the Pension Commission. I realized that the Commission was losing its credibility. The Commission had not really been thoroughly looked at from the early thirties. And a body of that nature, as a matter of principle, should never have that much power. Being quasi-judicial, it should never be allowed to go more than ten, fifteen years without a thorough review of what they're doing. You know, it was getting pretty independent, and telling almost anybody, including the government, to go to hell.

So I felt it was important to have this looked at. I had Justice Wood, from Regina, chair the ministerial committee.

It was important to get someone who would be credible to the veterans of Canada. The 1971 legislation resulted from the Wood Report, a complete revamp of the Canadian Pension Commission, the benefits to the veterans, and ultimately — not that I intended this — compensation to POWs. And the rest of this: better widows' pensions, and certainly a complete and very great improvement in the legislation for veterans' benefits, disability, hospitalization, and compensation for POWs.

As you know, all disability pensions are granted on a percentage basis. POWs get ten per cent if they were a POW three months or more, fifteen per cent for eighteen months. And over thirty months — and the thirty months was used because of the Dieppe POWs — then you get the full twenty per cent POW pension. Right now, on a married basis, that's $227.62[2] a month. On top of that, POWs qualify for all other disability benefits, over and above that.

I think that our veterans are treated better than any other veterans in the world.

Owen Deal I still think they should give us more. I still say that the first three months of being a prisoner of war was the worst. That's while they were interrogating you and keeping you in solitary. Anybody under three months can't get compensation. And the first three months when I was a prisoner of war was the worst. I was thirty-nine days in solitary.

I still have nightmares of prisoners of war. Like, I dream about being on the march, and the dogs. I can't sit and watch war pictures on TV.

This survey done by Doctor Hermann claims it shortened our lives, for every year we were prisoners, by five years. I think there's a lot more heart attacks and stomach troubles and things like that in prisoners of war than there is in people that served, or didn't serve, at the same age. Our death rate is quite high. Diabetes is bad among prisoners of war, too. Whether this was caused in the prison camp we can't prove, and this is why we can't get a disability pension for this sort of thing.

Howard Paillefer You know, old soldier's tales always gather additional gloss as you go through life. But I think it's made me treasure the freedoms we have. When that freedom is taken away from you, and the loss of your family and friends, it changes your outlook on life. I particularly treasure freedom, and the right to speak up and the right to go and do what I want to. And I think in Canada, we probably have the most free nation in the world for that kind of thing.

Ron Finn I just wound up appreciating the people that I knew, that I'd met, that I associated with, a great deal. To the point that I really resent this East-West problem that we have today. I just can't understand how this came about. We have the western people that Ontario picked on and the Ontario people who are sure the West is doing it to them now. This is just a bunch of malarky.

Harold McConnell We really had a strong sense, I think, of loyalty and pride in our own country. We learned to be very proud of Canada and the part it took in the war. We should be proud of Canada, after that Dieppe raid.

Canadians had a good name in England. And they were very highly respected by the Germans, and by the Dutch, and by the French. Maybe we weren't much to look at, but Canada really had a lot to be proud of.

And I think that if that pride came back to us now, it could solve a lot of our problems today.

Footnotes

1. Testing is being carried out by federal health officials for strongyloidiasis. This is a condition caused by a parasitic microscopic worm. This rare tropical parasite can be killed with drugs. Carriers may show symptoms such as itchy skin, stomach disorders, and an inability to gain weight. Strongyloidiasis is common in hot, moist tropical areas, such as southeast Asia, but it is virtually unknown in Canada.
2. As of March 4, 1982, when this interview was conducted.

The Ex-POWs

John Achtim joined the Manitoba government in 1948, the Department of Municipal Affairs. Since 1975, he has chaired Manitoba's Municipal Board, based in Winnipeg.

Al Aldridge went to work for the federal Immigration Department after the war. He is now retired and lives in Ottawa.

Bob Alldrick is a noted photographer in southern Ontario. He has his own photo business, located in Grimsby.

Daniel Almon is a professional engineer based in Halifax, where he is President of his own firm, Almac Agencies Ltd.

Ivan Anderson retired in 1979 after a career as a Customs officer. He makes his home in Calgary.

Bill Ashton has been retired for eleven years, following careers with the federal Department of Veterans' Affairs and the Manitoba Telephone System. Winnipeg is home.

Hayden Auld became a lumber wholesaler after the war. Now retired, he lives in Winnipeg.

Simon Avery spent thirty-six years as a civilian employee of the Department of National Defence. Recently retired, he lives in Hatchet Lake, Nova Scotia.

Ronald Barton is a resident of Toronto, where he is a supervisor in a sheetmetal shop.

Stan Baty apprenticed as a printing pressman in Winnipeg after the war. He is now retired and living in Edmonton.

Wilf Blewett is a resident of Ottawa, where he helps administer the RCAF Benevolent Fund. He remained in the armed forces for fifteen years following his return from the war.

291

Roy Bourne retired two years ago, after a career that spanned thirty-five years with the Alberta Liquor Control Board. When he is not travelling, he lives in Calgary.

Lucien Brunet plans to retire this year, after spending forty-four years with Canadian National Railways. Based in Montreal, he is a Prevention Services Analyst with CN's St. Lawrence Region.

Stan Bryant lives in Edmonton, where he is a fruit and vegetable inspector with the federal Department of Agriculture.

Henry Byrnes served a few months in the Korean War before being posted to Military Intelligence, where he remained until 1960. He then launched a new career in the British Columbia civil service, retiring in 1976. He lives on Vancouver Island.

Bruce Campbell has been an insurance salesman with Canada Life since 1954. He is a resident of Montreal.

Donald Campbell is a broker with Greenshields Inc. in Halifax.

Bob Charman became a pharmacist after the war. He is still working and living in Calgary.

Richard Clark went into the building business after the war. Now he is a stationary engineer at Queen's Park in Toronto. He and his wife Jean are actively involved in the National Prisoners of War Association.

Bob Collins has spent the past twenty-three years with Ontario's Ministry of Transport. He lives in Burlington.

Al Comfort is retired after a thirty-year career at Stelco in Hamilton. He lives in nearby Ancaster.

Cecil Cook has worked for thirty-three years with Simpson's Sears in Halifax.

Hector Cooper has had a checkered career since the war. He stayed in the navy until 1959, then went to work for Great West Life, where he spent thirteen years. He is now involved with warehousing in Halifax.

Claude Corbett is a resident of Delta, British Columbia. He was employed by the federal Department of Veterans' Affairs until his retirement in 1975.

John Cox lives in Mississauga, Ontario, where he has been employed the past twenty-five years by GT Sylvania.

Don Craigie went to work for the Health and Animals Branch of Canada Agriculture in 1945. After eleven years as a meat inspector, he moved to the Contagious Diseases branch. He retired in 1980. In 1967, he was awarded the Centennial Medal for "outstanding service" to the country.

Art Crighton retired recently as a Professor of Music at the University of Alberta in Edmonton, where he has been since 1949.

Tommy Cunningham worked in the Post Office in Calgary for thirty years. He retired more than four years ago.

Barry Davidson is in the insurance business in Calgary, where he has his own company, Davidson-Elves Agencies Ltd.

Jim Davies retired from the armed forces as a Lieutenant General in 1976. Based in Ottawa, he is Director of Government Affairs for the deHavilland Aircraft of Canada Ltd.

Arnold Dawkins spent more than thirty years in the federal civil service, prior to his retirement in 1978. He now lives on Vancouver Island.

Reginald Daye retired from Imperial Oil on a disability pension in 1968. He is a resident of Jeddore-Oyster Lake, in Nova Scotia.

Art Deacon ran a service station in Vancouver until 1972. He is now a salesman for Kerrisdale Lumber.

Owen Deal is actively involved in the Royal Canadian Legion and the National Prisoners of War Association. Before his retirement, he worked for twenty-five years at the Defence Research Establishment in Dartmouth, Nova Scotia.

Bert Delbridge went to work for the Winnipeg *Free Press* after the war, retiring as Circulation Manager in 1979. He also served as President of the Hong Kong Veterans' Association of Canada.

Tommy Dewar has been employed by the Canadian Imperial Bank of Commerce since 1950. He is now a supervisor in the bank's regional office in Winnipeg.

Bill Dignam sells real estate in Toronto.

Howard Donnelly sold giftwares for fifteen years before going into real estate. He is now retired and living in Edmonton, where he is President of the local chapter of the Hong Kong Veterans' Association of Canada.

Bill Douglas retired in 1980, after a thirty-five year career with CP Rail. He lives in Winnipeg.

Jack Dunlap went into pharmacy after the war, first in Edmonton, then in Banff, where he still resides. A widower, he retired in 1981.

Sam Dunn became an electrician after the war and joined the federal civil service in 1954. He retired in 1980 as an electrical foreman at Griesbach Barracks in Edmonton.

Gordon Durrant is a security official with the Calgary Exhibition and Stampede Board.

Ray Eaton is getting ready to retire after serving as an automotive mechanic with Air Canada since 1959. He is a resident of Dartmouth, Nova Scotia.

Sam Ebsary is a tax consultant in Sydenham, Ontario, where he lives with his lovely wife, Joan.

John Edelson runs his own investment counselling business in Calgary. He has no plans to retire.

Ross Elford recently retired as a District Operations Manager with Alberta Government Telephones. He spent thirty-seven years with AGT. His home is in Edmonton.

Geoffrey Ellwood retired in 1976, after spending thirty-six years in the army's Signal Corps. A resident of Dartmouth, Nova Scotia, he is now a part-time postal worker.

Harold Englehart worked at the Montreal *Star* for thirty-three years, until it folded. He is now retired.

Ray Epstein is a dentist in Halifax, specializing in pedodontics. He practices on a part-time basis and teaches at Dalhousie University.

Des Ewins is a construction superintendent with Bay Roberts in Toronto.

Brian Filliter is Traffic Manager at Trane Air Conditioning, where he has worked the past eleven years. He lives in Toronto.

Ron Finn is a stationary engineer with Tricil, a waste management firm in Hamilton. He lives in nearby Paris.

Aubrey Flegg remained in the armed forces for twenty-five years. He retired as a sergeant in 1967. He makes his home in Richmond, British Columbia.

Wally Floody lives in Toronto, where he has his own business.

George Gardiner retired in 1978 after a lengthy career with Shell Oil in Montreal. He lives in London, Ontario.

Harold Garland is getting ready to retire. He has been in the federal civil service for thirty-six years. He is an Assistant Deputy Minister with Revenue Canada in Ottawa.

Ken Gaudin has just retired as District Sales Manager for SKF of Canada. A resident of St. Lambert, Quebec, he is also Secretary-Treasurer of the Hong Kong Veterans' Association of Canada.

Donald Geraghty is Manager of Academic Book Caravans in Hamilton, a wholesaler of educational paperbacks to schools and libraries. He is also a member of Hamilton's Orpheus Male Choir.

Bill Gibson is an accountant with an insurance company in Halifax.

Malcolm Gillis is a Senior Estimator with Dominion Engineering in Lachine, Quebec. He is a resident of Chateauguay,

Quebec, where he and his wife have raised five daughters and two sons.

Allan Glenn went to work as a field officer for the Veterans' Land Act, where he remained until his retirement in 1973. He now dabbles in farming, but he lives in Edmonton.

Bert Gnam is getting ready to retire as a yard foreman with CP Rail in Calgary. He has been with CP for thirty-five years.

Elmer Graham retired from the air force in 1968, after a career that spanned twenty-seven years. A widower, he lives in Winnipeg.

Arnold Graves spent thirty-four years with Canada Packers. He is now retired and living in Greenfield Park, Quebec.

Gordon Gray became an orthopaedic surgeon in Edmonton after the war. He eventually got into the administration end of medicine at Charles Camsell Hospital before moving to the Workers' Compensation Board rehabilitation centre. He retired in 1978.

George Hailes has been retired since 1972, after a career with the Province of Alberta Social Services Department. He lives in Edmonton.

Wally Hair has been in construction-related work since the end of the war. He is currently employed at the Southern Alberta Institute of Technology in Calgary. He plans to retire soon.

Arnold "Skid" Hanes is a Commissionaire at RCMP Headquarters in Ottawa. Prior to his retirement in 1977, he spent thirty-five years with the federal Department of Veterans' Affairs.

Al Hannah is an Assistant Deputy Minister with Revenue Canada's Customs and Excise Department in Ottawa.

Gordon Harrison retired recently, after a career with the City of Calgary's Engineering Department.

Bill Haslam is in fire equipment sales in Vancouver. He makes his home in nearby Delta.

Doug Hawkes is retired and living in Calgary, after a career in real estate.

Clem Hawkins is recently retired. He spent the past fifteen years in maintenance at the University of Calgary.

Al Hayward is in business with his brother. For the past fifteen years, they've run The Dressmakers' Supply Company on Bay Street in downtown Toronto.

Alec Henderson became a construction superintendent after the war, but had to take an early retirement in 1965, for health reasons. He lives in Winnipeg.

Cliff Hooey has been a meatcutter for thirty-seven years. He works for Safeway in Calgary.

Ed Houston practiced law for twenty-five years after the war, before being made a judge. He is now a County Court Judge in Ontario, based in Ottawa.

Cliff Irwin became a well-known pharmacist in Calgary after the war. He is now retired.

Harry Jay joined the federal External Affairs Department in 1948, and has held a variety of posts around the world, including a stint as Canada's Ambassador to Sweden from 1973 to 1976. Ottawa is his home at the moment.

D.D. Johnstone farmed in Manitoba until health problems forced him to retire. He now lives in Winnipeg.

Gren Juniper has his own music store, Juniper's Guitar Studio, in Burlington, Ontario. He resides in Hamilton.

Stephen Kashton worked for twenty-three years as a machinist with the Department of National Defence. He retired in 1979 and lives on an acreage on the outskirts of Edmonton.

Gord King has been in wholesale floor coverings since 1947 with W.C. McMahon Limited in Edmonton.

John Kozakewich moved around quite a bit after the war, eventually going to work for Edmonton Telephones until his retirement in 1978.

Herb Krentz is a Technical Resources Officer with the federal Indian Affairs Department. He is based in Winnipeg.

Bill Laidlaw is retired and living in Vancouver, after spending more than thirty years as a Customs official.

Marcien Lafortune died in October 1982 at his home in Dougald, Manitoba.

Marcel Lambert is a lawyer, a former Rhodes Scholar, and since 1957 has been the Conservative Member of Parliament for Edmonton West.

Gilles Lamontagne is the Minister of National Defence. He's been in politics since the early '60s and in 1965 he became mayor of Quebec City, a post he held until 1977, when he made the transition to federal politics.

Bill Larin does a lot of travelling these days. He retired in 1980, after thirty years with Consolidated Sand and Gravel in Paris, Ontario.

Dallas Laskey is a Professor of Philosophy at Concordia University in Montreal.

Leo Lecky lives in Winnipeg, where he retired in 1975 after twenty-eight years in the Post Office.

Jim L'Esperance recently took his pension, at age sixty, after a thirty-eight year career with Canadian National Railways, in Winnipeg.

Arthur Low is a maintenance technician with the Ford Motor Company in Oakville, Ontario. He lives in Hamilton.

Don Lush retired in 1982 as President of Supreme Aluminum in Toronto. He spent forty-two years with the firm.

Bob Lytle lives in Winnipeg, where he has been an insurance adjustor for more than twenty years.

Don MacDonald has his own insurance agency in Winnipeg.

Donald Macdonald went into life insurance after the war. He stayed in it until 1961, when he switched to real estate. He is still in it, on a part-time basis, in Calgary.

Dave Mackey retired in 1979, after a long career in sales. He came out of retirement in 1980 to become Sales Manager for System 5 Fabricating. He lives in Hamilton.

Ralph Maclean has been with Cominco Fertilizers in Calgary for thirty-five years.

Peter Macleod went into the insulation business after the war. He has been retired for the past several years. He calls Toronto home.

John MacMullin spent thirty years with the Department of National Defence, retiring in 1981 as a stores supervisor. A resident of Dartmouth, Nova Scotia, he and his wife have nine children.

Alden Magnus is nearing retirement. He has been in automotives since 1945. He works for Nova, in Calgary.

Bill Maltman is semi-retired, with a small accounting business in Winnipeg. He still plays the bagpipes occasionally with the Queen's Own Cameron Highlanders band.

Al Martin has held a variety of jobs since the war. Presently, he is in the security business in Monterey, California.

Bob Masters flew with Pacific Western Airlines and the Canadian Coast Guard after the war. He is now an engineering and design consultant on Vancouver Island.

Alex Masterton is a professional engineer living in Vancouver.

Harold McConnell retired due to health problems in 1971 as a school caretaker in Edmonton.

Allister McDiarmid got into retail lumber in Winnipeg until his retirement in 1974. He still "dabbles," to use his word, in several small businesses to keep busy.

Jim McIntosh lives in Vancouver, where he's been in the federal civil service for the past twenty-two years. Right now, he works for Forintek Canada Corporation, researching wood products.

Phil Mechlair spent thirty-one years in automotive services in Winnipeg. He is now retired.

Alfred Moody recently retired after a number of years doing work for contractors in the Toronto area.

Don Morrison has been with Air Canada for over thirty years. Based in Toronto, he is the airline's Customer Relations Manager for the Central Region.

Forbes Morton went to work for Eaton's in 1947, and he has been there ever since. Home is in Edmonton.

Don Nelson is President of the Calgary chapter of the Hong Kong Veterans' Association of Canada. For the past thirty years he has been an automotive parts salesman.

John Nicolaiff retired in 1982 after thirty-five years with Environment Canada. He lives in Ottawa.

Carl "Soggy" Norton was a professional football player with Toronto and Ottawa before the war, but a car accident ended his comeback attempt with the Rough Riders after the 1945 season. He then joined the Ottawa Police Force, retiring in 1977 as a Detective Inspector.

Keith Ogilvie remained in the air force after the war, rising to the rank of Squadron Leader before his retirement in 1964. He then went to work for Revenue Canada until retiring in 1979. He continues to make Ottawa his home.

Bill Olver spent thirty-five years with the Metro Toronto police department. He now works for the Ontario Attorney-General's Department.

Bill Oxendale is retired now after careers in the army, lumber, and real estate. A political activist, he lives in Calgary where he paints in his spare time.

Howard Paillefer was Air Canada's General Manager for Alberta when he retired in 1981, after a career that spanned thirty-six years. He is now Executive-Director of the Calgary and District Foundation, as well as Past President of the Calgary Stampeder Football Club.

Lou Pantaleo has held a number of different jobs since the war. A resident of Toronto, he owns an apartment building in Brantford.

300

Ed Patrick worked for twenty-five years in the paint business in Toronto, and retired following a nine year stint in the administration of a girls' school. A part-time job with the Hospital for Sick Children Foundation keeps him busy these days.

Anthony Pengelly is in marketing management with Warner Lambert of Canada. Based in Toronto, he is the company's Director of Corporate Marketing and Community Services.

Keith Pettigrew joined Noranda Metal Industries in 1954. He is now Noranda's Western Canada Sales Manager, working out of Edmonton.

Jim "Pappy" Plant eventually joined the federal civil service, with the Department of Veterans' Affairs. He retired in 1974, and is enjoying life with his wife on their acreage near Calgary.

George Price is now retired and living in Regina.

Steve Putnam retired in 1982 after thirty years as a school teacher in Winnipeg.

Ed Rae lives in Ottawa, where he works as a graphic artist with the federal Department of Industry, Trade, and Commerce. Prior to that, he spent seventeen years with the Department of National Defence.

Fred Reich worked for the Post Office in Winnipeg for twenty-eight years. He is retired.

Dennis Richard had to take an early retirement in 1972 due to health problems. He spent thirty-four years as an engineer with Canadian National Railways in Halifax.

Derek Rix retired in 1971 after seventeen years with the Post Office. He lives in North Vancouver.

Russ Rogers retired in 1982 after twenty-nine years with Celanese Canada Incorporated. Edmonton is home.

Bill Rowbotham went into real estate in 1948. In 1963, he became a real estate appraiser in Calgary, and he has been at it ever since. He has no plans to retire.

Jim Sampson opened a sporting goods store in Winnipeg in 1957. Sampson's World of Sports now boasts three stores.

Stew Saunders sold shoes for thirty years, but for the past five years he has worked in sales at Supreme Aluminum in Toronto.

Bill Savage says he's "not retired, just tired." He was a steelworker in Winnipeg until 1979.

George Sendall is a semi-retired Anglican priest and can sometimes be found at St. Cuthbert's Church in Delta, British Columbia. He also resides in Delta.

Joseph St. Arnaud retired from the air force in 1968 with the rank of Lieutenant Colonel. He then went to work for Transport Canada, retiring in 1979. He now does consulting work on a part-time basis in Ottawa.

Earl Summerfield is a resident of Hamilton, where he lives after retiring from Stelco in 1976. He says all he does now is keep "DVA busy with examinations!"

Dempsey Syvret is planning to retire in the near future. He has been with Bell Canada in Montreal since 1946.

Fred Tanner went to work as a diesel mechanic after the war. He retired three years ago. A widower, he lives in Toronto.

Keith Tate lives in Winnipeg, where he's worked with the Land Surveys Branch of the Manitoba Department of Highways since 1947.

Roger Teillet is a former politician, having sat in the Manitoba Legislature for much of the 1950s. In 1962, he won the riding of St. Boniface for the federal Liberals. He later spent four years as Minister of Veterans' Affairs in the Pearson government.

George Thom is retired after thirty-three years with the Post Office in Calgary.

Sid Vale has had a number of jobs since the war. For the past several years, he has worked at the Lincoln Hotel in Edmonton.

Emile Van Raes recently retired after a thirty-five year career with Canadian National Railways in Winnipeg.

Roy Westaway has spent most of his career since the war in maintenance and construction. He is currently employed by Zochem, a manufacturer of zinc oxide, in Brampton, Ontario. He lives in Burlington.

Harold White was a policeman in Hamilton for thirty years. He retired in 1975 as a Sergeant, and now lives in nearby Stoney Creek.

Jack Whitley joined the air force after the war. Following a twenty-year career with the RCAF, he went to work at the Southern Alberta Institute of Technology in Calgary. He plans to retire soon.

Cal Willis is retired and living in Ottawa after spending more than thirty years in the federal civil service, first in Fisheries and then in Employment and Immigration.

Jack Willis was employed in the federal civil service for twenty-one years. He took an early retirement and now lives in Richmond, British Columbia.

Cecil "Red" Windsor went into physical therapy after the war. He later went to work for Eaton's in Winnipeg. Retired since 1973, he now lives in Calgary.

Fred Woodcock has dedicated his life to helping other blind people. He retired in 1970 from the Canadian National Institute for the Blind. He also helped form the Council of World Veterans' Federations. He lives in Grimsby, Ontario.

DATE DUE			
De 10 '85			
De 24 '85			
Jn 16 '88			
Se 30 9?			
Jl 13 15			
.			

170   CHRISTIE SCHOOL SUPPLIES LTD.